The Third Reich
on Screen, 1929–2015

ALSO BY BOB HERZBERG
AND FROM MCFARLAND

*Savages and Saints: The Changing Image of American
Indians in Westerns* (2015; paperback 2008)

Revolutionary Mexico on Film: A Critical History, 1914–2014 (2015)

Hang 'Em High: Law and Disorder in Western Films and Literature (2013)

*The Left Side of the Screen: Communist and Left-Wing
Ideology in Hollywood, 1929–2009* (2011)

*The FBI and the Movies: A History of the Bureau on Screen
and Behind the Scenes in Hollywood* (2007)

Shooting Scripts: From Pulp Western to Film (2005)

The Third Reich on Screen, 1929–2015

BOB HERZBERG

McFarland & Company, Inc., Publishers
Jefferson, North Carolina

LIBRARY OF CONGRESS CATALOGUING-IN-PUBLICATION DATA

Names: Herzberg, Bob, 1956– author.
Title: The Third Reich on screen, 1929–2015 / Bob Herzberg.
Description: Jefferson, N.C. : McFarland & Company, Inc., Publishers, 2017. | Includes bibliographical references and index.
Identifiers: LCCN 2016047081 | ISBN 9781476664262 (softcover : acid free paper) ∞
Subjects: LCSH: National socialism in motion pictures. | National socialism and motion pictures. | Motion pictures—Political aspects—History—20th century. | Nazis in motion pictures.
Classification: LCC PN1995.9.N36 H47 2016 | DDC 791.43/65843086—dc23
LC record available at https://lccn.loc.gov/2016047081

BRITISH LIBRARY CATALOGUING DATA ARE AVAILABLE

ISBN (print) 978-1-4766-6426-2
ISBN (ebook) 978-1-4766-2697-0

© 2017 Bob Herzberg. All rights reserved

No part of this book may be reproduced or transmitted in any form or by any means, electronic or mechanical, including photocopying or recording, or by any information storage and retrieval system, without permission in writing from the publisher.

Front cover: *Triumph of the Will* (1935 Germany) aka *Triumph des Willens* documentary (Contemporary Films/Photofest)

Manufactured in the United States of America

McFarland & Company, Inc., Publishers
Box 611, Jefferson, North Carolina 28640
www.mcfarlandpub.com

To my parents,
Harry and Helen, who survived the Shoah,
came to America, raised three children,
and Never Forgot…

Acknowledgments

And now comes that moment you've all been waiting for: That time when I have to thank those people without whom I couldn't have written this book. It's kind of like an Oscar acceptance speech without mentioning a social problem or the influence of my fourth grade teacher.

First of all, I'd like to thank Jenny Romero and the dedicated staff of the Special Collections Desk of the Margaret Herrick Library in Los Angeles (who work frequently with the Oscars) for their help in providing the studio files for my research; this includes budget sheets, scripts, Breen office correspondence, newspaper reviews, and ad copy for various productions. I should like to also thank the wonderful people at the Warner Brothers Archives at the School of Cinematic Arts at the University of Southern California. Also on my list is Dollie Banner of Jerry Ohlinger's Movie Memorabilia and the helpful staff of Larry Edmonds' Bookshop on Hollywood Boulevard for plenty of photographs from many Hollywood films depicting the Third Reich.

And last, but not least, I'd like to thank my beautiful Colleen as we just passed our twentieth wedding anniversary. I've played many films for her on many different topics (the usual mandatory viewing for researching my books), and this time she's had to view not only films featuring Nazi characters but World War II documentaries, including those showing the atrocities of the Holocaust which would upset many a viewer. She's seen it all and not flinched: the documentaries on Nazi rule, the clichés and contrivances of the World War II propaganda film, the not-so-subtle propaganda of the Soviet and Eastern European films and the Nazi Germany-set films populated by actors with all-too obvious British accents. I thank her for the patience, endurance and love which she's given me for far longer than the previous twenty years.

I hope you enjoy this work. Hopefully, my take on these films and the history behind them will inform and entertain you. It did for me, but then I'm kind of biased...

TABLE OF CONTENTS

Acknowledgments		vi
Introduction		1
I	Infection (1929–1937): Weimar-era filmmaking and the disease taking root in Germany	9
II	Rage (1938–1941): As Nazi aggression spreads across Europe, voices of defiance are finally heard	40
III	Inferno (1942–1945): America enters World War II as the combatants attack each other on-screen as well as off	76
IV	Final Solutions (1946–1954): Postwar Hollywood and Washington continue to ignore the Holocaust even as Nazi war criminals are hunted down on-screen	114
V	Airbrush (1955–1962): Both Hollywood and Germany rewrite history as it condemns Nazism while praising "good Germans" in war-themed films	136
VI	Meshugannah (1963–1980): Mad doctors, Nazi zombies, attempts to revive Hitler, death camp perverts and Ships of Fools	165
VII	Ghosts (1981–2015): Concentration camp children appear as next-door neighbors, we find out what it's like to be Hitler's secretary, and Nazi zombies return (with a vengeance!)	179
Chapter Notes		193
Bibliography		195
Index		199

INTRODUCTION

On May 2, 2015, celebrations began all over Europe commemorating the end of World War II on the continent. Though all would celebrate the victory of the Allies and the defeat of Nazism, it seemed that each country would commemorate the occasion in her own way, with slight variations that said as much about the particular nation doing the commemorating as well as the solemn occasion itself.

In a special session of Berlin's House of Representatives on May 2, 2015, German Foreign Minister Frank-Walter Steinmeier praised the Allied nations for turning a defeated Germany back into a democracy: "The hand that you reached out to us, we will never let go of. It is precisely we, perhaps even more than others, who must today take the responsibility of the preservation of a peacekeeping order."

Later that day, at a ceremony at the former Sachsenhausen concentration camp, a death camp specializing in "political" enemies of the regime, the foreign minister passionately declared that "Remembrance has no expiration date.... The crimes of the National Socialist regime are incomparable to any others. They make us shiver."

One of the leading lights of Germany's Social Democratic Party, Steinmeier also acknowledged the sacrifice of 10,000 Red Army soldiers captured in the Soviet Union and taken to Sachsenhausen to be murdered. Days later in the former Russian city of Stalingrad, now renamed Volgograd, he repeated the tribute to Red Army prisoners in a ceremony presided over by Russian President Vladimir Putin.

Echoing this theme, German President Gauck also paid homage to Soviet suffering under the Nazis. On May 2, 2015, at the Holte-Stukenbrock cemetery in northern Germany where hundreds of Soviet soldiers were buried, President Gauck addressed 20 officials from both Eastern and Western Europe. Condemning Nazi barbarities, the former pastor who served under the Communists in his native East Germany, focused his speech particularly on the horrors inflicted on Soviet prisoners of war. "They (Soviet prisoners) succumbed miserably to disease, they starved to death, they were murdered.... Just as the Jews ... were selected out, humiliated and murdered (and similarly) the handicapped and homosexuals, so too were the people of Eastern Europe defamed as inferior."

Though criticizing the West for ignoring Soviet sacrifices during the Cold War era, Gauck did also acknowledge the immediate imprisonment and mass murder of former Red Army prisoners at Stalin's orders once they returned to the Soviet Union, with outlandish accusations of desertion and espionage being the reasons for their internments.

In what seemed like a snub to everyone else's sufferings, Russian President Vladimir Putin ordered a triumphant military parade in Moscow's Red Square, featuring the nation's latest tank hardware; an unusually insensitive act considering that the rest of the planet was condemning Nazi militarism. The only leaders attending the parade were the (not duly elected) presidents of China and North Korea, as well as U.N. Secretary General Ban Ki-moon. Openly boycotting this display of military might were the democratic nations of Europe and the United States, angered by what they saw as Putin's Nazi-like aggression in the Ukraine. However, in the land where Nazism was born, German Chancellor Angela Merkel went through her own political balancing act: On the one hand, she stayed far away from what she felt was Russia's bellicose reminder of its military might, yet she also attended ceremonies opposite Putin at that very same Red Square days later to lay a wreath at the grave of Russia's Unknown Soldier.

Greece used the anniversary to demand war reparations from Germany to shore up its own economic collapse, a demand which was angrily rejected by the German government. However, in Eastern Europe, days after his visit to Holte-Stukenbrock, German president Gauck joined Polish President Bronislaw Koromoski at the peninsula of Westerplatte in the Polish city of Gdansk, the location of the first Nazi attack during their invasion of the country on September 1, 1939. Both leaders paid tribute to the less than 200 Polish soldiers overwhelmed by thousands of *Wehrmacht* troops in the initial storming of Westerplatte, as well as the Nazi murders of Poles during the Holocaust.

Meanwhile, in Israel on May 3, 2015, in solemn ceremonies attended by Israeli Prime Minister Benyamin Netanyanhu, President Reuven Rivlin and Defense Minister Moshe Ya'alon at both the Museum of the Jewish Fighter, as well as Yad Vashem, President Rivlin declared, "We mark here this evening seventy years since the victory of the free world over the Nazi beast, and pay tribute to the Jewish fighter who played part in this victory. Around one and a half million Jews served in the Second World War, around eight percent of the population, and around half a million of whom fell in battle."

While he was at it, Defense Minister Ya'alon used the specter of Nazi aggression to remind the world of a more immediate danger coming from Iran: "Seventy years later, we must remember that a country that openly discloses its intention to destroy another country—means it. A regime that supports terrorism and spreads it around the entire world—it is a necessity to act against it in various ways in order to stop its intentions."

Though the Israeli government used the anniversary to emphasize the courage of the Jewish soldier in wartime, it must also be noted that, while they acknowledged the suffering of Jews during the Holocaust, none of the other countries celebrating the fall of the Third Reich *ever* mentioned Jewish soldiers or partisans who also died during the conflict; an unusual omission during an event commemorating the defeat of the Jews' main enemies.

And so, the Days of Remembrance continued, from one corner of the world to another. In America, Britain, France and other democratic nations, the few surviving veterans of the war attended various ceremonies and toasted the fall of Nazi Germany, merging this celebration with new 21st century pleas for tolerance and inclusion. Here, we have a good example of various governments using a solemn occasion of decades past, such as that of the end of World War II in Europe, to not only condemn the barbarity of National Socialism, but also to further their own political and social agendas in the present day. Certainly, these dramatic ceremonies were as much a loud crowing of the Victors as they were a heartfelt and completely

Introduction 3

justified condemnation of the Vanquished. In fact, on most of the planet, and even in places where elections were nonexistent and iron-fisted rule was the order of the day, it was a given that Nazism was seen as a plague on mankind; an oppressive system based on a fantasy of racial superiority that promoted genocide of all those considered "inferior" and ruthless extermination of all perceived enemies of the regime.

Indeed, if this is the way politicians in these countries commented on the specter of Nazism in their various speeches and pronouncements in the 21st century, one can only imagine how the film industries of these nations portrayed the Third Reich and their numerous crimes against humanity on screen over the past ninety years.

Certainly, Nazis would continue to be the all-purpose villains on international movie screens for decades after the collapse of the Third Reich. From Europe to Latin America, from Asia to the United States, Canada and even Mexico, those who served the National Socialist system would pop up as villains in everything from espionage films to social dramas, their appearances recalling a history of brutality seldom seen in the 20th century. It was a given that Hollywood and most other filmmakers would use these figures of history as bigots and sadists whose malevolent presence always gave our heroes that little extra initiative to fight for truth and justice.

However, there were some nations who, if not exactly following the Nazis' racial doctrines to the letter, *did* have something else in common with them: For instance, their rabid anti–Semitism, along with other examples of mindless bigotry. Perhaps predictably, the only nations *not* celebrating the defeat of Nazi Germany and, by extension, the end of the Holocaust, were the Islamic dictatorships of the Mideast; the same people whose nations had previously harbored escaping Nazi war criminals and had given them sanctuary from Allied justice. As far as what these nations allowed their people to view on-screen, this ignorance of history, and Jewish suffering in particular, would never be more evident than the banning of the landmark Oscar-winning film *Schindler's List*.

According to the *Chicago Sun-Times* on March 3, 1994, a month after the film's U.S. release, Jawad Anani, Jordan's Information Minister, banned the film for allegedly showing "sympathy for the Jewish people." The minister then defensively added that "I issued orders to ban this film before it reaches Jordan. It is my own decision." However, it was obvious from the start that Anani was also very aware of the anti–Semitism of Jordan's royal rulers, King Hussein and Queen Noor, with the banning taking place even as the government toyed with the idea of quietly opening up diplomatic relations with Israel. In nearby Lebanon, authorities moved quickly to confiscate all advertising materials for the film before its planned export to the country. Consequently, even as *Schindler's List* continued to be a box office hit in the United States, Europe and Latin America, Muslim nations closed their doors to any import of the film. Though Islamic governments declared that they found the violence and nudity of the film repugnant, and freely used those reasons as their excuse for banning the film, it was obvious what really lay behind their decision. In their own blunt explanation for why they banned the film, Malaysian censors, echoing the government of Prime Minister Mahathir Mohammad, were quoted in the *New York Times* on April 7, 1994, as saying that *Schindler's List* wrongfully portrayed Jews as "stout-hearted" and "intelligent" and the Germans as "brutal."

The film's main villain, Amon Goethe, seemed to have found a spiritual twin.

At first, naively imagining that the Muslim nations would embrace *Schindler's List* as a comment on the genocide in Bosnia (and by extension, *all* genocides), director Steven Spielberg was shocked at their decision to ban the film. However, to his credit, he called these nations out, declaring to Bernard Weinraub of the *New York Times* in an April 1994 telephone interview that their actions were "rooted in anti–Semitism," and was, in fact, "an attack against Jews." Finally seeing the writing on the wall, his production company, Amblin Entertainment, announced that they had no plans to export the film to Saudi Arabia or Pakistan, places where Jews (as well as Christians, Hindus and homosexuals) were openly treated as inferiors and female empowerment was virtually nonexistent.

Schindler's List would not be the first film about the Third Reich and its various crimes to be controversial, or to inspire different points of view about Nazism from filmmakers, critics and the public around the world. Like the politicians of the various nations mentioned above, Hollywood and other filmmakers used their own artists to depict Nazism as the ultimate evil but also sometimes to further the various agendas of their own governments as well, usually with the end result emphasizing how much better their own political systems were than that of Hitler's Germany. "We spread no sawdust on *our* prison yards," the judge smugly tells the accused Nazi spies after sentencing them to "lenient" terms at the end of *Confessions of a Nazi Spy*.

Needless to say, during the 1930s and early '40s, off in merry old *Deutschland*, the Nazis used the German film industry to portray themselves as flawless gods and tolerated no other viewpoints during their 12-year reign (from the rise of Adolf Hitler to the chancellorship of Germany in January 1933 to the government's fall in the spring of 1945). During the 1930s and into the war years, German filmmakers, all under the direct orders of Reich Minister for Propaganda and Enlightenment Dr. Joseph Goebbels, would make sure that the phrase *Germany Über Alles* was going to be taken literally; from *Triumph of the Will* to *The Eternal Jew*, from *Ohm Kruger* to *Jew Süss*, from euphemism to blatant attack (albeit that blatant attacks were a cinematic approach Goebbels did not approve of), Nazi filmmakers praised the tenets of nationalism and racial superiority and condemned their enemies both within its borders and without (Britain, democracy, "International Jewry," etc.). To the Nazi filmmakers under Goebbels, arrogance, bullying and racial and international domination by Germans (and, if these films were set in past centuries, Prussians, Bavarians and various other Germanic states pre-unification) were seen as positive traits, with the "Aryan race" being threatened by countless enemies whose perfidy and bottomless cruelty must be fought by our Master Race heroes.

However, Hollywood had a slightly different take on Nazi Germany from the early 1930s to around 1939, but basically it came down to this: They ignored them. Or at least they ignored Nazi barbarism to the point of absurdity. It was indeed sad but true that, from the early 1930s on, the heads of the major studios, most of whom were Jewish, shockingly continued to cater to the Nazis' whims so that they could keep dealing with the lucrative German film market. For right up to 1939, months after the anti–Semitic pogrom known as *Kristallnacht* on November 9, 1938, the Hollywood moguls nervously kept the ties open to Germany if only in the forlorn hope that Hitler and the Nazis would eventually go and a more democratic and tolerant government would soon take control. This rather pathetic naïveté coming from producers whose people were usually sensitive to the scourge of totalitarian regimes only revealed the ignorance most of the world seemed to have of the Nazi Way. For even in a cultured nation like Germany, the Nazis stopped for no one; nor were they *ever* going to compromise, tolerate or accept anyone else's opinions but their own (for that matter, neither would Communists or Islamists).

Emphasizing this strident self-viewpoint, the Nazis had their very own Hollywood spokesman who pressured the moguls into listening to their complaints, as well as acting on them. In fact, it was because of German complaints of how they were portrayed on screen, many of which were filed by the Nazi consul general Dr. Georg Gyssling (whose offices were based in Los Angeles), that the studios cancelled projects that would have either attacked Nazi Germany or at least depicted it in a bad light. Sometimes backed by the anti–Semitic Joseph I. Breen and his Production Code office, Gyssling was able to bully the Jewish filmmakers (and even the *goyish* Darryl F. Zanuck at 20th Century–Fox) into kowtowing to German demands to withhold anything in their films that would be considered even the slightest criticism of the New Order. Appeasement in Washington and Europe was therefore now complemented by appeasement by the movers and shakers of the world's film capital.

Under Article 10 of the Code, entitled "National Feelings," the rule stipulated that "The history, institutions, prominent people and citizenry of all nations shall be treated fairly." And so, according to the Breen office's version of "fairness," no nation on the planet, which apparently included Nazi Germany, could be accused of oppression or brutality of its own people or anyone else by any Hollywood studio which had signed on to the Code. This rule, coupled with the moguls' almost neurotic desire to keep a fascist Germany as a business partner, became, to many righteous people, a kind of cinematic appeasement that would symbolize Hollywood's traditional reluctance to take a stand.

However, after Goebbels banned all Hollywood films by 1939 (films privately admired by both himself and Hitler) because of the involvement of too many Jewish artists, the moguls took a different tack. Belatedly taking note of the world's rage (the non–Islamic world anyway) over Nazi outrages like *Kristallnacht*, Hollywood's Jewish studio heads started to make anti–Nazi films, ignoring the increasingly shrill complaints of the previously bellicose Dr. Georg Gyssling. Certainly, if one wanted to make a detailed list of those studios who still dealt with Nazi Germany, one wouldn't have to dig too deep. It seems that out of the major studios who continued to deal with the Nazis into 1938, Paramount, 20th Century–Fox and Louie Mayer's MGM still sold films to Germany, with Warners admirably severing relations with them back in the early 1930s when the Jewish manager of their Berlin office was chased down and beaten to death by Nazi thugs. Soon after, Harry Cohn's Columbia would also sever ties to Germany, with United Artists and, in 1937, Universal, following suit. After Pearl Harbor and the Nazi declaration of war on the United States, with the backing of the Roosevelt administration, the cinematic depictions of "the New Germany" took a 180-degree turn. In early 1941, director William Wyler was ordered by Mayer to back off on attacking Germany in his latest film project, *Mrs. Miniver*. Yet just a few months later, the now-humbled mogul rescinded the order, telling the helmsman he didn't care *how* much he attacked Germany. This view would be taken up with great enthusiasm all through the war years. Attacking the Nazi system of government in Warners' *Confessions of a Nazi Spy* in 1939 would soon become an all-out call for destroying Nazi Germany and all its leaders by 1942, and continue in the same vein for the next three years until victory was achieved in the spring of '45.

And so it was that Hollywood took a stand—though typically, it was half-assed. The film industry would portray Nazism as an enemy to be destroyed, the foe of democracy and freedom and the Rights of Man. Unfortunately, this attack on National Socialism would neglect to mention their chief victims. Indeed, all through the war years (and many years after that), Hollywood's Jewish moguls would ignore the sufferings of their own people and, in collusion with the anti–Semitic Breen office, make Jews disappear from the screen in much the same way the Nazis airbrushed out of view the past contributions of Jews to German society all through their reign. However, in an example of equal-opportunity neglect, the producers also made sure that any references to the mass murder of Slavs, Gypsies and homosexuals (this last group never *once* mentioned throughout all the years of Breen's Production Code office) were also missing from Hollywood's usual cinematic condemnations of Nazism. Indeed, in wartime films like *Hitler's Children* and *Hangmen Also Die*, you'd think that every country occupied by the Nazis was populated only by straight, non-ethnic Christians.

However, there were some antidotes to this ostrich-like ignorance. Paramount's *The Hitler Gang* of 1944 freely showed the rising Nazi Party using Jews as a scapegoat to Germany's economic problems; Chaplin's *The Great Dictator* showed, even in a comic way (if such a thing was possible), Nazi persecution of the Jews, despite the fact that the fictional villain was called "Hynkel," and he was dictator of "Tomania"; and Leo McCarey's *Once Upon a Honeymoon* showed compassion for its persecuted Jewish characters in an otherwise sharp comedic attack on Nazism.

Perhaps because the Nazis were such extreme and dangerous characters in real-life, trying to depict their penchant for brutality on American screens pushed Production Code dictates to the limit. Indeed, only our own native gangsters came close to depicting the Nazis' violence on screen, yet even *they* were never shown to be as cruel as Hitler's Swastika-wearing thugs. As the years passed, the image of the Nazi storm trooper evolved into not only a universally hated figure but a cultural icon whose presence made its way to hundreds of movies.

Filmmakers came up with a wide variety of depictions, portrayals, euphemisms, references, subtle attacks and out-and-out caricatures of the Nazis and their barbarities that still endure to this day. There are the clichéd villains of Hollywood's *Casablanca*, *All Through the Night* and *Mrs. Miniver*; the schlocky mad scientists of *She Demons*, *The Frozen Dead*, *Shock Waves* and *They Saved Hitler's Brain*; the based-on-history mass murderers of *Hitler's Madman*, *The Hitler Gang* and *Operation Eichmann*; the coming plague of evil in films set before the war like *The Mortal Storm*, *Ship of Fools* and *Cabaret*; the heroic saviors of their nation in *Triumph of the Will* and *The Eternal Jew*; a shadowy horror in *Address Unknown* and *Strange Holiday*; the euphemistic bloodsuckers opposite the real ones in the wartime-set *Son of Dracula* and *Return of the Vampire*; the all-consuming soldiers of evil in Soviet films like *Professor Mamlock* and *The Fall of Berlin*; the barbarians whose rise was helped along by organized religion and big business in East Germany's *Council of the Gods* and *The Gleiwitz Case*; the sympathetic soldiers and sailors of *A Time to Love and a Time to Die*, *The Sea Chase* and *The Enemy Below*; the corrupting influence perverting formerly good characters in *Apt Pupil* and *Swing Kids*; the twisted perverts of *The Damned* and *SS Girls*; the psychotic serial killers opposite the mass murderers of the Nazi system in *The Lost One* and *The Night of the Generals*; the genocidal maniacs of *Schindler's List*; and the what-if historical fantasies of *The Great Dictator*, *The Magic Face* and *The Hindenburg*.

For more than eighty years, we have seen the many faces of the Third Reich on screen, in documentaries, newsreels, and especially fictional stories ranging from comedies and musicals to war films, horror and science fiction (and even westerns!). A great many of these films comment as much about the filmmakers and the nation the film originated as much as they do Nazism itself. They also comment on the times these films were made, from the 1930s to the present, as National Socialism evolved from its infancy as a fledgling party of crackpots and fanatics to a fully entrenched fascist government to a postwar warning from history. Hollywood and other filmmakers would use the image of the brutal Nazi as an all-purpose villain in escapist adventures set during and after the war; but just as often use him to attack the evil he symbolized, and by extension, the forces within humanity that would cause them to act as if others were less than human.

In the following pages, you will see how various nations depicted the ultimate evil to befall the 20th century, from its inception to the present day. I reveal the background of many of these productions through studio files, internet sources, the works of noted historians of both film and World War II, and quotations from several novels and plays that were the bases of the various films featuring Nazi characters. You will see how the political systems of various governments depicted National Socialism and the enormous influence they had in terms of script, direction and even casting. Some productions courted controversy behind the scenes, with the hot topic of the revelation of Nazi atrocities leading to discord behind the cameras. In the case of the German films of the Nazi era, sometimes the perceived disloyalties of those involved led some to an early and tragic end.

Not only will you read about the Nazis' regard for cinema, as exemplified by Adolf Hitler and his propaganda minister Joseph Goebbels, but the off-screen activities of other notorious figures, such as Josef Stalin, Heinrich Himmler, Reinhard Heydrich, Ernst Röhm, Adolf Eichmann and Joseph Mengele, and how their own lives inspired the making of some of these films. In the world of entertainment in both Hollywood and Europe, you will read about not only cinema icons like Orson Welles, Fritz Lang, Marlene Dietrich, Peter Lorre, Conrad Veidt, Leni Riefenstahl and Emil Jannings, but underrated refugee filmmakers like Frank Wisbar, Robert Siodmak, Douglas Sirk and Anatole Litvak, who had their own axes to grind against the Third Reich. On the enemy side, I also go into the various works and ultimate fates of those artists who provided their talents, willingly or not, to the Nazi propaganda effort on film: people like Ferdinand Marian, Veit Harlan, Werner Krauss, Hans Albers and (again) Emil Jannings.

Not forgotten will be an examination of rarely-known Bs: films like *The Magic Face, The Strange Death of Adolf Hitler, The Hitler Gang, Address Unknown* and *Hitler's Madman*; as well as schlock "classics" like *She Demons, The Frozen Dead* and *The Boys from Brazil*.

For myself, perhaps the barbarities of the Third Reich resonate with me far more personally than with most people. My own mother and father were survivors of Nazi concentration camps, and most of their families, especially the older ones (including both sets of my grandparents) perished during the Holocaust. For me, this book is not so much a labor of love, as an act of remembrance, and a tribute to their sacrifice.

In the following pages, you will read not only how a cultured nation like Germany could elect a government of genocidal killers, but how the cinematic world viewed these killers in their various guises and at various times. And more to the point, you will see how these films became not only escapist entertainment but historical documents to consult again and again, and become a constant reminder to all of us that the civilized world allowed this evil to go as far as it did.

I

INFECTION (1929–1937)
Weimar-era filmmaking and the disease taking root in Germany

> "You Nazis are like the microbes of some dreaded disease…"
> —Peter (Anton Wolbrook), *The 49th Parallel*

There are those in the world of cinema who look back at the years of the Weimar Republic, praise all their classic films and instantly pigeonhole them as prophetic cinematic attacks on the Third Reich.

Even a few years ago, in a retrospective at the Museum of Modern Art titled *Weimar Cinema, 1919–1933: Daydreams & Nightmares* that was held from November 17, 2010, to March 7, 2011, the almost neurotic need to link the silent films of Fritz Lang, F.W. Murnau and G.W. Pabst to the rise of Nazism was all-too obvious. In the program advertising the films to the public, MoMA proclaimed: "The extensive program reaches beyond the standard view of Weimar cinema—which sees its tropes of madmen, evil geniuses, pagan forces, and schizophrenic behavior as dark harbingers of Hitler—by adding another perspective: that of the popular German cinema of the period."

Of course, this neglects to explain America's own attraction to "madmen, evil geniuses and pagan forces" as Hollywood churned out the sometimes grotesque material associated with Lon Chaney, Sr., or our obsession with the rising genre of gangster films (with Chaney sometimes playing both gangster *and* monster). Perhaps this perspective is colored by the then-current status of specific combatants in the recent Great War. Chaney's mutilated, yet soulful, creations were borne of a victorious America; the obsessive and chaotic figures of Cesare the Sleepwalker, Nosferatu and Dr. Mabuse were creatures of a defeated Germany.

Still, the logic was stretched a little *too* far. Was Cesare a symbol of National Socialism's zombie-like obedience to a Führer? Was Nosferatu a symbol of the bloodsucking plague of National Socialism? Were Orlac's murderous hands the unwitting tool for carrying out the will of the New Order?

German writer Heinrich Mann (older brother of the more famous Thomas Mann) certainly had no illusions about the growing Nazi menace. An author who attacked Germany's sacred cows decades before the Nazis came to power, Mann's work almost seemed to be preparing his fellow countrymen, as well as those outside Germany, for the evil to come.

Like many a socialist who attacked the rich and powerful, Mann was the son of a rich and powerful man; in this case, grain merchant and Senator Thomas Johann Heinrich Mann. Born in Lübeck, Germany, on March 27, 1871, Heinrich would become a writer of essays at 20 and publish his first novel at 22. After his father's death, he, his mother and the rest of the Mann clan moved to Munich, and finally to Berlin, the hub of the German literary community. His father's inheritance helped make him financially independent as his career grew, first as an essayist, then as an author and editor. Not having to work for a living, his books, of course, attacked the bourgeois; in this case the movers and shakers of the Second Reich led by Kaiser Wilhelm II, or what today we'd refer to as the "military-industrial complex." Popular with the leftist intelligentsia, but hated by those in the Kaiser's government, Mann would take flight to Italy, France and Switzerland. Without the Kaiser's bluenoses looking over his shoulder, voluntary exile only whetted his taste for literary controversy.

Then came his most famous novel in 1904 (some sources say '05): *Professor Unrat*, literal translation: Professor Garbage (or, if you will, a pun on a German word for excrement); that's when the novel was not being called Professor U*nrath*, Small-Town Tyrant. The central character was a rather curt and misogynist schoolmaster in a small German village. A no-woman man, Unrat (or Un*rath*) fairly detests the opposite sex and instead finds comfort in *control*, and surrounding himself with monotonous, yet razor-edged, precise routines timed practically down to the second: rising from bed, traveling to school, arriving there, and then teaching the sometimes unruly German youth of the early 20th century, he goes about his status quo existence with all the passion of a Krupp factory Bessemer converter. Everything works great for the basically good but nasty professor, until some of his charges show up late for class, thus causing the headmaster to find the source of their late-night carousing. Since the students are freely displaying a postcard with a scantily clad woman on it, a scantily-clad woman who is actually no fantasy, but one who really exists and is singing at a dive not too far from the school. Enter trampy nightclub singer Rosa Frohlich, a woman who makes Sally Bowles look like Sister Bertrille. In record time, the woman-hating professor is himself staying out late and cavorting with Rosa and her sleazy friends. Before you can sing *Falling in Love Again*, Unrat (or *Unrath*) abandons his profession and all he loves (or what passes for it) to be with Rosa, thereby losing his home, his job, and pretty soon, his mind.

The novel was seen then, as it is now, as a slam at the bourgeois, with Mann rather cruelly stating that the professor, a pillar of middle-class respectability and prestige, deserves his corruption and painful downfall, a downfall helped along by society's have-not underclass. Though written at the beginning of the 20th century, in Mann's novel we see the seeds of class conflict and anti-authoritarianism that would be popular in the cinema of the Weimar years. However, Mann, like his contemporaries, had no crystal ball; they could not see into the future, where thousands of goose-stepping Unraths would appear wearing swastika armbands and murder literally millions all for the sake of control, from allowing only the most perfect human beings to exist, right down to making the trains run on time.

Though keeping the novel's basic theme, Ufa, Germany's premier film producers during the Weimar period and into the Hitler era, made several changes to the story before they put it on celluloid. Though seen as a classic today, Fritz Lang's *Metropolis* (and its huge budget building cities of the future) practically bankrupted the studio. The resulting turmoil in the boardrooms of Ufa paved the way for the elevation of right-wing financier Alfred Hugenberg as a principal owner of the firm. Certainly it's hard to mention the topic of Nazism and the

I. Infection (1929–1937)

men who supported it during its rise without focusing on the career of Alfred Hugenberg, a former government official and major power-broker who harbored a love for authoritarianism decades before the Nazi Party was even formed.

Already an experienced economist and president of several agricultural societies (as well as being an official in the Prussian Ministry of Finance), in 1909, Hugenberg entered the world of business as chairman of the supervisory board of Krupp Steel. As chairman of the most powerful steel manufacturer in the world (and in later years, major financial backer and supplier of Hitler's war machine), Hugenberg strengthened the Krupp dynasty and helped build the steel giant into a major backroom power-broker in the Kaiser's government, making him, more or less, the same type of German success story Heinrich Mann had been attacking in his novel, *Der Untertan* (in English: *The Patrioteer*; filmed in East Germany in 1951 as *Man of Straw*). After his acquisition of several newspapers, magazines and telecommunication companies, these various firms would, of course, produce the news or inform the public in the *exact* manner Alfred Hugenberg wanted them to. Indeed, it was said that Hugenberg's influence in Germany's mass media was due to the public's "taste for the mediocre, their lack of civic courage, their intellectual dullness, and their gullibility."[1] With unerring purpose and complete confidence in his cause, he used these corporations as tools to call for the destruction of the democratically elected Weimar Republic.

Politically a liberal in his early years, he turned radically right-wing by the time of Germany's entry into World War I. A leading light of the rightist Fatherland Party, Hugenberg openly called for German territorial expansion and an increase in anti–Semitic policies. Like many nationalists, Hugenberg was violently opposed to the Treaty of Versailles and the Young Plan (named after American financier Owen D. Young), which Germany approved of in a referendum in 1929. A successor to the Dawes Plan of 1924, the Young Plan was a *slight* reduction of the payments of war reparations Germany owed the victorious Allies after World War I, some 132 *billion* gold marks reduced by only 20 percent (or 8 billion American dollars in 1929; 110 billion dollars in 2016). Needless to say, with the backing of militarists like former war commander Paul von Hindenburg, DNVP chairman Alfred Hugenberg, and a rising politician named Adolf Hitler, the German government paid no more than 8 percent of its reparations to the Allies for the horrors it had brought onto the world. By 1933, with Hitler the newly installed German chancellor, the agreement would be declared null and void.

In March 1927, with Ufa studios owing huge sums to Hollywood's Paramount and MGM for financially assisting them in the 1920s (especially weathering the costs of Fritz Lang's usually over-produced films, not counting the expensive *Metropolis*), Hugenberg took over Ufa, not only to save the company from financial ruin, but to make sure that the films they produced extolled Truth, Justice and the German Way. Or, as Hugenberg himself declared when he took over the reins of Ufa, he promised to "preserve for the national outlook this German cultural institution that has become so valuable."[2]

Working fast, Hugenberg and his partners bought up all the stock Paramount and MGM had in Ufa, giving the autocratic media baron a major voice in any direction the studio would take. In a few short years, Hugenberg would not only consolidate his media empire, with Ufa being a major jewel in his crown, but he would be one of the Nazis' most important backers, excusing their excesses and turning their brutalities into acts of heroism on screen and in print. This included granting (albeit reluctantly) Nazi control of all newsreel coverage, making SA atrocities look like business as usual in the New Germany. "He was (a) hopelessly reactionary and politically ambitious magnate," said film historian Peter Gay, "animated by insatiable political passions and hatreds masquerading as convictions."[3] Gradually, Jewish employees of Ufa soon found themselves out of a job as massive firings took place under Hugenberg's reign.

Suddenly, a film version of a novel attacking the bourgeois looked like a pretty sour proposition to newly minted board members seeking to curry favor with their strident new company chairman. There was further dissension when Hugenberg took a second look at the film contracts and discovered that *Professor Unrat* (or *Unrath*) was written by leftwing author Heinrich Mann. The media mogul thought he was getting *Thomas* Mann, the more popular Mann brother who had so recently won the Nobel Prize for literature in 1929. Talented Ufa chief Erich Pommer quickly moved to calm down Hugenberg enough to stop him from cancelling the whole project. To fulfill German and Hollywood star Emil Jannings' commitment to Ufa, the media baron authorized the purchase of Mann's 1905 novel, obviously not fully understanding just what he had purchased; or for that matter which author's work he was buying.

Looking back on the subject of the casting of Lola-Lola with some hindsight, perhaps the strangest candidate for the part was a woman who would soon become an icon for film propaganda, as well as a major reason why National Socialism became an acceptable form of government and way of life for millions of Germans. In 1930, Leni Riefenstahl was a veteran film actress who had made her debut in 1926 as a dancer in a film whose title could be seen as a harbinger for the Nazis' pursuit of physical perfection: *Ways to Strength and Beauty*. Riefenstahl's career as a starlet in Weimar Berlin was not going any further than that of dozens of ingénues haunting studios like Ufa; that is, until she met geologist/filmmaker Dr. Arnold Fanck. A natural explorer and lover of nature, Fanck was the father of the uniquely German film subgenre known as the Mountain-Climbing Film (In Quentin Tarantino's *Django Unchained*, Christoph Waitz' bounty hunter explains that in German folklore, there's going to be at least *some* mention of a mountain!). A tall, gangling dark-blonde with a perpetual stern look on her face to hide the fact that she was not a very expressive actress, the Berlin-born Riefenstahl had made half a dozen or so of these mountain-climbing films all through the late 1920s silent period and right into the early talkies. Her roles in these rural works rarely changed in the four years before the casting calls went out for *Der blaue Engel* (*The Blue Angel*). Riefenstahl played either a virginal mountain-climbing shepherdess, a virginal mountain-climbing skier or, in a stretch, a virginal mountain-climbing mountain-climber. Under the guidance of Dr. Fanck, the athletic Riefenstahl, doing most of her own stunts, climbed mountains, forded streams and basically played the symbolic unattainable virginal girl of the wilderness that our handsome Aryan hero desires from afar. And though many of these films were excellently shot by Dr. Fanck, an actress wasn't really going to further her career if all she was known for was how well she handled a rope and pulley.

That Leni Riefenstahl *never* got over the fact that Marlene Dietrich got the prized role and not herself, was obvious. What seemed more pernicious, however, was her implacable jealousy of the woman whom she always felt usurped her rightful place as a star in the Hollywood firmament. This borderline hatred included the usual spreading of nasty stories decades after events took place. There exists documentary footage, with interviews of the actress/director claiming that Dietrich had her banned from the set. She also ridiculously insisted that director Josef von Sternberg was paying more attention to *her* rather than Marlene, a fantasy bordering on mania. Of course, gleefully outliving everyone else who could disprove her allegations, Riefenstahl was able to spin any self-serving, outlandish tale she wanted, with Dietrich being a major target of her attacks.

Yet in the years to come, there might have been more to the iconic director's enmity than mere jealousy over lost stardom or a lost opportunity with a would-be lover. Leni Riefenstahl's image was that of a scrubbed, clean Teutonic girl of nature, whose whole life seemed to exist in a never-never land of tall mountains, lush forests and deep valleys. Marlene Dietrich's screen image would forever be (with only slight variations) that of the cabaret-singing, world-weary, vulgar and slutty everywoman who'd seen too much, loved too much and lived a life surrounded by cigarette smoke, a constant flow of liquor and numerous one-night stands in a dog-eat-dog world where (to quote Mae West) goodness had nothing to do with it. The two actresses, one a director, the other a singer, were more than just rivals whose careers happened to be on the rise in a Weimar-era/pre–Nazi Germany. The two artists symbolized the duality in the screen image of German women, and perhaps *all* Germans as a dictatorship took hold and the country headed for war and disaster for the second time in less than three decades.

See what the boys in the back room will have: Marlene Dietrich (in top hat, with unknown extras) in *The Blue Angel*, one of the Weimar Republic's greatest films. In later years, the singer/actress would become an implacable enemy of Nazi Germany.

Indeed, it would be the supreme irony that it was Marlene Dietrich, the woman who personified the slutty, imperfect, world-weary whore on international screens who would become, due to her own basic decency, an active and enthusiastic supporter of America's "arsenal of democracy." Though somewhat of a perfectionist herself, Marlene saw only trouble when the Nazis graduated from street brawls and muscled their way into the *Reichstag*. A bisexual, she had many gay and Jewish friends and knew what lay in store for them if Hitler took control of Germany. Added to this rage against National Socialism, one can only imagine how Marlene must have felt when she discovered that her own sister was a Nazi as well, a discovery that caused her to cut off all ties with her sibling and angrily deny her sister's existence to the end of her days (including her heated denials, while never being seen on-camera, in Maximilian Schell's fascinating documentary, *Marlene*).

When *The Blue Angel* was released, as everyone knew, it made a huge star of Dietrich, and Paramount signed her to a long-term contract; though not all were pleased with Marlene's well-deserved stardom. Invited by Erich Pommer to a screening of the film in Nice, Heinrich Mann was asked what he thought of it. Rather bitterly, the aging socialist author remarked that posterity would now remember him only "because of the naked thighs of Miss Dietrich."[4]

Emil Jannings hated her by now and, partly because of the attention he felt she was stealing from him, spitefully left Paramount and returned to Germany to make films. As National Socialism took hold, he would become, like Dietrich's catty, mountain-climbing rival, a major backer of the Totalitarian Way, starring in propaganda films whose only consistent themes were the beauties of National Socialism and a bitter condemnation of everything else, particularly World Jewry and the United Kingdom.

As for Leni Riefenstahl, the fame she envisioned for herself would be coming to her in just a few short years. And thanks to her, one of the most evil regimes on the planet was given a cinematic showcase with which to sell itself and its corrupt ideas to the world.

But the Nazis weren't in yet; and while the Weimar Republic tottered between anarchy and dictatorship, a German author's greatest work would spark a bitter controversy between the forces of free expression and those of fascist censorship.

"Within ten minutes, the cinema was a madhouse!"[5] So proclaimed Dr. Joseph Goebbels in his diary for the night of December 5, 1930. The reason for the future propaganda minister's euphoria was due to the day's events at a movie house in Berlin then showing a recently imported American film; said film would win awards and prizes all over the world, including the Academy Award for Best Picture; the reason said venue was a "madhouse" was due to the violence and chaos he himself helped to inspire.

All Quiet on the Western Front was not the first antiwar film, but it became, up to that time, the most powerful. Though the screenplay was written by (including adaptations and additional dialogue) playwright Maxwell Anderson, Del Andrews and silent screen veteran C. Gardner Sullivan, with uncredited work by director Lewis Milestone, the work was based on a novel by a German veteran of the "Great War" named Erich Maria Remarque.

Born Erich Paul Remark in Osnabrück, Germany on June 22, 1898, Remarque had had his original French name changed to "Remark" by his grandfather. After attaining adulthood, Erich would return the spelling of his last name back to the French version and dispense with his middle name of "Paul" and adopt his mother's middle name "Maria" as his own. Conscripted into the German army in 1916, at the age of 18, Erich's army experiences were basically

Fascist-in-waiting: Emil Jannings as the strident teacher who is brought down by Marlene Dietrich's cabaret singer in *The Blue Angel*. Though written after the turn of the century, Heinrich Mann's novel could have been seen as a warning against totalitarianism. Jannings himself would later become a major star of Nazi cinema.

unremarkable until he was transferred to the Western Front ten days before his 19th birthday. From all reports he fought bravely until a French artillery barrage left him with shrapnel wounds in the left leg, right arm and neck. He would spend the rest of the war recuperating in a German military hospital.

He had written novels all through the 1920s, without finding any publishers, until 1929 (some say 1928) when his first novel, *All Quiet on the Western Front*, was published. It quickly became an international bestseller, with Hollywood's Universal Pictures quickly purchasing the film rights. In a meeting with the author, Lewis Milestone promised him that the film version would retain the novel's antiwar tone, as well as its bitterness against the Kaiser and other German militarists. In fact, Universal president Carl Laemmle, a German Jew who fought his way up from haberdasher and nickelodeon owner to movie mogul, also insisted upon this approach. Added to this dedication to realism was the decision to keep out any romantic interludes, as well as make the entire film without music so that neither would distract audiences from its a 16ntiwar theme.

It premiered in Los Angeles on April 21, 1930, and then opened in New York City eight days later; after it "opened wide" on August 24, it became a box office smash. Its commercial and critical success was indeed unusual for a film with such a depressing theme, but it obviously touched a nerve with war-weary audiences around the world. With nothing to show for their "victory" but packed cemeteries, the democracies now also had to deal with a worldwide Depression, with once heroic war veterans now having to sell apples on street corners a little over a decade after their triumphs on the battlefield.

However, before the film could be exported to Germany, Carl Laemmle, Sr., and Jr., and other Universal brass expected trouble. Laemmle Sr. knew full-well the German character more than anyone in Hollywood, having spent much of his life there as both a victim of anti–Semitism and a man closely acquainted with German militarism and its accompanying arrogance and bullheadedness. Playing *All Quiet on the Western Front* to universal (no pun intended) acclaim for audiences in America, England and France was one thing, but how would *the losers* take it?

Before its targeted export to Berlin in early December, the Laemmles got in touch with the German general consul in San Francisco, Baron Otto von Hentig, and invited the diplomat over to Universal City for a private screening of the film. Thanks to the input of Baron von Hentig and the German chargé d'affaires in Washington, certain scenes were cut and others were trimmed for a special edition of *All Quiet* to be shown to German audiences only. Then, on November 22, the film was finally approved by the German censorship office. The new German-approved version had some noticeable differences from the version viewed by the victors. For one thing, the antiwar rhetoric was toned down, as well as the hardships of trench warfare, with the mud, grime, poor food and disgusting sanitation facilities sliced out of the film. But the film's most controversial cut was a smattering of dialogue directly indicting the Kaiser for the war. As the troops are having a breather between French bombardments, the subject comes up on who started the war in the first place. At first, the soldiers are all too ready to lay the blame on the Allies. Then, one of the men comes up with a truly innovative answer:

1st Soldier: I think the Kaiser wanted a war.
2nd Soldier: I don't see that. The Kaiser's got everything he needs.
1st Soldier: Well, he never had a war before. Every full-grown emperor needs one war to make him famous. Why, that's history![6]

So there it was. A little too simplistic perhaps, but plain as the spike on a junker's helmet. Certainly, the explanation circumvents German militarist tradition (with a soldier like General Paul von Hindenburg alone having left his family and gone off to a Prussian military academy at the tender age of 11); as well as the assassination of Archduke Franz Ferdinand and the all-too-real ethnic and religious hatreds between Austria-Hungary and Serbia that allowed the various combatants to use the conflict for territorial gain and imperialist expansion.

Still, when the edited film finally premiered at Berlin's *Mozartsaal* (Mozart Hall) on December 4, 1930, the reaction was totally unexpected, even by Universal officials and Hollywood journalists scattered throughout the audience. Unlike the thunderous applause of audiences at practically every showing of the film in America, France, England and other free nations, the Berlin audience was "too stirred and moved to either disapprove or applaud," according to the unnamed reviewer in the December 12 issue of *Variety*.[7] After remaining seated for what seemed like an eternity, they finally roused themselves out of their seats and silently filed out of the theater, reportedly too stunned to speak. Seeing this reaction as wholesale approval of the film, a reporter for *Film Daily* wired back his editor in New York on December 11, 1930, that "[I]t does not appear likely that any untoward demonstrations will result."

That's what *he* thought.

The next day was quite different. The Berlin police who had been expecting trouble were curiously missing-in-action the next day when Joseph Goebbels and a platoon of SA men showed up at the Mozart Hall on December 5. It is said that the Nazis had bought some 300 tickets for a showing of *All Quiet on the Western Front* just so they could interrupt the showing (ironically providing the film, and its makers, a good-sized profit). Goebbels stood up and cried out *"Judenfilm!"* Standing in the balcony (the egomaniacal Goebbels didn't seem the type to merely take a seat in the orchestra), he proclaimed again *"Judenfilm!"* which, of course, needs no translation. The storm troopers quickly pelted the audience with stink bombs and sneezing powder; they released mice throughout the theater and papered the house with pro–Nazi leaflets; except for the leaflets and the stink bombs, they used every means of attack that would later be used on screen by the Three Stooges. Still, some of the chaos was emphatically *not* amusing, such as the physical assault on certain members of the audience the attacking Nazis had decided *looked* Jewish. "The police are powerless!" crowed Goebbels in his diary that night. "The embittered masses are violently against the Jews,"[8] he claimed, without noting that the "embittered masses" were mostly burly, brown-shirted thugs of the SA who had actually bought tickets.

The reaction stunned Carl Laemmle. He was aware of German bullheadedness in accepting blame for the prosecution of the war, but he did not expect a wave of violence in a civilized theater in cultured Berlin during the tenuous reign of the Weimar Republic, much of that violence obviously triggered by anti–Semitism. Even the canny Laemmles, as well as many of the Jewish officials at Universal, as well as much of Hollywood in general, had not yet come to terms with the phenomenon of Nazism. No political movement up to that time, with the possible exception of Fascist Italy and Imperial Japan, had conducted themselves like murderous gangsters (Stalin's Russia and the Islamic nations also showed contempt for democracy, but unlike the fascists, they usually committed their atrocities quietly, out of the world's view).

It was said that Carl Laemmle was a fighter, a canny, feisty little man who fought the odds and rose to a position of prominence in the entertainment industry, and who didn't take enemies lightly. He was one of the leaders of the rebellious movie moguls who fought like demons against Thomas Edison and his infamous Trust which sent goons to harass film production on the East Coast; this, of course, caused many of them to set up shop in sunny Southern California, with the father of Universal Pictures being one of the first to lead the charge. Yet the old man's reputation for courage takes a hit when one calls to mind his reaction to the Nazis' violent attacks on the film. Though he would compassionately take in dozens of German Jews persecuted by the Nazis during the 1930s and give them jobs at his studio,

Laemmle was still hoping against hope that the film would touch his fellow countrymen in his native land. Indeed, they *were* touched, but not in the way he intended.

The next day, the subject of the film was brought up for a contentious debate in the *Reichstag*, with Adolf Hitler being the loudest of the many politicians protesting its showing; he was soon joined by the German Nationalist Party, which was slightly to the *left* of the Nazis. In the days ahead, the SA returned to the Mozart Hall, as well as other venues around the country, bringing along their usual stink bombs, mice, leaflets and psychotic behavior. And soon their loud, bellicose voices were being joined by others. On December 9 the German Federation of Cinema Owners and the main student association of the prestigious University of Berlin attacked the film, though presumably without explosives or hungry rodents. Two days later, five German states submitted petitions to ban the film.

And the reaction was not confined to Germany alone. Upon the release of the film in Vienna on January 7, 1931, a mob of several thousand Nazis attacked the Apollo Theater where the film had just premiered. Though guarded by a cordon of 1500 policemen under the control of the fascist government of Chancellor Engelbert Dollfuss, they were soon overrun by the National Socialists. Detonating stink bombs under seat cushions inside the theater, the Nazis followed up with attacks outside as well, with dozens of vehicles, including several streetcars, being torched by the mob; shop windows were also broken and several mounted policemen were assaulted. All at once the Nazis had caused an uproar that, in later years, could be viewed as just the beginning of the violence. In Germany, the attacks had hit only the nation's Jews; now, thanks to a film that was an international hit, the Nazis' violence was on full display for all the world to see. It frightened many of the Hollywood moguls, with one of the most fearful being Carl Laemmle.

The little fighter who had stood up to adversity did not react with rage to this new attack. His reaction would be tragically typical for the Jewish (and non–Jewish) Hollywood moguls of the coming years. He and others officials at Universal, desperate to save the film and keep up friendly relations with Germany, held meeting after meeting with German censors. Universal promised to cut the film yet again; German censors, soon to wield great power under the coming Nazi regime, held Laemmle's offer in contempt. The studio was willing to do *anything* to have the film play in Germany.

The negotiations dragged on between the studio and the German Foreign Office, with the latter taking their sweet time and in no hurry to approve a film they had such disdain for; indeed, they seemed to enjoy Laemmle's misery and desperation. Then, in August 1931, after Universal had made many, *many* cuts to the film, the Foreign Office finally agreed to show the film in Germany; that is, under *one* condition: All the branches of Universal Pictures in every part of the world where the studio had exchanges would have to make the *exact same cuts* to every copy of the film shipped to these branches. For Laemmle and his associates who believed passionately in the film's antiwar message, it was a bitter pill to swallow. The studio had originally just deleted offending sequences in Germany alone; *now*, Laemmle's powerful, award-winning antiwar masterpiece would be gutted, not only in Germany, but in every part of the world where German consulate officials could personally go to the theater and check that the cuts were made; if there were any shenanigans, they could quickly report back to the Foreign Office that the deal was off. Needless to say, many of the nations this newly edited version played in included the democracies that had beaten Germany so soundly years before. *All Quiet on the Western Front* now became far quieter than originally planned.

And even *this* didn't please the Germans, with the Supreme Board of Censors finally banning the film. Of course, this meant that the film was still being shown, but with the draconian cuts insisted upon by the German Foreign Office, the representative of a government which, remember, was *not* yet controlled by the Nazis, indicating Germany's continued refusal to accept blame for a war they helped to start. For the time being anyway, the Nazis, the nationalist street thugs who were growing in popularity, had won the Film War.

Unfortunately, Universal's kowtowing to the German government and its arrogant censors was only the beginning. The disemboweling, and finally, banning of *All Quiet on the Western Front* was the first shot fired in a war Germany maintained against the film industries of all freedom-loving nations, particularly Hollywood, which the soon-to-be-victorious Nazis would view as a haven of Jewish corruption and decadence. Now with the image of Germany at stake, the Nazis threatened a cutoff of all business dealings with the film capital. Unfortunately, the results of all these bellicose threats were all-too predictable: The moguls, most of whom were Jewish, responded meekly and accepted the Germans' demands for cuts to any film deemed to be detrimental to the German character, as well as films which did not follow the precepts of Nazi racial dogma.

However, nine years after its tumultuous debut in Berlin, *All Quiet on the Western Front* would have an interesting afterlife in the same year that saw the armies of both Nazi Germany and the Soviet Union storming into Poland. Re-issued by Universal in 1939, the film now began with a prologue; a narrator honored the memories of the young German soldiers of the First World War and emphasized that they were *not* to be confused with the Nazi barbarians currently overrunning Western Europe. Then, after the ending with Lew Ayres reaching for the butterfly and getting a bullet for his trouble, Universal inserted a clip of the Nazi book-burnings of May 10, 1933, with the same narrator announcing that one of the books thrown into the fire was the controversial antiwar classic written by a brave veteran of the Great War, Erich Maria Remarque.

Since their inception as a political movement, the Nazis had wanted to control both the imagery and the very memory of the First World War, with much selective revisionism in order to stoke Germany's rage for being "stabbed in the back" by homegrown traitors. Though *All Quiet on the Western Front* was indeed a film made by the victors showing the futility of the vanquished to go to war against them (none of the victor nations would dare make an antiwar film showing the futility of *their* soldiers going into battle), the film's export to Germany revealed that the Nazis, the nation's new militarists, were willing to do *anything* to be the true authors of the German image, even if they had to rewrite history to do it.

In the years ahead, now safely residing in Switzerland (and then in 1939, safely residing in Hollywood), Remarque would return to the world of the German soldier in battle, but added to this image would be novels set during the Second World War and a scathing portrait of Nazi barbarity.

Meanwhile, one of Germany's greatest filmmakers would soon have his own problems with those fanatics who shamelessly cried, "*Deutschland über alles!*"

With a filmmaker like Fritz Lang, the theory that his final films made during the Weimar Republic were all cinematic harbingers warning the world of the Nazi terror to come would get its full play mostly from the imperious Lang himself. A liar and fabricator even on his best days, Lang would never challenge film critics and students who saw the child murderer in *M*, the social and economic chaos in *Metropolis*, and especially his 1933 *The Testament of Dr.*

Mabuse, as stern warnings against a Nazi dictatorship. Pertinent to this claim is the following commentary from no less a film historian than the German writer Otto Friedrich in his *Before the Deluge: A Portrait of Berlin in the 1920s*, comparing Peter Lorre's child murderer and those killers who would soon dominate the German government:

> It was indeed a curious misunderstanding, but, in a way, it was not a misunderstanding at all, for some of the most horrifying Nazis of the coming decade were not the brawlers of the SA, but the Peter Lorre figures, neatly respectable, a little effeminate, and driven by uncontrollable demons. In the course of a few years, such men were to take power, and the Nazi regime was to reverse the very meaning of law and order. The criminals were to rule and the innocent were to be punished.

Unfortunately, Friedrich's assertions that the Nazi elite were all like the child murderer in *M* were erroneous to say the least. Unlike Lorre's killer, who was driven to kill by "uncontrollable demons," the Nazis knew *exactly* what they were doing, with a well-organized plan for mass extermination of innocents that made a mockery of those on-screen murderers who killed because "they couldn't help it."

For Fritz Lang, however, Nazi-like callousness and brutal behavior to his own cast and crew were just the perks of power for being a groundbreaking filmmaker. There are dozens of tales of his sadistic cruelty; such as actress Brigitte Helm *really* getting burned on the stake in *Metropolis*, despite Lang's ignoring her distress; or his pushing Peter Lorre down a flight of stairs to make him look appropriately beaten and haggard for his final confession scene in *M*; or the coldblooded ignorance of animal safety which resulted in the deaths of horses in both his German films and his Hollywood westerns; or his use of live ammunition during the many shootouts in *The Testament of Dr. Mabuse*; or his seeming hatred for actors in general, especially women (Henry Fonda detested Lang's treatment of actors, and he came to Gene Tierney's defense when the helmsman called her "a little bitch" on the set of *The Return of Frank James*).

Paramount in the *auteur's* volatile personality, however, was the ability to fabricate stories which elevated his own standing, denigrated those he did not like, and ass-kissed the powers that be, all for the sake of his career. But then, *everyone* in Hollywood did this, back then and especially today. However, unlike proven liars like Howard Hawks and John Ford, Lang could weave a story which emphasized his personal opposition to National Socialism and show what an icon of artistic freedom and political democracy he was, especially since he stopped making films in Germany at the time the Nazis took power.

Film historians and journalists would quote, *ad nauseum*, the story of Lang having a life-changing meeting with Dr. Joseph Goebbels at the Propaganda Minister's office in March 1933; how Goebbels had just banned *the Testament of Dr. Mabuse*; how Goebbels and Hitler *loved Metropolis* and *Die Nibelungen* (a film which, according to Lang allegedly quoting Goebbels, caused Hitler to "break down and weep"[9]); how Goebbels was ready to offer Lang the post of chief of the entire German film industry; and especially how a frightened Lang decided right then and there in Goebbels' office to leave Germany; and inevitably how he left that night by train to Paris with the clothes on his back and little or no money.

Though many film writers would take this story of courage and sacrifice as gospel, other saner folks noticed how little details in Lang's life-changing Escape from Nazi Germany kept changing with each retelling; how the carpet in Goebbels' office kept changing color, how the hands of the big clock outside his office kept going from two to three to four and then back again, how Goebbels' words, including his grand offer, kept changing, though apparently not

I. Infection (1929–1937)

Herr director: Fritz Lang (forefront) was one of Germany's greatest and, unfortunately, most sadistic directors. An out-and-out liar, he would fabricate a tense meeting with Dr. Joseph Goebbels, who would ban his masterpiece, *The Testament of Dr. Mabuse*.

the Propaganda Minister's effusive praise for Lang the Filmmaking Genius ("Your qualities as a filmmaker are so exceptional!"[10] Goebbels gushed, according to Lang); how, after said offer was made, Lang claimed to Goebbels that he was "tickled pink,"[11] and another time that he was "somewhat dazed"; how much Lang was sweating when Goebbels' offer was made (Lang went from "sweating" during one interview to "drenched"[12] in another); or how the amount of the currency Lang had on him when he took his escape train kept changing after conductors punched his passport (another time it was station guards).

Certainly, with a little probing into Lang's career at the time (post-meeting with Dr. G), one will notice that Lang never once relates this story to anyone, including the press, until 1942 or '43, years after establishing himself in Hollywood. The U.S. was now at war with Nazi Germany, and what better way to ingratiate oneself in a new country than to dream up some cock-and-bull story of heroism and courage which demonstrated that you were an early fighter against the nation your new country was now at war with?

The story, first thought to be true, started to come apart when journalists would investigate it decades later. For one thing, Joseph Goebbels, though a liar, hate-monger and all-around rat's ass, was a very detail-oriented man who, more than any other activity, was punctilious about one thing, and that was his Diary. In fact, examining the many volumes of his diaries, at no point in his tome is an important meeting with Fritz Lang ever mentioned; nor, when he did mention Lang, was there any such entry about offering the director the post of czar of the entire Nazi film industry. Nor was Lang's passport ever stamped at all for March of 1933, around the time he told of his fateful encounter with Goebbels and his escape from Germany. In fact, it would be proven that Lang was still residing in Berlin (despite quick trips to Austria, Belgium and England, and finally, a trip to France on June 23) until his passport had a final exit visa stamped on it on July 31, several months *after* his miraculous "escape." In that time, Lang made enormous exchanges of foreign currency, perhaps indicating some kind of permanent move out of Germany, but not the quick clothes-on-his-back desperate flight from the Nazis that was part and parcel of the typical American wartime film, whether directed by Lang or not.

Lang cameraman Fritz Arno Wagner told film historian Gero Gandert about riding in a limousine with the director around the time the offer from Goebbels was allegedly made. According to Wagner, Lang, who had related the offer to his cameraman, suddenly turned to him and asked, "Should I accept?"[13] According to this story, the offer *was* made, but this hardly sounds like the frightened man sweating bullets in Joseph Goebbels' office who decided to flee the country and lose all his possessions. Director-writer Gottfried Reinhardt said of Lang, "He tried to stay. He was a dishonorable man, a totally cynical man. I don't think he gave a damn about (the Nazis') politics."[14]

Film historian William K. Everson wrote in his *Classics of the Horror Film*: "Its [*The Testament of Dr. Mabuse*] claims to anti–Nazi content have, in any case, been exaggerated. In wartime, Lang, with the original no longer available to dispute him, indulged in a combination of hindsight and showmanship to describe his propagandist 'message' in terms which suggested a far more outspoken anti–Nazi undercurrent."

Sixteen years later, an article in *Der Spiegel,* published on November 26, 1990, backed up Everson's claims. In the article, the magazine's editor, Willi Winkler, wrote: "Lang knew exactly, his whole life long, how to style his own myth. His biggest success was the Goebbels number. He was the only witness."[15]

Indeed, the self-hating Lang, who always claimed he was Catholic, only *once* mentioned his being half Jewish to enhance his story with Goebbels. Claiming that he told the propaganda minister that he was half Jewish, he has him reply, uncharacteristically, that "*I* will say who is Jewish."[16] And though it was true that Goebbels could be somewhat broadminded about film professionals of "mixed race" (like the half Jewish Emil Jannings and director/actor Reinhold

Schünzel), so long as they toed the Nazi line (Schünzel, emphatically, did *not*), it's highly doubtful the career-minded Lang would have mentioned his actual heritage, especially when he emphasized to journalists in the years ahead that he had so much to fear from Goebbels and the offer he made. The real reason Lang left Germany, wrote Winkler, was "hurt male pride."[17]

Obviously, this was a touchy subject Lang did *not* want to get into. Though once in America, he would slam his ex-wife Thea von Harbou for being pro–Nazi (which she was) and that she divorced him because he was "not Aryan," Lang did not admit the existence of a Jewish mistress named Lily Latte. Nor did he mention the fact that, prior to the divorce, he had not been sleeping with his wife for a year, or the fact that it was *he* who filed for divorce, not von Harbou. Another detail he never bothered to mention but which infuriated him nevertheless, was the fact that von Harbou, ardent Nazi scenarist that she was, had an Indian lover named Ayi Tendulkar. After the divorce was final, she would turn the dark-skinned man towards Nazism, but, because he was obviously not Aryan, they had to marry secretly. (Though one would think that being nonwhite would be a barrier to collaborating with Nazis, the surprise was that several black actors had appeared in pro–Nazi films at the time, if only as representatives of non–Aryan "decadence"—black jazz musicians in *Hans Westmar*, black characters among the Arabs of *The Adventures of Baron Munchausen*, the insultingly stereotyped African tribesmen of *Ohm Krüger*. And let us not forget that the Nazis formed Muslim SS legions in the nations of Eastern Europe and the Mideast to fight the Allies and aid in the Holocaust, an inconvenient fact Muslim nations refuse to acknowledge to this very day.)

If anything, Lang's own rage at being displaced sexually in his wife's affections by a man of color obviously upset him. (For his production of *The Return of Frank James*, it was noted that his only contribution to a script he had nothing but contempt for was to change a description of African Americans from "pickaninies" to "colored people").

More discrepancies appear in Lang's alleged meeting with Goebbels when the subject of *The Testament of Dr. Mabuse* is brought up. Goebbels had banned the film because, according to him, "it proves that an extremely determined group of men, whether they seriously want to or not, are perfectly capable of unhinging, no matter which State, by using violence." And though Goebbels might have missed the irony of his National Socialist regime's deploring the use of violence to take over a country, his reasons go totally against Lang's claim that the film was banned because it was anti–Nazi. If anything, Goebbels deplored revolutions of any kind (except maybe Nazi ones) and personally made sure that no German film would depict them in a positive light. To the propaganda minister, Mabuse and his gang were not only criminals in a supposedly crime-free Germany, but anarchists who desired to take control of the State, a good enough reason for even American censor Joseph Breen to ban a film or at least cut it to ribbons.

In *The Testament of Dr. Mabuse*, the criminal mastermind is seen as a ghostly presence controlling the head of an insane asylum; or, according to Lang, the possessed man is portrayed as a Hitler figure who, in turn, controls his criminal disciples from afar; Mabuse has even left his papers behind (his "testament") which might be seen as a kind of Hitlerian plan for conquest like *Mein Kampf*. Still, Lang had yet to explain how he was making an anti–Nazi film when his own pro–Nazi wife did the screenplay. In 1938, years after he banned *The Testament of Dr. Mabuse* and Lang had settled in Hollywood, Goebbels spitefully said of the film that he was "struck by the dullness of its portrayal, the coarseness of its construction, and the

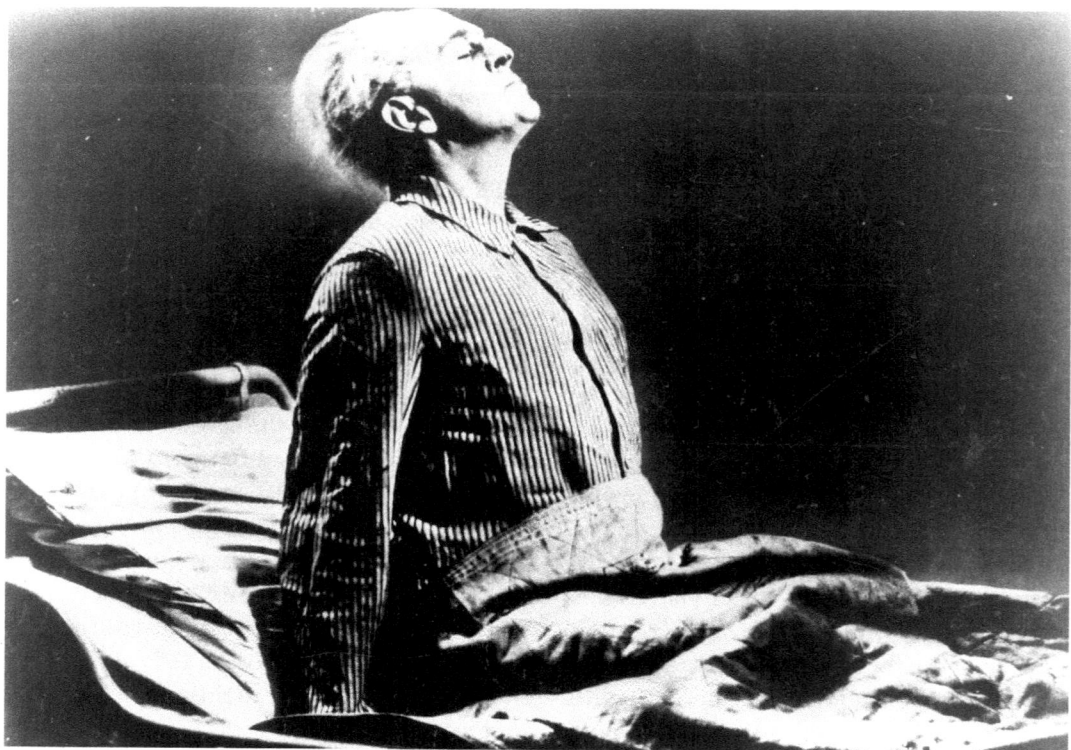

Führer envy: Fritz Lang would always claim that Dr. Mabuse (Rudolph Klein-Rogge, pictured here in *The Testament of Dr. Mabuse*) was a cinematic stand-in for Hitler, and purposely rewrote history to make himself look anti–Nazi to his new patrons in America.

inadequacy of its acting."[18] "Dullness," "coarseness" and "inadequacy" aside, the propaganda minister *still* ran the film, uncensored, in his own private screening room for specially invited guests whenever he had the opportunity. Apparently, something about an unearthly spirit commanding the head of a madhouse to initiate a nationwide crime wave appealed to the Nazi government's chief fabricator.

With *Testament* banned in Germany in 1933, Lang went to France and, under orders from producer Seymour Nebenzal (a Jewish filmmaker who would flee to America and later give us *Hitler's Madman* for PRC) shot a French-language version (*The Will of Dr. Mabuse*). During the early 1950s, Lang re-edited an English-language version of *The Testament of Dr. Mabuse*, abruptly "Americanizing" the dialogue (the detective's desire to go to the opera was changed to "the fights"[19]) and inserting references to Nazi doctrine that were obviously *not* part of Thea von Harbou's original script.

In the years to come, now settled in wealthy, prosperous and very sunny Southern California, Fritz Lang would give the audiences of the free nations his own unique portrayal of National Socialism, depicting them not necessarily as blatant monsters, but as, more often than not, part of a vast, shadowy conspiracy to take over the world. In Lang's anti–Nazi wartime films, paranoia hovers over the scene like a dark cloud; and the actions of the hero are never as fascinating as the presence of Nazi spies in black overcoats and felt hats lurking in the shadows, as well as those in official positions who aided and abetted them in their evil tasks. Emphasizing the paranoia angle, Lang used the figure of the Nazi agent as the monster in civilian garb; the blind man in *Ministry of Fear*; the "harmless" old woman guarding the kidnapped female scientist in *Cloak and Dagger*; the silent man with the umbrella in *Man Hunt*. Only in *Hangmen Also Die*, where the Nazis are out-in-the-open occupiers of a conquered nation, is the paranoia of killers hiding in shadows absent. In this film, the Nazis are not men in the shadows; in occupied Czechoslovakia, they are running the show. However, in *Hangmen*, their murderous behavior is channeled into presiding over a stifling fascist bureaucracy where death warrants are stamped by the hundreds and bored SS interrogators initiate torture sessions with all the emotion of a civil clerk closing the drawer of a file cabinet.

In other words, in Lang's imperfect universe of fear and paranoia—a milieu where nothing was as it seemed, a world where Nazi agents became the tools of a criminal conspiracy that a Dr. Mabuse would've been proud of—"The S.A.'s rightful place is in the streets and not on the cinema screen."[20] This statement was made by Dr. Joseph Goebbels on May 19, 1933, before the Reich Chamber of Culture, concisely spelled out his opinion (which was usually made into law) of putting blatant tributes to National Socialism, and especially its thuggish guardians, on German screens. He was particularly incensed by the release of films like *SA-Mann Brand* and *Hitlerjunge Quex*, pro–Nazi tributes to Hitler Youth members "martyred" to the Cause. Goebbels had always preferred subtlety and euphemism to express the triumph of Nazism; in this way, he had always insisted that German filmmakers view the works of Communist filmmakers like Eisenstein to get their messages across without hitting the audience over the head (seen today, however, though *Battleship Potemkin* and *October* are brilliant filmmaking, their attempts at propaganda are clumsy and *still* hit you over the head). The third of this trio of Hitler Youth films would, nevertheless, top the first two. Titled *Horst Wessel*, the film was a tribute to Hitler Youth squad leader Horst Wessel, who was shot dead by Communists at the age of 23. He also reportedly co-wrote what many Nazis referred to as "the Horst Wessel song," a corny little ditty praising the "movement."

Born in Bielefeld, Westphalia, Germany on October 9, 1907, Wessel was the son of a Lutheran minister. Many conflicts between father and son would be triggered by Horst's refusal to follow the old man into the ministry. In fact, the young man's head was anywhere but the church. At the tender age of 15, Horst joined the German National People's Party youth group. Pro-rightist and militarist, Horst and his comrades frequently got into street battles with the youthful members of the leftwing Social Democratic Party. Later, he'd expand his fascist horizons by joining the more violent *Black Reichswehr*. Despite his tendency to do his fighting in the streets rather than a courtroom, Wessel enrolled in the law faculty of Friedrich Wilhelm University in Berlin. The enrollment might have impressed his God fearing parents, but young Horst's interests still favored the brass knuckles over the law book. Considered "too radical" for them, the German National People's Party kicked him out.

Losing little time in finding another paramilitary group that suited his goals, Horst finally joined the National Socialist German Workers' Party, aka the Nazis, in 1926. Before he even reached 20, he joined the Nazis' military wing, the *Sturmabteilung* (aka "Storm Detachment"), the dreaded SA. Right away, Wessel hit it off with the new *Gauleiter* (or district leader) of Berlin, a driven little man with a clubfoot named Joseph Goebbels. Wessel showered praise upon the future Minister of Propaganda and Enlightenment: "There was nothing he couldn't handle. The Party comrades clung to him with great devotion. The SA would have cut itself to pieces for him."²¹ Wessel would not live to see Goebbels be part of the conspiracy to cut the SA itself into pieces on the Night of the Long Knives on the morning of June 30, 1934, but that would be many years later.

Goebbels gladly returned the compliment, and appropriately elevated Wessel's importance in the SA. He sent the young man to Hitler Youth study groups in both Germany and Austria, "study groups" basically meaning tactical military maneuvers and combat training so that a Hitler Youth member can handle himself in a street brawl. In 1929, Goebbels appointed him as a "Street Cell Leader" of the Alexanderplatz Storm Section of the SA. In September of that year, Wessel met Erna Jänicke, an 18-year-old prostitute and the two became lovers, finally moving in together in a sleazy apartment building in Berlin. The landlady, a corpulent woman named Elizabeth Salm, took an instant dislike to the young fascist; one of the reasons for this might have been that her late husband had been a Communist. Another reason was that Wessel was tardy with the rent; this despite the rumor that the newly appointed street cell leader was making money on the side by pimping his love out to the flotsam and jetsam of Berlin.

Fed up with Wessel's arguments, which probably included some political ones as well, Salm had her own ideas for dealing with her deadbeat tenant. It is heavily rumored, and quite possibly true, that the left-leaning landlady turned the key on Wessel, with Communist Party members quickly alerted to the presence of the rising Hitler Youth member. The situation finally came to a head on January 14, 1930, when two young members of the Communist Party went to Salm's building, knocked on the couple's door and, when Wessel opened it, shot him in the face. The Hitler Youth leader hovered between life and death in a Berlin hospital for the next five weeks until he finally died on February 23 of blood poisoning.

On January 17, Berlin police quickly grabbed Communist Party member Albrecht Höhler as the assassin. Identified by Jänicke as the triggerman, the young Communist was soon sentenced to six years in prison for the murder. After Wessel's death, the young SA leader would be lionized by the growing Nazi movement as a martyr to the cause, with Goebbels being the loudest and most passionate in his praise of the dead youth and virulently condemning his Communist murderers. Years later after Hitler assumed power, SA men dragged Höhler out of his cell and murdered him; from all reports the sight was not pretty, indicating a massive beating before his execution.

Hitler Youth members had been killed in battles with Communists before, but Wessel was the most famous; it was a given that, after the Nazis took power, there would be a film version of his life. Directed by the little-known Franz Wenzler, *Horst Wessel* went before the cameras of the new Nazified German film industry in the summer of 1933. Wenzler *does* do an exceptional job during the film's many street riot scenes which are shot more or less realistically. The government had offered Leni Riefenstahl the chance to direct it, but, believing the material beneath her, she turned it down. With preparations for the filming of *Triumph of the Will* on the horizon, she concentrated on a project she could be far more enthusiastic about.

Hitler himself had asked horror/fantasy author Hanns Heinz Ewers to write a book on Horst Wessel, and when the film version was green-lighted, Ewers also did the screenplay. Certainly, there should be something said for the fascinating career of Hanns Heinz Ewers, a talented author many had favorably compared to Poe, and especially his career vis-à-vis the Third Reich. Perhaps the choice of having an author known for writing horror stories do a book on a dead Hitler Youth member was odd, but Ewers had actually been a good friend of

Wessel's for many years, especially since it turned out that the two had gone to the same pro-nationalist student fraternity (though, obviously because of the difference in their ages, not at the same time).

Born in Düsseldorf, Germany, on November 3, 1871, Ewers would become the German version of H.P. Lovecraft and Edgar Allan Poe. His stories were scary, bizarre, violent, and at times, extremely sensual. He was an actor and director who had attempted to start his own theater company, but the group met with heavy censorship (it was rumored that Ewers material might have been a little *too* violent for the turn-of-the-century stage). He wrote a trilogy of novels featuring a kind of occult-oriented protagonist named Frank Braun, the first of which was published in 1910 called *The Sorcerer's Apprentice*.

It was the second in the trilogy, however, that forever put his name on the horror literature map. Titled *Alraune*, the film dealt with the creation of an evil woman, the spawn of a hanged murderer and a prostitute, helped along by the use of a "mandrake" plant and a little dabbling in the laboratory of a shady scientist named Professor Ten Brinken. Despite the hazy and questionable hocus-pocus behind the material, there was no doubt that Ewers authored a story that took the Frankenstein idea much further than it had gone previously. As far as the author was concerned, Alraune was more than a horror story. All through his life, Ewers was a dedicated follower of Nietzsche and a student of the eugenics movement. It would not be too far from the truth to see the elitist author as using the horror genre to further the idea of creating a Perfect Being, an idea which would have lots of play two decades after the book's publication when the growing Nazi movement would openly proclaim the same goal.

An enthusiastic believer in the cinema, Ewers had written the screenplay of *The Student of Prague* in 1913, marking the film debut of horror film icon (and frequent Nazi film actor) Paul Wegener. Ewers would continue to write for the silents until his political activities took precedence (he traveled widely drumming up support for Germany during the First World War). Not long after Hitler took power, Ewers would make yet another Faustian bargain with the men who controlled Germany.

In the meantime, however, "the new Edgar Allan Poe" was about to see the film version of his book debut in front of Party big shots in Berlin. Set for its world premiere on October 9 at the Ufa Palast theater, everyone, especially the filmmakers, were aghast when they received word that very morning that the film was banned. According to associate producer Dr. Ernst Hanfstaengl (who also co-wrote the music for the film): "The premiere was arranged. The invitations had gone out. Everyone in Berlin society from the Crown Prince down was to be present, and suddenly Goebbels forbade the film to be shown. This was too much. A lot of money had been tied up in the project and now ruin stared us in the face."[22]

Goebbels, who cared little about ruin staring *anyone* in the face, seemed to have triumphed in a vicious pissing match with other Party bureaucrats. He had publicly made his theories of film in the New Germany crystal clear to anyone who cared to listen: National Socialism was too great a movement to be portrayed on stage or screen. This included his much-quoted view that the SA, the then-premiere enforcement arm of the Nazis, should not be "marching on the stage or screen, their place is on the streets. Such an ostensible show of National Socialist ideology is no substitute for real art."[23]

Certainly, Germany's Jews, who felt the full impact of Goebbels' insistence on keeping the SA on the streets, saw nothing "artistic" in being racially profiled by representatives of the "great movement." Still, Party big shots, pro–Nazi journalists and Horst Wessel groupies were appalled at the middle-aged propaganda minister suddenly morphing into a pouty teenage girl at her own sweet-16 party. Yet there it was; with the former frustrated writer imposing his views on "art," not only on hapless filmmakers, but on Party officials who dared to think they could encroach on *his* territory. After the death of the Weimar Republic, the rules on what was allowed on German screens were already written in Nazi stone. Under the new dictates governing both the news media and the entertainment industry, not only was Joseph Goebbels the *only* man alive who could appoint Germany's censors, especially concerning what was to be shown on stage or screen and broadcast on the airwaves, but his rules stipulated that his office could ban all films "calculated to endanger all State interests, or public order, or to offend National Socialist moral, artistic or religious sentiments or endanger respect for Germany abroad or her relations with foreign countries."[24] Certainly, in five years' time, *Kristallnacht* would do a lot more to "endanger respect for Germany" than any film banned by Goebbels' propaganda ministry. But that was years away. For now, in the fall of 1933, Goebbels' fight for full control of the new German film industry resulted in a personal victory for him, but left much controversy in its wake.

Forced to respond to his critics (this was early in the regime's reign, when Goebbels could still be criticized without fear in 1933), the propaganda minister said in an interview with the Reich newspaper *Licht-Bild-Buhne* on October 19, 1933: "The figure of Wessel in this film did not correspond to the wonderful memory that the German public have of this great National Socialist."[25]

Though it is certainly debatable just *what* the German public exactly thought of this young, goose-stepping street thug, the next order Goebbels expected Hanfstaengel and the filmmakers to follow was as plain as day. Goebbels not only insisted on massive cuts in the film, but a title change as well. And so, *Horst Wessel* was now renamed *Hans Westmar* (this was when the film was not referred to under its full title, translated in English as *Hans Westmar, One of the Multitude, a German Life Tragedy in the year 1929*). Particularly gone was a sequence showing his composition of the *Horst Wessel Song*, which was reputedly based on a little ditty sung by North German fishermen. Redubbing changed Wessel's name to Westmar and other characters now called the leading man Hans instead of Horst. Instead of being about a "great National Socialist," the film was the story of an earnest young German who works for the expansion of national pride by his membership in the SA.

Our story begins when Hans (Emil Lohkamp) welcomes two friends, an expatriate German businessman and his cute daughter who have just returned from a trip to America. Hans himself had just returned from a Hitler Youth training camp in Vienna where the young man had a smashing time. However, one night when he takes his friends out to a German nightclub, he is stunned by the changes in his country under the Weimar Republic. The décor is American, the signs in the place are in English, the club's dancers are Spanish, and worse yet according to the doctrines of the New Germany: The musicians are black. In fact, when the bandleader mutilates the lyrics of the patriotic *Die Wacht am Rhein* to the style of an American jazz tune, Hans shouts at them to stop. "This is no longer Germany!" he cries, leaving the place in anger. Later, he and an SA comrade visit the cemetery of German World War I veterans and mourn, not only their sacrifice, but the decadent country Germany has become thanks to the influence of the victors. We also assume that the cemetery has no *Jewish* veterans of the war, since Hans and his SA pal would not be mourning *their* sacrifice.

Trying to influence others to go the Nazi Way and support Adolf Hitler, Hans' and his comrades' main enemies are the Communists. The brainwashing in this film is pretty obvious; Hans and his young friends in the SA are blonde and clean-cut, dress neatly, and are sincere, full of humor and are physically attractive. The Reds, however, are a motley bunch of slobs in plain and dirty working clothes, mostly dark-complexioned and ethnic. They never smile, constantly smoke cigarettes (Hans and his friends *never* smoke or drink) and will lie, cheat and murder to gain power; unlike, of course, the Nazis. They are also led by a big, ugly, frightening-looking Russian called Kuprikoff (the big, ugly, frightening-looking German actor Paul Wegener). In fact, emphasizing the ugliness of the lead Communist villain, the periodical *Der Film* referred to his character as an "Asian Commune Golem" on December 16, 1933.[26] In this way, and fully exploiting Wegener's reputation as Germany's premier king of horror (as well as a talented, distinguished actor of the stage and screen), the producers emphasized Kuprikoff's homicidal qualities. Bulging with money sent by Moscow in order to promote Red Terror as a wonderful and fulfilling way of life, Kuprikoff is willing to betray even loyal comrades to promote Moscow's agenda.

Needless to say, in accord with Nazi dogma, the Communists in this film are also dominated by Jews. Ramping up the insulting stereotypes, the film makes ample use of a weasly little man in a derby and topcoat with a spade beard, standup collar and pince-nez glasses named Kupferstein who incites the Communists to start riots, yet hides under a table when a fight erupts between storm troopers and Reds in the Communists' hideout. Through it all, the Communists call out the "Nazi scum" and hold up signs proclaiming "Death to Nazis," the exact same things Nazis had demanded of their own enemies. In fact, *Hans Westmar* would be one of the first films in the cinema of the New Order where the Nazis' propaganda would project their own hatred of their enemies onto film characters playing their enemies; in other words, a macabre mirror image in which the Nazis' own loathing and hatred would be projected onto Jews, Slavs and Communists, with Germans portrayed as either virtuous heroes or innocent victims. By 1940, the Nazis' demonizing images would also include the British.

Hoping to influence young workers to join the Nazis, Hans decides to give up his studies and rub elbows with the workers in East Berlin's Communist-dominated working class district by becoming a cab driver. Warned by Communist idealist Carmillo Ross (Heinrich Heilinger) to leave town, instead, Hans becomes successful recruiting workers to the Nazi cause. This angers Kuprikoff and the rest of his badly-dressed comrades, and they decide to do what villains like them have done in all cinema history: Order the hero's violent death. In the meantime, Hans rescues a working girl named Agnes (Irmgard Willers) who has a Communist father (who is, of course, a drunk) who beats her. After Hans has given her money, he does not suspect that the Commies have ordered Agnes to spy on him; however, she finds herself liking the young storm trooper and soon rejects the group. Finally, fingered by their landlady, Hans is mortally wounded by Red agents when he opens the door to Agnes' apartment (however, he is not pimping her or living with her; theirs is a platonic relationship, at least according to this film). Though guarded at the hospital by his SA friends, Hans dies anyway. At his funeral procession, Communists loudly shout down the marching Nazis, with many of them clenching their fists in an angry Bolshevik salute. However, when Ross, already disgusted with the Reds' murderous agenda, views the procession of proud, clean, young Hitler Youth, his raised fist gradually changes to a Hitler salute. Even in death, Hans has won.

Taking note of the film's climactic reconciliation between storm troopers and working class Germans, the now-Nazified cinema magazine, *Der Film*, commented:

> The German worker is not bad, he has been manipulated by foreign elements (Jews) and even so-called "Germans" who have to force the people into a foreign *Weltanschauung*. However, the worker has rediscovered his Germanness, and it is a fool who does not pardon him today. But there shall be no pardons for the intellectuals who have tried to bring about the downfall of the Third Reich.[27]

After the 1933 releases of *Hans Westmar*, *Hitlerjunge Quex* and *S.A. Mann-Brand*, Nazi cinema now acted like the Nazis themselves did not exist. Heeding Goebbels' call (or more likely, *demand*) that storm troopers stay in the streets and not on the screens, Germany's film industry would stay far away from stories that blatantly promoted National Socialism and instead, by euphemism and historical comparison, bolster Nazism and its doctrines through escapist entertainment.

However, to Goebbels' eternal frustration, there would be but one more film that put National Socialism front and center, not by showing the sacrifices of a martyred young storm trooper, but by promoting the political party that now controlled the country, as well as the man who led it.

In fact, the film was not even a fictional drama, but a documentary which introduced

Triumph of the Ill (No, it's not a typo): Though *Triumph of the Will* was a clearly staged "documentary," thousands of Nuremburg residents *still* came out to cheer Hitler and the new Nazi regime.

I. Infection (1929–1937)

to the world a new filmmaker. Considered by many, even to this day, a groundbreaking work, this mammoth production is still controversial for its unflinching praise of pure evil....

"As soon as our own propaganda admits so much as a glimmer of right on the other side, the foundation for doubt in our own right has been laid...." So said Adolf Hitler in a statement that could have been commenting on the only feature-length propaganda film made during his 12-year reign that centered almost totally on himself. Shot at the time of the Nazi Party Congress in Nuremburg in late 1934, this so-called documentary "was a staged production from its opening scenes right down to its final shots."[28] It's the one film which brought Leni Riefenstahl the fame she craved, but it also marked her as a pro–Nazi pariah for the rest of her long life.

For many years, long after the Third Reich lay in smoldering ruins, Leni Riefenstahl would always claim that she was *ordered* to direct *Triumph des Willens* (*Triumph of the Will*), the classic, and now infamous, feature-length "documentary" using the 1934 Nazi Party convention to promote Adolf Hitler, the Nazi Party and the New Germany, in that order. However, to truly understand the working methods, as well as the personality, of Leni Riefenstahl, we would have to examine the back story of the *first* film for which she was credited as director.

Our story, full of sound and fury and plenty of "*zieg heils*," begins in 1932, when actress Leni Riefenstahl decided to branch out from her mountain-climbing film resume (and away from *über*-geologist, Dr. Arnold Fanck) and become her own producer and director. Dr. Fanck

Propagandist: *Triumph of the Will* propelled Leni Riefenstahl to international fame—and would damn her for the rest of her life as a promoter of the Nazi regime and all the atrocities that came in its wake. Denying that she knew of the Holocaust, during the war, she used Gypsy concentration camp prisoners for the film version of the operetta *Tiefland*.

and others had already given her much input on filming her previous mountain adventures, but now she was going to put a little more fantasy and melodrama into her new film, *The Blue Light*. It was based on a 1930 novel by Swiss author Gustav Renker called *Bergkristall (Mountain Crystal)*, a novel which rock maven Dr. Arnold Fanck was well familiar with. In fact, the geologist/filmmaker quickly realized not only that Riefentsahl had decided to use it as the basis for her new film but that she never bought the rights to it. In Renker's novel, a painter visiting a Swiss village discovers a mysterious blue light emanating from some caves high up in the mountains, which, as it turns out, come from some beautiful crystals. Claiming that "everything that happened [in the film] came from my head,"[29] Riefenstahl also added that her story was an old Dolemite legend. Despite her sometimes feverish claims, Dr. Fanck saw through her naked thievery and refused to give his support to the project.

Nevertheless, Riefenstahl kept Renker's entire story, more or less, the way it was, with one glaring addition: The character of a half-wild, primitive mountain girl named Junta, to be played by her. In Riefenstahl's story, only Junta can climb up to the high caves and see the mysterious blue light; everyone else that's tried to find the blue light has fallen off the peak to a horrible death. Because of this power to actually see the blue lights and survive the experience, thick-headed villagers see her as a "witch," an epithet more than one collaborator had surely thrown at Ms. Riefenstahl, or perhaps something that rhymes with it. Certainly, her treatment of her co-workers on this film bears out the previous sentence.

Having never directed a film before, Riefenstahl realized that she needed help, and needed it *badly*. Despite Dr. Fanck's disapproval of her project, she snagged the geologist/filmmaker's usual cameraman, Hans Schneeberger, as well as Fanck's other crew members; she charmed the important Hungarian-Jewish (and Communist) film critic Béla Belázs into directing the scenes she wasn't in; and she was forced to approach the producer of her first film as a dancer/actress, Heinrich Richard (Anglicized as "Harry") Sokal, to get his H.R. Sokal Film Company to back the project. With Belázs gladly agreeing with the co-directing proviso, the part-time helmswoman then begged Dr. Fanck to view her film and give her editorial advice; in fact, he ended up cutting the film at his country villa.

When Riefenstahl visited her former mentor to view the film, with its many, *many* cuts, she claimed, "…I nearly *died* because he had taken apart my film. Everything was changed. I went into shock. I fell down crying."[30]

Dr. Fanck did not refute her story; however, he added a few embarrassing details she conveniently left out: "She got hysterical. She was very, very excited. The room next to the cutting room was the dining room and she went in there and rolled on the carpet, completely hysterical. I went into the kitchen, got a bucket of water and poured it all over her."[31] Not exactly the image a major director would want anyone to bring up during a film study class.

Still, after the mandatory calming-down, she supposedly listened quietly as he taught her how to edit scenes with movement, a talent even the formerly wet Riefenstahl was forced to admit. "I learned cutting from him. I saw how he did it." Still, she would outrageously grumble years later, "Dr. Fanck was my slave because he loved me. But after that, he went against me in hate."[32]

Going against people in hate was soon going to become the Riefenstahl Way. When *The Blue Light* premiered on March 24, 1932, at Ufa's Palast theater, she claimed that "Berlin critics outdid one another with their accolades."[33] Not exactly. Most Berlin critics, especially those that cherished the Weimar democracy like the *Berlin Tageblatt*, panned it, calling it

I. Infection (1929–1937)

"phony romanticism,"[34] which, in fact, it *was*. Having formed Leni Riefenstahl Produktions with the hope of getting as much profit from the film as she could (and cutting out any profit to Harry Sokal for his sizable investment in the film), Riefenstahl also withheld any monies going to her overworked collaborators, especially co-director Béla Belázs.

Though referring to Belázs many years later as one of her great friends (to prove that she was not anti–Semitic), a letter exists, written in her hand, granting power of attorney to, of all people, Julius Streicher. As any student of Nazi history knows, Streicher was the editor of the violently anti–Semitic "newspaper" *Der Stürmer*, a periodical whose Jew-baiting caricatures rivaled Henry Ford's *Deerborn Independent*. Immature and thuggish, even on his best days, Streicher was appointed Gauleiter (district administrator) of Franconia, which included Nuremberg (as an upcoming party functionary, Joseph Goebbels had the all-important post of Gauleiter of Berlin). It would have been a bit of a stretch had Riefenstahl not known the man whom she magnanimously had given power of attorney over legal matters. Or, as her letter clearly states: "I grant to Herr Gauleiter Julius Streicher of Nuremberg—publisher of Der Stürmer—power of attorney in matters of the claims of the Jew Bela Belacs [sic] on me."[35]

None of her collaborators received payment from showings of *The Blue Light*, but the insult Riefenstahl would deliver to her former collaborators was compounded when the film was widely reissued by the Propaganda Ministry of Joseph Goebbels in 1938, the year of *Kristallnacht*. Now with a Nazi government firmly in charge, the New Order was not going to forget loyal Friends of the Reich. This influence was never more apparent than in the film's startling new title credits. Totally ignoring any inkling of the existence of Renker's source novel, the new credits now proclaimed that *The Blue Light* was "A mountain legend told and shaped into images by Leni Riefenstahl."

However, back in 1933, one man *had* seen *The Blue Light* and remembered it. He saw the woman who was at the heart of the film as a noble heroine, a lone woman battling the ignorance of the masses when it was obvious to all who had seen the film that *she*, and only she, knew the right way of doing things. He identified with this persecuted and obviously superior woman, who, though a non–German character, was an Aryan in every other way. Martyred because of her superiority (Junta falls to her death at the end of the film), she seemed to know the forbidden truth that the rather dense villagers were never privy to.

Adolf Hitler thought often about *The Blue Light*, just as he remembered the woman who played the stridently superior heroine and directed (or, rather, claimed she fully directed) this inspiring film. He *had* to meet her. Coincidentally, eyewitnesses at the time would claim years later that Riefenstahl, after reading some passages of *Mein Kampf*, would exultantly shout, "I *must* meet this man!"[36]

A devil's pact was about to be struck…

To view *Triumph of the Will* today is not a rewarding experience. Drowning in obscenely pro–Nazi imagery, with swastika banners unfurled and waving at the viewer practically every minute of the film's close to two-hour running time, audiences are not as repulsed by the film's persistent visuals as they are bored to tears. Perhaps this is because we had been inundated with Nazi imagery and Hitler's demagoguery so many times in the past eighty years since the film's German release on March 28, 1935, that we had become jaded to what we now know are a pack of lies. A groundbreaking, if abhorrent, work to students of film; a self-congratulatory propaganda success to the Nazi state; and a hideous atrocity to the world's democracies, *Triumph of the Will* has survived as a kind of grotesque yardstick for documentary filmmakers; this despite the fact that not one thing in the entire film is real and that everything in it was staged for the cameras with infinitesimal care.

Joseph Goebbels despised hit-you-over-the-head propaganda, and he disagreed strenuously with Hitler's decision to film the 1934 Nazi Party Congress in Nuremberg. But, as usual, what the Führer wanted, the Führer got. It is also part of the legend that Goebbels was *really* furious that Hitler brought in Leni Riefenstahl, whose previous claim to fame had been playing mystical mountain maidens, and stealing money and film credits from her Jewish collaborators. And though the latter would have been all right in Dr. Goebbels' book, he did not like his purview invaded by what he saw as a *Fräulein* amateur. Much of this legend had been spread, with little variation, by Riefenstahl herself, the lone survivor of the Hitler era to live to tell the tale. Yet her assertions of Goebbels' jealousy, as well as charges of what today we would call sexual harassment, were made in sharp contrast to what the propaganda minster himself wrote in his diaries. Indeed, there are times he even feels respect and grudging admiration for Riefenstahl.

For instance, in a diary entry of June 11, 1933, as preparations for the film were started, Goebbels writes of his so-called rival: "She is the only one of all the stars who understands us."[37] This quote alone flies in the face of Riefenstahl's constant claims that she was naïve as to matters of politics. Indeed, Riefenstahl was quite familiar with the Goebbels family, having befriended both him and his wife, the long-suffering Magda, since the late 1920s. The future propaganda minister even attended the December 1929 screening of her early talkie mountain-climbing epic *Die weiße Hölle vom Piz Palü* (*The White Hell of Pitz Palu*). As he wrote in his ubiquitous diary on December 1, 1929: "Also in the film is Leni Riefenstahl. A splendid child, full of grace!"[38]

However, decades after Goebbels' suicide, the former splendid child full of grace would charge that the propaganda minster was groping her at the Berlin opera on May 16, 1933, during a performance of *Madama Butterfly*. A guest of Goebbels and Magda, Riefenstahl sat next to him and, she would claim years later, after the lights went out, the Minister of Propaganda and Enlightenment thrust his hand up her gown. Unfortunately, Riefenstahl would have us believe that, despite this outrageous attack, with his own wife obviously sitting on his other side, that she apparently had no problem collaborating with Goebbels and his ministry on her purported film. Certainly, Joseph Goebbels, even if he was not a Nazi, would be no one's idea of a gentleman at any time of his controversial life. He cheated on his wife Magda with abandon, and his offices, where he dined with beautiful German actresses, would be renowned for being part-time boudoirs. Being the one man in charge of every aspect of the film industry, Goebbels refined the term "casting couch," with promises of stardom to any ambitious actress who was willing to sleep with him; and a blunt denial of employment to any principled *Fräulein* who refused his advances. In fact, his approach was no different from that of the Zauncks, Mayers, Warners or any other Hollywood mogul of the time (or, for that matter, *today*) who used the casting couch to either make or break an attractive performer.

Yet for Riefenstahl to claim repeatedly that Goebbels tried to molest her at the time such an important project was being prepared, was just another example of her rather pathetic attempts to distance herself from the Nazi regime by personally demonizing one of its main figures (again, this was not hard to do).

With full government backing, she had been told by Hitler that the sky was the limit,

I. Infection (1929–1937)

and that no expense was too high for what she, the director, wanted. According to her Wikipedia page, the film ultimately cost some 280,000 *Reichsmarks* (110,000 U.S. dollars in 1934; $1,540,000 in 2015).[39] Always saying in later years that she was *ordered* to do the film, her claims were blown out of the water when Goebbels and others remembered her enthusiasm for what the propaganda minister referred to at the time as "the Hitler film," the still-untitled work that would showcase the Führer and the Party. Indeed, when Goebbels offered her a chance to make a film about murdered Hitler Youth member Horst Wessel, Riefenstahl turned it down. If she was indeed *ordered* to direct *Triumph of the Will*, one would fully expect some horrible backlash against her for this alleged lack of cooperation. However, if anything, Riefenstahl was now a privileged member of the Nazi elite, and Hitler himself was a fervent admirer. Her refusal to direct the Horst Wessel project emphatically did *not* prompt the SS to show up at her house and drag her by the hair to Dachau. She herself had not turned down the Wessel film because she disagreed with its politics, but because she thought the material was beneath her talents.

Instead, Riefenstahl had no problem accepting an offer by the government to film the 1933 party congress, eventually released as *Sieg des Glaubens* (*Victory of Faith*). Unfortunately, there seemed to be abundant footage of SA chief Ernst Röhm throughout the film. Since Röhm and much of the SA leadership had been murdered by the SS on Hitler's orders on the Night of the Long Knives in June of 1934, *Victory of Faith* was going to lose face, mainly Röhm's. When Hitler ordered that his former comrade-in-arms never be mentioned, printed about, nor have his image shown in public, it was an all-too predictable conclusion that all copies of *Victory of Faith* (which apparently *did* make money when first shown) be destroyed; though somehow the only existing copy was smuggled out and kept somewhere in England. Reportedly, Hitler was uncharacteristically uncomfortable on screen, though it might have been equally obvious that he was *really* uncomfortable having to share the screen with his jackbooted SA rival for attention.

With *Triumph des Willens,* the Führer was going to make sure that *he* was the star of this new production. Riefenstahl was to be a tool in this effort of glorifying Hitler and the Party, and since she was already a fan, she would be a more than willing tool. It is again the legend that Riefenstahl was given some fifty assistant directors, and that even these A.D.s would all have *their* own assistants. Or was it fifty *cameramen* with their own assistants? In reality, Riefenstahl's film crew consisted of an eye-popping 172 people, which included 10 technical staff, 36 cameramen and assistants (operating in 16 teams with 30 cameras), nine aerial photographers, 17 newsreel cameramen, and *they* would be assisted by a crew of 12 technicians, 26 drivers, 37 security personnel (SS and regular Nuremburg police), four labor service workers and two office assistants; to top it all off, many of her crew dressed in SS uniforms to blend in with the crowd.[40]

The film opens with on-screen titles:

On the 5th of September 1934
20 years after the outbreak of the World War
16 years after the beginning of German suffering
19 months after the beginning of the German rebirth
Adolf Hitler flew again to Nuremberg to review the columns of his faithful followers.

Therefore the lies start even as the audience barely has a chance to get to their seats. Notice the titles proclaim the "outbreak of the World War" rather than identify who started it; notice the absolute refusal of Germans (even those who did not care for the Nazis) to accept responsibility for the war; notice the whiny claim about "German suffering" without even the slightest acknowledgment of any other nation's suffering; notice the phrase, "German rebirth" is meant to convey how wonderful things are now that the Nazis are in charge; and notice the reference to Hitler "again" flying to Nuremberg, a rather grudging admission that *Triumph of the Will* is a kind of sequel to the mysteriously vanished *Victory of Faith*.

At rise, we see from the cockpit of an airplane flying in the clouds. The plane carries Adolf Hitler, high among the clouds like the god he always thought he was, to Nuremberg for his party's congress. Hundreds of cheering people are at the airport giving the Nazi salute and welcoming him. Then it's a motorcade through the streets, again lined with cheering crowds. Riefenstahl shoots close-ups of smiling little Aryan children, who are also raising their arms to salute him, all as thunderous music is heard on the soundtrack. In his car, and later when he arrives at the *Hotel Deutscher Hof*, Riefenstahl shoots Hitler from every conceivable angle; this is interspersed with close-ups of the faces of SS bodyguards watching the crowd, but not looking *too* mean for the camera.

The parades and repetitive displays of Nazi regalia continue, with Riefenstahl segueing to a Hitler Youth camp, where these future concentration camp guards engage in much homo-erotic physical byplay and good-natured roughhousing, all while smiling for her camera and visually proclaiming how wonderful it is to be young, alive and National Socialist. Indeed, more than one cable documentary on the Nazis' rise to power have used these clips as an "example" of the large number of gay men in Ernst Röhm's SA.

The playing of pageant music is the *only* sound we'll hear in this film for the first 24 minutes until Rudolf Hess finally addresses the throngs at the start of the convention. Riefenstahl wisely cuts down the speeches of the various Nazi officials to brief sentences, and though most of what they say is the same general empty platitudes about a victimized Germany rising from her misery yet again, a few of their comments are worth noting. Certainly it's hard to keep a straight face when Sepp Dietrich proclaims: "Truth is the foundation on which the power of the press stands in the world. And that it reports the truth about Germany is the only demand that we place on the foreign press."

Then we have Julius Streicher, the man whom the director of this film had given power-of-attorney, stridently proclaiming, "A people that does not protect the purity of its race goes to seed!" Throughout Riefenstahl's film, it seemed that all the participants (at least from what we can tell from the finished film anyway) restrained themselves from spouting the typical Nazi racial dogma, except, that is, for the usually bellicose editor of *Der Stürmer*. However, Streicher was always a man who goose-stepped to the beat of his own drummer.

Then we have the bizarre figure of Hans Frank. A truly scary-looking man (many on the dais were), Frank's strident pronouncements about the law in Hitler's Germany were indeed chilling coming from a seasoned attorney who should have known better. However, in his speech, the future military governor of occupied Poland (called more commonly "The Butcher of Poland") proclaimed: "These rich laws can assure you, national comrades, that your life and existence is safe, in the National Socialist State of order, freedom and law!"

Viewing this film decades later, one is reminded that most of these men would die violently, with a lion's share of the speechmakers, including Frank and Streicher, returning to Nuremberg 11 years later for their own hangings.

Indeed, when Hitler does speak, it's almost anticlimactic. His speech, starting quietly and mounting in emotion as he goes on, is the same series of pious, self-congratulatory nationalist platitudes his own men had just delivered. Through all of it, however, usually when the Führer is not speaking, Riefenstahl trains her camera for close-ups on only the most handsome and rugged faces of SS men, police officers and Hitler Youth she can find on the periphery of the crowd. Apparently, anyone with a scar or facial deformity of any kind need not get in front of her lenses.

Later on, Hitler will give another speech to thousands before a huge swastika-bedecked platform specially designed by his Minister of Armaments, Albert Speer. And so, it is at Speer's direction (*not* Riefenstahl's) that pits were dug in front of the speaker's platform so that she could get the shots she needed, while camera tracks were blatantly laid out in front of supposedly spontaneously-enthusiastic crowds so that she could get the close-ups of adoring followers all through the Führer's speech. When her shots predictably turned out to be of inferior quality (co-directing *one* mountain-climbing film does not an *auteur* make), Party big-shots again mounted the platform and re-did their speeches as the crowd *again* applauded enthusiastically as if they were hearing them for the first time. Sometimes, the director and her bellicose actors "cheated" and recreated lines from their speeches or individual actions in a well-lit studio.

At the end of it all, Riefenstahl had some 61 hours of film, which she labored over night and day to condense into a less than two-hour time frame. Riefenstahl hired a crew that consisted of some 172 technicians, a number that made Louie Mayer's MGM look like PRC. However, despite her use of hundreds of people, Riefenstahl would still insist years later, "The idea that I helped plan [the film] is downright absurd."[41]

Maintaining that she was only a filmmaker for hire, not a propagandist who believed in what was transpiring before her own eyes, Riefenstahl declared that *Triumph des Willens* was "A pure historical film ... it is film-vérité. It reflects the truth that was then in 1934, history. It is therefore documentary. Not a propaganda film."[42]

Pointing out the fact that Riefenstahl held sway over every single aspect and detail of the production (which included an enormous amount of tech personnel at her immediate beck and call), author/activist Susan Sontag maintained: "Anyone who declares Riefenstahl's films as documentary, if documentary is to be distinguished from propaganda, is being disingenuous. In *Triumph of the Will*, the document (the image) is no longer simply the record of reality; 'reality' has been constructed to serve the image."[43]

Triumph of the Will premiered on March 28, 1935, at the Berlin Ufa Palast Theater and, with the full backing of the State, was a box-office success that played for months. Riefenstahl won in all the award categories sanctioned by the Nazis, including the German Film Prize and the Venice Biennale (a gold medal given to notable filmmakers by fascist Italy); however, she even won the "Grand Prix" award at the World Exhibition in Paris in 1937.

Certainly, by the time the war broke out, and not having to worry about paying royalties to an enemy power, the Allies freely pirated sequences from *Triumph of the Will* to show to their own audiences. However, the various ways they used the clips would *not* have pleased either Riefenstahl or her Nazi backers. For instance, the British stole clips of Hitler from the film and dubbed in the comical tune *The Lambeth Walk* onto the soundtrack every time he moved. It is said that Resistance fighters in occupied countries sneaked into theaters and inserted the British clips mocking Hitler's walk onto the projectors of unsuspecting pro–Axis projectionists. The results were almost always the same: SS men fired their Lugers into the screen and then took the poor projectionists away, presumably never to be heard from again. Predictably, when Joseph Goebbels saw the clip, his reaction was almost as violent, shouting profanities at the British and viciously kicking chairs out of his way (we assume, with his *good* foot).

In 1960, clips from *Triumph* would turn up in a *real* documentary, the Swedish-made *Mein Kampf* by Erwin Leiser (his first film as a director). Born in Berlin in 1923, Leiser fled to Sweden with his family and prospered as a journalist, author and documentary filmmaker. Of course, none of this impressed the embittered Leni Riefenstahl, ex–Nazi, ex-filmmaker and ex-jailbird (the Allies had put her in prison for four years for her role as a Nazi propagandist, despite her loud protestations to the contrary). Deep in debt, she unsuccessfully sued *Mein Kampf's* distributor, Minerva-Film, for copyright infringement, demanding 100,000 marks and 10 percent of the profits. Interesting that she was claiming ownership of a film, a documentary yet, that she always maintained she did as a work-for-hire. Minerva mocked her claim, stating that they "had no need to buy anything from the beneficiaries of the Third Reich in order to make a film about that Reich."[44] Still, Leiser's work was a smash hit in Germany and much of Europe (it would make money in the United States as well when it was released on April 21, 1961). Briefly, Riefenstahl was able to secure an injunction stopping distribution of the film in Germany. Not wanting to dampen their overwhelming cinematic triumph with the money-grubbing ravings of a Nazi propagandist (who also makes an unauthorized appearance in said film), Minerva-film elected to wash their collective hands of the matter and paid Riefenstahl 30,000 marks for their German distributor and another 5,000 for the Austrian unit.

The West German government, however, unlike Minerva-Film, was not benefiting from a showing of *Mein Kampf*, and had no reason to pay off Riefenstahl. In fact, the laboriously slow wheels of West German justice were not going to grind any faster for a woman who had once supported a hated regime, if only for the fact that the newly democratic Germany steadfastly refused to recognize copyrights on films produced by the Third Reich. Finally, West Germany's highest court ruled that *Triumph of the Will* was produced by the government of the Third Reich, not Riefenstahl (as the credits clearly state); therefore, she was not the copyright holder. Furious at what she called a "miscarriage of justice,"[45] she continued to be embittered by the experience, totally missing the paradox that she had publicly repudiated everything in *Triumph of the Will*, yet was still eternally proud enough of her involvement to want to receive compensation for it.

Meanwhile, as Riefenstahl stewed, Erwin Leiser's *Mein Kampf* continued to be a huge international hit. For its filmmakers and their fight to reveal the truth about Nazi Germany, a *real* Triumph of the Will...

The change in Germany's political climate *did* prompt Hollywood to produce films tackling the subject during the 1930s, but these projects were met with resistance. *The Road Back, Three Comrades, Hitler: Beast of Berlin*, all set in Germany, with the first two film projects gutted to the point of absurdity and the last *never* seeing the light of day. Thanks to the immense pressure put onto the moguls and the Production Code office by German consul Dr. Georg Gyssling and the quick capitulation by said moguls and the Breen office, *any* project set in Germany, even World War I–era Germany, was dead on arrival, or at least devoid of any honesty concerning the country's rather neurotic need for totalitarian governments. By the time Leni Riefenstahl came to Hollywood in November 1938 to drum up American distribution for her highly overrated, overlong and boring *Olympia*, her timing was, let us say, a bit off. When her ship docked in New York, there was barely enough time for the smoldering cinders of burning synagogues to go out in the aftermath of *Kristallnacht*. The nationwide pogrom was happening even as she was out at sea; by the time she got to a Hollywood dominated by Jewish moguls, she was more at sea than she thought. Finally, outraged by *Kristallnacht*, the moguls kept their studio doors closed to her, with only the viciously anti–Semitic Walt Disney giving her a tour of his studio (Disney would also later welcome Nazi engineer Werner von Braun and use his studio to promote the now-respectable war criminal). Typically, once Riefenstahl returned to Germany, she blamed the Jews for her ostracism in Hollywood.

In the meantime, as the world was rapidly going to hell, some people on the other side of that world seemed to show the guts that Hollywood lacked to attack the Third Reich.

II
RAGE (1938–1941)
*As Nazi aggression spreads across Europe,
voices of defiance are finally heard*

> "…We must be the great arsenal of democracy."
> —President Franklin D. Roosevelt, December 29, 1940

In the mid to late 1930s, as Hollywood struggled to produce anti–Nazi screenplays that would not be shot down by either the moguls not wanting to anger Germany, or the Breen office not wanting to besmirch a nation that persecuted its Jews, thousands of miles away in forbidding and cold Moscow, at least one filmmaking industry was not going to be kowtowed into dropping its own anti–Nazi projects.

To the Soviets, it was a given that they were not anti–Nazi because they sympathized with the Jews or any other people victimized by the Third Reich. In fact, the two movements, Nazism and Communism, though politically and economically incompatible, were in reality fairly close. Both Germany and the Soviets used terror and mass murder as a means to accomplish their goals, leading, in their respective ways, to the task of finding their own "perfect" citizen which would symbolize the triumph of their movement. For the Nazis, it was the "Aryan superman"; for the Bolsheviks, it was the "Soviet man," an alleged champion of the proletariat and avowed enemy of capitalist imperialism. Needless to say, both human symbols were ludicrous, and often it was a trip to a concentration camp or gulag (Soviet concentration camp) for anyone foolish enough to show their imperfection in these totalitarian states. All in all, though both Hitler and Stalin had grudging respect for each other, their governments were typically populated by gangsters fighting over disputed territory; both nations would relentlessly attack each other in the press, on radio, the theater, and, of course, film.

Though the Soviets had been making anti–Nazi and anti-capitalist films for many years, few, if any, would make an impact with international audiences since the Communists' neurotic desire to have their usually bellicose film characters make pompous speeches instead of showing any kind of positive action put moviegoers to sleep (as did many a play written by Communists for Broadway audiences, most of them with astonishingly short runs). However, one such play *did* stand out among the many that closed early, an uncompromising attack on Nazi anti–Semitism called *Professor Mamlock*.

Opening on Broadway on April 13, 1937, *Professor Mamlock* was a hit with Communist

Party members, as well as local Jewish audiences and others who relished a brutal attack on the Hitler regime. Written by Communist Jewish author Friedrich Wolf, the play closed after 76 performances on July 10, 1938, less than two months before the film version, with a screenplay by Wolf, was released in the Soviet Union. However, perversely, the timing of the film's American release could hardly have been better: November 7, two days before start of the Nazi pogroms known as *Kristallnacht*. Amkino, the Soviet purchasing agency charged with releasing films into the United States, cunningly targeted the film for Jewish neighborhoods around New York City, with extra showings for the predominantly Jewish and left-leaning neighborhood of Brownsville, Brooklyn (it is rumored that the film played to packed audiences at Brownsville's "Peoples' Theater," a movie-house once located at Saratoga and Livonia Avenues that specialized in showing left-wing and Soviet films—a long way from its former function as a synagogue).

Wolf was an interesting character. Born on the Rhine on December 23, 1888, he was the son of a Jewish merchant. A student of philosophy and art history, the young man made medicine his goal; as Germany entered World War I, he became a ship's doctor and was able to make port at places like Greenland, Canada and the United States before its own entry into the war. After his ship returned to Germany, the pacifist-minded Wolf became a field doctor for his country's troops on the Western Front. The carnage that he personally witnessed stayed with him and the experience hardened his resolve to fight against wars of all kind.

Like so many disillusioned by the militarism of the Kaiser and his junkers in the government, Wolf became a Communist in 1918, joining all manner of left-wing organizations that called for the downfall of capitalism; ten years later, he officially joined the Party. Working with unconventional theater professionals who sought to push the envelope in the arts, Wolf also chose to write material that sparked controversy in the then-tottering Weimar Republic. In 1929, he and his friends in the Party staged *Cyankali*, a work that addressed the issue of abortion. Perhaps on the strength of this production, Wolf was suddenly arrested and it was thought he actually *performed* them (though writing took up a great deal of his time, he was still a practicing physician). In early 1932, he helped form the Communist agitprop theatrical company *Spielstrupp Sudwest* in the city of Stuttgart for the purpose of staging even *more* controversial works.

At no time during these days of the dying Weimar Republic did the aspiring leftist doctor/playwright come near the popularity of either Bertold Brecht or Kurt Weill or the controversy of *The Threepenny Opera*; in fact, very few had ever heard of him—except perhaps the new regime which had so recently taken control of the country. Since he was both a pacifist and a healer, it is extremely doubtful that Wolf took part in the numerous street brawls between Communist gangs and their new enemies, the rising National Socialists. It was not as if Friedrich Wolf was not a fighter who kept up the struggle in his own way. He would always claim that he was inspired to write the autobiographical *Professor Mamlock* shortly after the Reichstag fire (at other times he said the *day of* the Reichstag fire). According to him, *Professor Mamlock* was supposed to premiere for Gustav Wangenheim's theatrical company, *Truppe 1931*. However, pressure from the new Nazi regime forced its cancellation, though this is unsubstantiated.

There is, however, some evidence that an early version of the play, called *Dr. Mamlock*, addressed far more Jewish issues than many Europeans of the day cared to address. One controversial topic was the character of Simon, a hospital worker who became a Zionist and who wanted the persecuted Mamlock to leave Germany and immigrate to pre-independence Israel. Though this plot point was reportedly still in all Hebrew and English-language versions of the play, Simon's Zionism was removed from the German-language version. This was done *not* at the behest of the ruling Nazi authorities, but by Germany's Communist Party, who was clearly uncomfortable with the idea of Jews controlling their own destiny. An unsigned review of the play submitted to the Party's exiled leadership in Moscow attacked it for "emphasizing the race struggle, while the class struggle remains in the background. The Party's role is not sufficiently presented."[1] Interesting that these Communists, like the Nazis they attacked, *also* saw Jews as a "race" whose concerns were not worthy of addressing.

Ironically, the play, now under the title *Der gelbe Fleck* (*The Yellow Badge*) would make its stage debut in anti–Semitic Poland on January 19, 1934, at the Warsaw Yiddish Art Theater. It was soon translated into Hebrew and was performed in Tel Aviv on July 25 under the title *Professor Mannheim*. Finally, the first German-language production was mounted in Zurich on December 8; unfortunately, Swiss Nazis disturbed the performances by using the same tactics their brethren used in Germany and Austria in 1930 during the showings of *All Quiet on the Western Front*. The Swiss government sent riot police to protect the actors during the performances; a benign act considering Switzerland's later cold-blooded appropriations of the life savings of Jews murdered during the Holocaust.

Professor Mamlock was even set to be performed at London's Westminster Theater in 1935, but the country's traditionally anti–Semitic Foreign Office pressured the producers to close. Though no reasons were officially given for the cancellation, it was quite possible that the Foreign Office was uncomfortable with the play's themes of Zionism that called for Jews to go to Israel, a no-no to the British authorities who still ran the country and hoped to curry favor with the region's Arabs (the British Foreign Office continued wearing blinders into the war years as they high-handedly ignored their own intelligence reports concerning revelations of the Holocaust).

However, with a change in the world landscape by the late 1930s, the play crossed the Atlantic into America where, with an English translation by Anne Bromberger, it landed under the aegis of the Depression's Federal Theater Project; and then, under its subgroup, the Jewish Theater Division, it finally hit Broadway on April 13, 1937, and played 76 performances.[2] Though the play was banned by fascist elements in the Swedish government who feared pressure from the Nazis, it was still performed in other cities around the world.

Lauded in Moscow, Stalin gave his endorsement to a film version, though, needless to say, the play's Zionism and dialogue about the Bible and Jewish history would be ruthlessly cut out; *Professor Mamlock* was to be a play attacking Nazis, *not* a work that made Jews proud of their heritage. In 1934, Wolf emigrated to the Soviet Union and helped co-write the screenplay for the film version (produced by the government-controlled Lenfilms); co-directed by two Jews, the Soviet helmsman Adolf Minkin and Austrian émigré Herbert Rapoport (a refuge from Nazi terror). Despite its pro–Communist blather, the film is still powerful in its cinematic attack on Nazism; one of the few at the time.

Interestingly enough, the story begins, not on January 30, 1933, the day Hitler came to power, but on the day of the Reichstag fire weeks later. Professor Mamlock (noted Russian actor Semen Mezhinskii; spelled Semyon Mezhinsky in the IMDB website) is a decorated veteran who, like many a German Jew of the time, fought bravely for his country during the Great War. As in the play (and Wolf's own life) he is a doctor who is married to a non–Jewish

II. Rage (1938–1941)

woman, Frau Mamlock (E. Nikitini). The professor, who, like his wife, seems not to have a first name, is a brilliant surgeon, a healer who takes no money from poor patients; a humanist whose only enemy is bacteria and illness; he is beloved by his patients and the staff at his clinic, at least most of them. Preoccupied with performing a great service to humanity, he is ignorant of the Nazi infection spreading under his very nose and around his beloved Germany even as he fights those other parasites beneath his microscope.

Only his revolutionary son, Rolf (Oleg Zhakov), a charter member of the Party, sees the danger, not only to his family, but to the whole country. Father and son argue violently, and when Mamlock challenges his son to respect science by asking whether Pasteur and Koch are enough for him, his Red son responds in a bellicose manner, "No! Pasteur, Koch, Marx and Lenin!" The shock in this Communist production is that the line doesn't have Marx and Lenin being mentioned *ahead* of the two scientists. One thing leads to another and soon Rolf is seeking quarters with his fellow proletariat.

However, Rolf's Communist words soon ring true (in a Soviet production, could it be any other way?), and Mamlock senior soon finds that the Nazi plague has spread to his fellow staff members at the clinic, with one zealous pro–Nazi doctor kicking Mamlock out of the institution. With storm troopers backing the renegade surgeon's new power, Mamlock is forced to wear a white smock blackened by the word *Jude* scrawled on it. As the SA parade the cultured surgeon out on the street as if he were a captured animal, Minkin and Rapoport (who also wrote the screenplay along with Wolf) pan their camera at the crowd of Germans watching with intense disapproval. Here, it is implied that, since the people are seen by the Soviets as "the proletariat," they automatically condemn every single thing the Nazis did. Again, in the fantasy world of the Communists, all those who became Nazis or supported them *must* have been rich capitalists who never worked a day in their lives, totally ignoring the fact that the Nazis started as the National *Socialist* party, with millions of "the proletariat" flocking to join them. This convenient lie was noted by film historian Thomas Doherty on pages 192–193 in his insightful *Hollywood and Hitler: 1933–1939*:

> The party-line valorization of the German working class makes the Nazis seem more like an invading army than an expression of popular will. In the elaborate underground network operating around Berlin, seemingly every German except those in brown-shirts embraces the communist cause. Just where did all those marchers at the Nuremburg rallies come from? According to *Professor Mamlock* and contrary to the Nazi slogan, the German *Volk* are not with the Reich and the Führer.

Returning home after the humiliation of being paraded in the streets, the defeated doctor considers suicide. However, back at the hospital, a Nazi big-shot is suddenly taken ill and needs an emergency operation. Since all the other doctors apparently have no surgical skills at all, the hospital's new pro–Nazi administrators beg Mamlock to perform the operation. Offered a new smock, the newly defiant Jewish doctor insists on still wearing the garment smeared with the word *Jude* on it. Successfully performing the operation, however, will not suddenly awaken the Nazis to a new and beautiful world of tolerance for others. In fact, as soon as his usefulness is over, Mamlock is *again* persecuted for his religion; ordered out of the hospital, he wanders in a daze down a corridor until a shot rings out and his body is thrown into a hospital bed to die. But the good doctor is not dead; in fact, rising from the dead like Lazarus, he goes over to the hospital's balcony and, though wounded, addresses the crowd. Passionately, he exhorts the people to rebel against the fascist "plague." Predictably, the SA machine-guns him until he shuts up. Meanwhile at some underground Communist cell, Rolf joins his comrades in their fight against the Nazis and raises his fist in a Red salute. The ending is the exact opposite of the Nazi-produced *Hans Westmar* of four years ago; in that film, a Communist Party man raises his fist against parading Hitler Youth, only for his arm to stiffen in a Hitler salute. These two films would have made a hell of a double feature.

Almost universally praised, especially by David Platt in the *Daily Worker* on January 2, 1938 ("the most significant picture of the year!"[3]), *Professor Mamlock* was also one of the few films to come out of the Soviet Union that was granted a seal by Joseph Breen's Production Code Administration. "The film is a powerful anti–Nazi story with some incidental boosts for Communism," wrote Francis Harmon, Breen's man on the East Coast.[4] However, cleared by the Breen office did not necessarily mean it was clear sailing for *Professor Mamlock*. Both anti–Soviet and pro–Nazi isolationist groups influenced local and state censorship boards to either ban the film or limit its showing. In fact, a box office smash in the Jewish areas of New York and Los Angeles, *Professor Mamlock* was banned by the Chicago Board of Censors, as well as Pennsylvania, certain venues in the south and other places where sympathetic Jewish characters were *not* a common sight on screen.

However, it was not as if the Soviets had a sincere desire to present a pro–Jewish film. Though the entire sequence of Mamlock's operating on a Nazi boss, getting shot and then dying while making his balcony speech was added to the film (Wolf's play ends with Mamlock committing suicide after being kicked out of the hospital), the Stalinist regime controlled every aspect of the production to make sure its content slammed the Nazis, not helped the Jews. Communist censors refused Wolf and his collaborators the chance to emphasize Mamlock's Jewishness, except, that is, when he was being cursed by anti–Semites or manhandled by storm troopers. For instance, in the play, Wolf has Mamlock openly proclaim that he identifies himself as "an old soldier, as a democrat, and as a Jew,"[5] the last two seen as words the regime was *not* comfortable putting before Russian audiences. Wolf's play also has Mamlock take pride in the heroism of Jewish biblical heroes like David and Samson.

Though the film's message called for tolerance of other peoples, off-screen, foreign-born filmmakers Minkin and Rapoport were mercilessly followed by the NKVD; this included the usual Bolshevik harassment of ripping open their mail, searching their rooms and basically making Nazi-like nuisances of themselves. The author also had his problems in the workers' paradise; despite the fact that he was a Communist, Wolf was also a Jew, something the Stalinist regime wasn't going to forget despite its own public pronouncements attacking Nazi anti–Semitism. The NKVD reported that the author "routinely conducted anti–Soviet conversations, expressed a desire to leave the U.S.S.R. and said that in our country there is no freedom, but only repressions."[6]

A mere nine months after *Professor Mamlock* was released, the Soviets and their National Socialist "enemies" signed their nonaggression pact in August 1939. After Wolf's complaints about the Soviet Union's lack of freedom, Party bureaucrats were threatening to deport the playwright back to Germany where the Gestapo was, to put it mildly, eagerly awaiting his return. Fortunately, this did not happen. In fact, after the war ended and Wolf finally left the Soviet Union and returned to Germany (the Communist Eastern half), he was allowed to contribute to the screenplay for the antifascist and anti-capitalist *Council of the Gods* in 1950, while at the same time filling the post as East Germany's ambassador to (also Communist) Poland between 1949 and 1951.

Wolf died in Berlin on October 5, 1953, at the age of 64. In a tragic postscript to *Professor*

II. Rage (1938–1941)   45

Mamlock, Stalin would enact his own brand of anti–Semitic persecution of Jewish doctors in the early 1950s, the so-called "Doctors' Plot," with arrests and pogroms that would make Mamlock's shame in wearing a smock with *Jude* on it tame by comparison. There are many historians who believe, with good reason, that Stalin was going to use the Doctors' Plot as an excuse for triggering a second Holocaust of the Jews, and that extermination camps were actually being built in Siberia for the task (that is, extermination camps added to the ones the Soviets already had). Fortuitously, it was only Stalin's death on March 3, 1953, that permanently halted the plan.

Friedrich's son, Konrad, became a noted director in East Germany and even made a film version of his father's anti–Nazi play. In fact, like the Soviet film industry at the time, the East Germans would constantly use the Nazis as an ancient enemy from the past; *Professor Mamlock* would be made into TV movies in both 1958 and 1960, with Konrad Wolf's remake released in 1961. Actor Wolfgang Heinz, who had acted in *Nosferatu* way back in 1922, would be cast as Mamlock in both the 1960 TV-movie *and* the 1961 film version.

Perhaps the supreme irony of *Professor Mamlock* in the wake of the signing of the Nazi-Soviet Pact was an incident that occurred at the 1939 New York World's Fair. Needing a good film to represent the best of Russian cinema for the exposition's Soviet exhibit, the Stalinists sent over *Professor Mamlock*. However, by the time Molotov and Ribbentrop signed the Pact, the anti–Nazi picture was suddenly withdrawn from entry and replaced with a film about Lenin. When quizzed by American reporters, a Soviet official arrogantly claimed that it was "just a routine change in program!"[7]

In the meantime, at the height of cooperation between Nazi Germany and the Soviet Union in mid–1940, MGM released a film about another family and its intellectual head coming of age in the Nazi state. Based on a novel by British author Phyliss Bottome, the film did one better than *Professor Mamlock* in calling for a condemnation of Nazi ignorance while simultaneously suppressing the ethnicity of the film's Jewish characters.

"I would not put in Freya's mouth the word: 'Non-Aryan' instead of Jew."[8] So wrote author Phyliss Bottome to MGM producer Sidney Franklin in a letter dated February 7, 1940. The crux of the letter dealt with scripted scenes from the studio's newest delving into the burgeoning subgenre of anti–Nazi pictures coming of Hollywood in the wake of German conquests abroad. A dedicated, passionate spokeswoman for tolerance and decency in the wake of the growth of totalitarianism, Bottome was a prolific novelist and short story writer. Both a student of psychology and an educator who taught students on its importance in life (with one of her students being an eternally grateful Ian Fleming), Bottome was married to Alban E.D. Forbes, a diplomat, passport control officer and full-time agent for MI6 who was in charge of the Austrian-Hungarian-Czech station. After their extended stay in Germany in the late 1930s, Bottome published *The Mortal Storm* in October 1937, obviously, *not* in Germany, but in England. Much of her story about a peace-loving German family and its Jewish patriarch during Hitler's rise to power came from her own experiences witnessing the horrors of life in Nazi Germany.

MGM bought the rights to the novel practically before the ink was dry on the galleys, with script drafts cranked out as the 1930s came to a close. Loyal to the novel, the final script retained scenes showing great compassion for the persecuted Jews of Germany.

The plot deals with a German family headed by the beloved Professor Roth (Frank Morgan), a German Jew married into a *goyim* family consisting of his wife (Irene Rich), cute daughter Freya (Margaret Sullavan) and son Rudi (Gene Reynolds). Their friends are: Freya's beau Fritz (future "Jim Anderson" of *Father Knows Best*'s Robert Young), Otto (future "Elliot Ness" of *The Untouchables*' Robert Stack), Erich (future WB TV producer and director William T. Orr), and last but certainly the most miscast, Martin Breitner (James Stewart). In the film, the story begins on the professor's 60th birthday (Morgan was 49, but looked much older). Despite the fact that at least two biographies of Jimmy Stewart (one written by Donald Dewey and another written by Michael Munn) claim that the film version of *The Mortal Storm* never mentions its setting is Germany but instead "somewhere in Europe," the completed film plainly opens with a title that says: "January 1933. A small university town at the foot of the Alps in southern Germany."

Believing that everyone has forgotten his birthday, Roth is stunned to find that the entire school is there in the main auditorium to wish him a happy 60th. Typically, when Stewart's character wishes him a happy 60th, despite being a young German farmer, he hems and haws like Jefferson Smith. Soon, the prof is at home with the entire cast for a birthday dinner and enjoying himself; unfortunately, Roth has the great misfortune of having his 60th birthday on January 30, 1933, the day Adolf Hitler is elected chancellor of Germany.

Already battle lines are drawn, with Roth, his wife, Freya and Martin worried over Hitler's assumption of power and the others happy that the New Germany will stop for no one. Soon, Roth becomes frightened by the changes around him. Earlier, he had taught that blood types from people of different cultures and races are all the same, but after Hitler takes power, the very same lesson provokes cries of outrage from his students, who are now garbed in Hitler Youth outfits complete with swastika armbands. Led by storm trooper Holl (a small role, but a chilling performance by future song-and-dance man Dan Dailey), Roth's class is boycotted.

In a tavern, when an old teacher (who, it is implied, is a Jew) refuses to "Heil Hitler" along with the others, he is attacked by a mob led by Holl, though Martin comes to his rescue. Later, after Martin walks Freya home, he himself is attacked by men who had once been his friends (of course, being Jimmy Stewart, he fights back). Soon, the disgusted Freya breaks it off with Fritz and swings her affections over to the principled Martin. If one finds Jimmy Stewart unconvincing as a German, they had yet to see Maria Ouspenskaya, insanely cast as his *mom*. Indeed, with her as his mother, one wonders where he got his Pennsylvania drawl.

Eventually, as Nazi controls tighten, Roth, referred to by his former friends as a "non–Aryan" instead of a Jew, is kicked out of his teaching position by colleagues who had once cherished him. Expulsion is one thing, incarceration is another; and soon the formerly beloved professor is arrested and put into a concentration camp (which, as portrayed in this Hollywood film, seems to be nothing more than a local jail). On the orders of Gestapo chief Hartmann (one of the most enjoyable Teutonic scoundrels ever seen on screen, anti–Nazi German actor Rudolph Anders), storm troopers hunt for Martin. Soon, an SA platoon led by Franz (future blacklister Ward Bond) is sent to the Brietner farm.

Unfortunately, a girl helping them named Elsa (Bonita Granville, years before her own encounters with Nazi torturers in *Seven Miles from Alcatraz* and *Hitler's Children*) honestly admits that she is weak and panicky and that under even the *slightest* threat to her safety, she'll squawk like a canary. Soon, Freya and her mom and Rudi are taking a train to Innsbruck, Austria, where the fugitive Martin is staying. Unfortunately, Freya is detained for allegedly attempting to smuggle one of her father's papers about equal blood types out of Germany and she is arrested as Rudi and her mom continue on to Innsbruck.

II. Rage (1938–1941)

Staredown: Unlikely Germans James Stewart and Robert Young in a publicity shot for the film version of Phyllis Bottome's *The Mortal Storm*. Off-camera, MGM studio brass removed all mention of the word "Jew" from the film.

Soon, Roth is reported to have died of "a heart attack," with the angry Freya not believing the official report. Released by Hartmann, but not allowed to leave Germany, she returns to the Breitner farm and finds Martin, whom she is now in love with. It's soon decided they'll escape through a mountain pass on skis and into freedom in Austria, a scenario that would have gotten a huge laugh from the supporters of Chancellor Englebert Dollfuss, who ran the country as a fascist dictatorship (Dollfuss was eventually assassinated by Nazi agents in July 1934).

Unfortunately, the couple has the misfortune of revealing their plan to the wuss Elsa, who, after a little physical manhandling by Franz and company, turns the key on Martin and Freya. With a reluctant Fritz in charge of the pursuers, the chase ends with Freya mortally wounded, yet Martin is able to ski with her body across the border to Austria. Back at the abandoned Roth home, when Otto expresses happiness that Martin can now live in a land in which you can say what you please (in Austria?), Erich slaps him and leaves. It is heavily implied that the experience has changed all of Roth's former students, who will never again be the same.

Here, in 1940, with Nazi Germany on the verge of annexing all of Western Europe, was a blatantly anti–Nazi film where freedom is cherished and dictatorship is seen as wrong. Unfortunately, we also see something else: A film brave enough to attack Nazism, but *not* anti–Semitism. Hollywood's, and particularly Louis Mayer's, timidity never seemed to be

Cold comfort: Margaret Sullavan and James Stewart about to ski their way to freedom in *The Mortal Storm*. The German Foreign Office warned the cast against making the film.

more obvious than in the removal of a scene which clearly identified Professor Roth, not only as a Jew, but a *proud* one at that.

A major scene that had already been shot had young Rudi come home and tell his mom and Freya that classmates refuse to sit next to him and some have even thrown rocks at him. He is further mystified when his headmaster gives him a form to fill out titled Proof of Aryan

Descent, with a subsection titled Percentage of Jewish Blood. Showing the form to the professor, the boy is confused, asking worriedly, "I'm not a Jew, am I?" Then Roth goes into his own heritage and how proud he is of being a Jew and reciting names of great Jews of history who changed the world for the better; all in all, he hopes that Rudi will be brave and mention his own Jewish blood proudly on the form. "Our race ... outlived persecution. God willing, we shall outlive the injustice and cruelty of these bewildering days," Roth says. When the script containing this scene was sent to Phyliss Bottome, she wrote to producer Sidney Franklin, expressing dismay that Rudi was not as proud of being a Jew as he should have been.

Unfortunately, the producer was having his own problems. Reportedly sympathetic to the victims of Nazi persecution, Franklin himself was personally disgusted by the trappings of the Hitler regime he would see every time he visited the set and hated to be reminded of such evil still existing in the world. In a meeting with Louie Mayer, he asked to be relieved of his duties. And so, to the world's eternal regret, the reins of production would be handed over to British producer-director Victor Saville. It is to be noted that the script draft with the scene between Roth and Rudi had already been approved, not only by studio brass, including Mayer, but the traditionally anti–Semitic Joseph Breen and his bigoted minions at the Production Code Administration. When Franklin was in charge of production, the scene had been shot, with director Frank Borzage, as well as all the actors involved with the scene, including Gene Reynolds and Frank Morgan, visibly moved by it. Then one day in either late March or early April, something changed. As Gene Reynolds recalled it in an interview for the documentary *Imaginary Witness: Hollywood and the Holocaust*, "The producer, I recall, coming down to the set, and he says, 'We cut that scene, and you'll notice that in the whole film nobody ever says 'Jew.' It's 'non–Aryan' but nobody ever says 'I am a Jew,' 'He's Jewish,' and so forth.' And he said that with a certain amount of pride."[9]

Asked whether new producer Saville was responsible for the removal of the scene, Reynolds said,

> I do recall him smiling and pointing out how kind of clever he was.... But I don't think for a moment that this was done without counsel with L.B. Mayer and (Eddie) Mannix and whatever heavyweight producers there were that I'm sure were consulted. I'm sure they were very into this.
> Certainly Saville could not have done it on his own. He'd have to have it approved. So it went to L.B. But I don't know who advised him, or whether it was him alone.[10]

Reynolds and the other actors would realize that the line-chopping was just beginning. Moving fast, producer Saville ordered his screenwriters to slash all lines mentioning the Jewish people; and whenever possible change the words "Jew" or "Jewish" to "Non-Aryan." And so, thanks to a pompous, conceited new producer and a timid studio hierarchy, including the usually bombastic Louie Mayer, the impact of Bottome's condemnation of Nazi anti–Semitism, no less powerful than that shown in *Professor Mamlock*, would be watered down to the point of absurdity. Now, according to the film, Nazis were bad because they persecuted a lovable family and kept two young lovers apart, *not* because they persecuted Jews. In fact, in the advertising for the film, including the coming attractions, emphasis was put on the reteaming of Stewart and Sullavan, trumpeting them as "the popular sweethearts from *The Shop Around the Corner!*"[11] Instead of standing up to the scourge of National Socialism, Stewart and Sullavan were now depicted as young lovers merely trying to stay together during difficult times.

However, the cowardice did not end with Saville and Mayer's disemboweling of Bottome's novel or the change in focus from Nazi brutality in the ads to young lovers in trouble. According to Robert Stack:

> One morning a representative from the Swiss consulate showed up on the set in a vested suit and announced that he'd been told by the Germans to tell us that *Confessions of a Nazi Spy* and our picture would be remembered by Berlin after they won the war. I didn't give a goddamn about what they were going to remember, and that was the attitude of Jimmy, Maggie the director Borzage, and most everybody else.[12]

Jimmy Stewart basically backed up Stack's reminisces, though with one major difference: Stewart remembers that they were visited by, not the Swiss attaché, but "a representative from Germany," and it was he who had told the studio that "after the war was won by Germany, they would not forget our picture."[13]

Indeed, as it turned out, whether the man was Swiss or German, the Nazis took the film's production and its attack on them *very* seriously. Shortly after *The Mortal Storm* was released in June 1940, Goebbels banned all MGM films from being shown in Germany, making Mayer's studio the second-to-last Hollywood company to have its films banned (Paramount was still having their films shown in Germany, but soon they too would be blocked from exporting their products to the Nazis). In America, *The Mortal Storm* did disappointing business. All in all, it looked like most Americans detested Nazism, but as yet had no interest in half-hearted condemnations masquerading as love stories.

As *The Mortal Storm* and other films proved, the Breen office certainly tried all it could to block efforts to show the evils of Nazi Germany, with the repeated mantra of "hate pictures" being hurled at the producers of such films as late as mid–1940 (Breen would accuse Fox of making "hate pictures" when they produced Fritz Lang's anti–Nazi thriller, *Man Hunt*, in 1941). One such project set to be filmed for Columbia was *The Man Who Killed Hitler*. Typically, Breen's usual response was to approve the project, *then* remind the filmmakers how touchy the subject matter was, which meant that Breen's PCA actually did *not* approve of the project. In a letter to Columbia head Harry Cohn, dated May 27, Breen wrote:

> In this connection, it will be necessary for you to keep clearly in mind that provision of the Production Code, which states that the history, institutions, and prominent citizenry of foreign countries "must be treated fairly." The several scenes indicating, or suggesting, the shockingly brutal treatment of German citizens at the hands of Nazi soldiers, or officers, will have to be handled with the greatest possible care, not only because of the demand of the Code that the German government officials "be treated fairly," but in order to escape the suggestion of unnecessary brutality and gruesomeness.[14]

Cohn got the idea: The project was canceled.

Here we see an interesting situation: As the roundup and deportation of Europe's Jews was beginning in earnest, and as Nazi armies had conquered much of Western Europe and the *Luftwaffe* was dropping bombs on English cities, Joseph Breen was worried about Nazi Germany being "treated fairly."

Certainly, the Nazis themselves had no such hesitation in mentioning Jews as the focus of their rage; and in September, a mere two months after the release of *The Mortal Storm*, the country's Nazified film industry released one of its ugliest, hate-filled efforts before rapidly brainwashed German audiences. Based on a novel by Lion Feuchtwanger, the Nazi film version twisted the original's sympathetic Jewish hero into a brutal stereotype that was meant to justify the Final Solution. Veit Harlan said in a January 20, 1940, interview with *Der Film*: "Here I am depicting original Jewry as it was then and as it even now continues unabated in what was Poland. In contrast to this original Jewry, we are presented with the Jew Süss, the elegant financial advisor to the Court, the clever politician; in short, the Jew in disguise...."[15]

Joseph Süss Oppenheimer was a German Jew born in Heidelberg in 1692 (some sources say 1698). The nephew, and later stepson, of banker Samuel Oppenheimer, young Süss followed the family tradition and became a wizard at finance, one of the few fields open to Jews in the German states at the time. His talent as a banker and financial genius came to the attention of Duke Karl Alexander of Württemberg. Chafing under the dictates and restrictions of the Diet, the duchy's council who held sway over the palace budget, the free-spending Duke sent emissaries to the ghetto to see Süss to arrange a loan (Jews were not allowed outside their ghettos into the larger Christian-held provinces). Impressed with his knowledge of finance, the Duke appointed Süss the duchy's financial advisor and "Court Jew" (an inflammatory title as viewed centuries later). In record time, Süss not only straightened out the Duke's finances, which were generally in a shambles, but he added to the treasury with a series of what the citizens of Württemberg would consider draconian taxes and levies. The financial windfall not only added immeasurably to government coffers, it incited the eternal enmity of the local Christian populace, never at any time fond of the notion of paying taxes to a Jew.

Freely spending, drinking and fornicating like a drunken sailor with a three-week pass, Duke Karl Alexander ultimately got a heart attack and died. With the loss of the financial advisor's protector, the Diet instantly arrested Süss, their mortal enemy who they thought had usurped their power (in reality, their incompetence and personal corruption kept the town's treasury pretty much empty). Süss was quickly accused of every charge in the book, and perhaps some that were made up for the occasion: Fraud, treason (there was no proof that he was ever a traitor to Germany), embezzlement, accepting bribes, and perhaps worst of all in the eyes of the villagers: having relations with gentile women, many of whom happened to be Ladies of the Court. And though no woman he ever came in contact with, Court lady or not, ever denied Süss Oppenheimer's obvious charms, the Diet could not prove *one* of the many charges levied against him. The Jewish community put together all the money they could scrape up to buy his freedom, but the Diet would not hear of it. Sentenced to death, Süss was offered several chances to convert to Christianity, but he refused. His powerful last words before he was hanged on February 4, 1738, were "Hear O Israel: the Lord is our God, the Lord is One."

The incident inspired an 1827 novella by Wilhelm Hauff, but it was a sure thing no one in the 20th century would have heard of it until Jewish author Lion Feuchtwanger turned the Süss Oppenheimer story into a novel in 1925. Feuchtwanger used the incident as a sharp attack on anti–Semitism in his own time, as a well as a Shakespearean-like tragedy of diverse characters, both Jewish and gentile, who were caught up in their own obsessive drives and imbued with all too human weaknesses. The novel sold well internationally and in 1934, German-born Jewish producer-director Lothar Mendes directed an intelligent and sensitive film version of Feuchtwanger's novel, called *Power*.

With anti–Nazi German refugee Conrad Veidt cast as Süss Oppenheimer, the Duke's financial advisor is seen as a charismatic, intelligent and personable Jewish protagonist who not only aids the Duke in his spending whims, but also strives to get the Jews of Württemberg an entry into the gentiles' hallowed halls of power. Though Süss is undeniably seductive to the various *shiksas* of the Court and he uses altruistic motives to help his people, things go awry when the Duke rapes his pretty daughter; she is found drowned later. Filled with the desire for revenge, Süss agitates to get the duchy on the verge of war and seeks to stress the Duke's already weakened heart. Ultimately, the Duke dies of a heart attack and Süss is arrested. Before his death, he is told that he has a Christian mother, a fact that would nullify the death sentence (for having "relations" with Court *shiksas*), but the courageous Süss refuses to convert, and instead he goes to his death singing praises to the God of Israel.

Meanwhile, in Germany, it is said that a no-account hack writer named Ludwig Metzger became obsessed with the tale, and was indeed furious when Lion Feuchtwanger wrote his bestselling novel on the subject and Lothar Mendes made the film version in England. A rabid anti–Semite who had no problem later joining the Nazi Party, Metzger tried to pitch the project to the new Nazi-controlled Terra Films in 1939, which, surprisingly, turned him down. Boldly, he approached the Ministry of Propaganda and spoke to one of Goebbels' aides, who, after running the idea through his boss, responded with an enthusiastic yes.

It seemed that Goebbels fairly hated any pro–Jewish works coming out of England and America (of which there were pitiably few anyway) and spitefully gave orders to steal the ideas for these films (copyright infringement never bothered totalitarian states) and make anti–Semitic versions. A good example of this would be when they turned Fox's 1934 *The House of Rothschild* into the anti–British, anti–Semitic *Die Rothschilds* in 1940. With his typical obsessive drive, Goebbels authorized a budget of 2 million Reichsmarks and gave the project top priority. Realizing that the government needed more films that would make the public hate Jews and give the Nazis a pretext for the Final Solution to come, Goebbels envisioned a film which rejected the blunt and crude Jew-baiting of *The Eternal Jew* into a far more sophisticated cinematic condemnation of the Chosen People.

It is said that *no one* in the German film industry wanted to have anything to do with the project; this, of course, was claimed long after Germany lost the war. Nevertheless, despite his many vehement protests that Goebbels forced him to make the film, Veit Harlan was considered the Nazi film industry's top director. He had aided and abetted the Nazi propaganda effort, and he would have no problem making snide little anti–Semitic comments in the film's many publicity materials. He even had no problem casting his wife, box office star Kristina Söderbaum, to play the lead (he would claim that Söderbaum threatened to return to Sweden to avoid making the film; as anyone can tell who's ever viewed the film, apparently Goebbels' generous salary gave her a change of heart). Actor after actor would allegedly turn down the role of Süss Oppenheimer, including stage giant Gustaf Gründgens (as a "pet" of Göring, the Reichsmarschall kept the actor in his comfortable theatrical surroundings and far away from Goebbels' film propaganda efforts).

The spin of the Nazi dice finally came up snake-eyes and pointed toward theatrical matinee idol Ferdinand Marian. Though not Jewish himself, the actor apparently had no problem associating with the Chosen People; his ex-wife was Jewish and he had a half–Jewish daughter from the marriage; his second (and present) wife had been married previously to a Jewish man and it was said that Marian and his wife hid her ex-husband in their home to protect him from the Gestapo. Nevertheless, Harlan, who survived the war and lived to tell the tale afterwards, seemed to take pleasure in slamming his star and everyone else, but, of course, himself, involved with the production (paging Fritz Lang!). He claimed that Marian did not refuse the role because of its anti–Semitism, but because he saw himself as a *"bon vivant"* whose career would be ruined if he played Süss. What Harlan did *not* mention was that the actor probably was concerned for what would happen to his half–Jewish daughter and his wife (who had obviously had, like the Süss Openheimer of the 1730s, previous "relations" with a Jew). Reluctantly, the actor accepted; he was reportedly paid handsomely, but it was obvious that no amount of money was going to wipe away the guilt and torment he felt upon taking the demeaning role.

It is said that Werner Krauss was personally anti–Semitic and that he had no problem with the Nazis' racial agenda; though apparently his own son rejected this bigotry and married a Jewish woman. Seeking a way out of the film, Krauss demanded that he play all the Jewish roles; unfortunately, Goebbels agreed with his demand, giving the former Dr. Caligari a chance to portray the aging Rabbi Loew (the benign Rabbi Gabriel in the novel), rewritten here as a grasping stereotype, and Süss' confidante Levy, a slimy little toad who delights in making the various Christian characters in the film suffer. Ultimately, the anti–Semitic actor had Goebbels issue a statement declaring that Krauss was not of Jewish blood, but "playing a part as an actor in the service of the State." Later, Goebbels issued a disclaimer stating that all actors playing the roles of Jews were of "pure Aryan blood."

Typically, Harlan cast his beautiful blonde-haired, blue-eyed Swedish wife Kristina Söderbaum as the Christian heroine who gets raped by the film's "despicable Jew." Promoted all through the Nazi years as the ideal of "Aryan womanhood," Söderbaum had made more than one film in which she falls for the wrong kind of guy, gets laid, and ultimately has to commit suicide to expiate her sins, with the method of suicide usually, though not always, drowning herself in some obscure ravine outside of town. This caused German audiences to refer to her as *Reichswasserleiche*, translated as "the drowned corpse of the Reich." In *Jew Süss*, the actress holds onto her cherished title with a vengeance.

The film had Harlan and his screenwriters (which included Harlan), whether under Goebbels' instructions or not, freely pirating scenes from *Power* and coming up with their own anti–Semitic take on them. The Jews worshipping in temple, which marks the beginning of *Power* (including some powerful singing from a cantor), becomes the unruly ritual of an alien race in Harlan's *Jew Süss*. When the Duke's emissary visits Süss for a loan, the Jewish entrepreneur has no problem showing him a vault-load of jewelry and granting him a loan—but at a price. Süss decides to shave off his beard so that he'll look more gentile when he goes to his appointment with the Duke. However, in a hurry to get to the palace, his buckboard gets into an accident and turns over; he is rescued and given a ride by the beautiful Aryan maiden Dorothea Sturm (Kristina Söderbaum), who happens to be the daughter of the head of the royal council, the same one who refuses the Duke's demands to stage a ballet in his honor or pay for him to have a bodyguard. She is engaged to composer Faber (Malte Jaeger). In a previous scene at Sturm's home (the council head is played by Eugen Klöpfer), we see the couple's happiness and their family living a life of plenty and contentment in the Duchy.

However, Dorothea's meeting with Süss is a harbinger of disaster to come, as he is definitely attracted to her, though, of course, not in a clean *gentile* way. When she asks where he's from, Süss responds that he's a citizen of the world, a response which baffles the not-too-bright *Fräulein*, but makes sense in Nazi-speak: To Harlan and the filmmakers, Süss is symbolic of the rootless Jew who belongs nowhere and has allegiance to no land at all; in other words, a natural usurper and parasite.

After meeting the Duke (former Communist Party member and Nazi film star Heinrich George), we soon see that Süss' idea of repaying the loan is not only to elevate his own position within the Duke's realm but to get the ban on Jews broken so that they can enter Württemberg proper. In record time, the Duke's new financial advisor levies taxes on the *goyim* of Württemberg, the burdens of which practically bankrupt the Duchy and provoke the citizenry into acts of defiance and armed rebellion. When the local blacksmith attacks Süss' coach with an ax, the financial advisor orders the man's hanging. Süss has also played on his boss' sexual appetites, and after his ballet, young girls are invited to be ogled (and possibly more) by the lecherous Duke and his financial advisor, an arrangement that appalls Faber, Sturm and all the other "righteous gentiles."

When Süss tells Sturm that he wants to marry his daughter, the father refuses and instead quickly has her married to Faber to thwart Süss' designs on her. Angrily, Süss and Levy frame Sturm and the council as conspiring against the Duke, causing him to dissolve the Diet and have Sturm arrested. Since Faber is also leading the rebels and happens to be married to the object of his desires, Süss has the composer arrested and tortured (considering that Faber is a vicious anti–Semite anyway, one can hardly feel much sympathy for his plight). When Dorothea comes to beg Süss' mercy, the sleazy financial advisor tells her only *one* thing will make him release her husband, and then demonstrates this by making a grab for the attractive Aryan. With Faber's cries heard just across the way, ultimately Dorothea finds herself on Süss' bed with him climbing on top of her as the scene fades. In record time, Faber is released, but at a price, as his wife, the Drowned Corpse of the Reich, is soon found drowned.

Carrying her still-dripping corpse to the Duke and Süss, Faber calls for the royal to have his financial advisor arrested. Violently refusing, the Duke works himself up into getting a fatal heart attack. Now, with absolutely no legal right to do so, the mob has Süss arrested. Sentenced to death, not so much for any crooked dealings, but because he had relations with an Aryan woman, Süss is put into a human-sized birdcage and raised above the ground (not only does Harlan steal the way Conrad Veidt died in *Power*, but even steals the film's final tableau with the hanging occurring at night with snow lightly falling in the courtyard).

The film, fully promoted by Goebbels' propaganda ministry, and on a budget of 2 million Reichsmarks, would make back its cost and extra besides with a profit of 6.5 million Reichsmarks, having been seen by some 20 million Germans. Released in Germany purposely on November 8, the second anniversary of *Kristallnacht*, *Jew Süss* had already received the top prize at the Mussolini-controlled Venice Film Festival on September 8, 1940. *Reichsführer SS* Heinrich Himmler ordered that *Jew Süss* be shown to all SS personnel, concentration camp guards, and especially non–Jewish areas dominated by the Reich where Jews were about to be deported to the East. Lion Feuchtwanger was horrified by what Harlan and his Nazi bosses had done to his novel, and angrily called the film *Scandwerk* ("a shameful work"). Still enraged, the author wrote a letter to all seven actors in the film who played prominent roles, though we can safely assume that three of these letters were written needlessly since Werner Krauss allegedly played four roles.

Though the film justifiably brought Lion Feuchtwanger's blood to a boil, *Jew Süss* would provoke the same reactions to German audiences, but for far different reasons. According to reports filed by Reinhard Heydrich's SD, whose agents had attended showings of the film in cities all over Germany, *Jew Süss* inspired something far uglier: "Among the scenes especially singled out—apart from the rape scene—is entry of the Jews and all their bags and baggage into Stuttgart. In fact, this scene has set off *demonstrations against the Jews* during the showing of the film. In Berlin, for example, people shouted, 'Ban the Jews from the Kurfurstendamm! Throw the last Jews out of Germany!'"[16]

In a report filed by SS unit III/1 of the Strasburg Security Police, the unknown writer relayed an even more violent response:

> The events on the screen are so realistic that audiences are constantly provoked to comment and shouting—an indication that the Party's educational work on the Jewish question is taking effect. "Dirty pig Jew!" "You Jewish swine!" "Filthy Jewboy!" are comments often heard, particularly from women; and the rape scene, linked as it is, with the only just bearable torture scene, really outrages people.[17]

The unknown SS reviewer continues by writing that "Heated discussion of the film continues outside on the street...." However, most of these "discussions" seemed to take place while these critics brandished lead pipes, clubs and fists. It was reported approvingly by SS personnel that Jews were assaulted by both teenage and adult Germans shortly after seeing the film, with regular police units looking the other way.

Just before his own war crimes trial in Hamburg for contributing to the Nazi propaganda effort with anti–Semitic films, Veit Harlan wrote a letter, dated July 22, 1948, to German-born American rabbi Dr. Joachim Prinz that was not so much an apology as an obvious plea for mercy. Nevertheless, the document, written to a rabbi concerning the fact that he made a blatantly hateful tract, only proved that the anti–Semitic helmsman *still* did not get it:

> In this trial, I am least afraid for my own person. But however the trial goes, it is my deep conviction that it will bring misfortune, misfortune for Jewry, misfortune for the German people, misfortune for the victorious Western Allies in their efforts to reconstruct the shattered foundations of a democracy which is to be based on the concept of human tolerance....
> I will not talk in this letter of the pressures which were exerted on all artists. I will assure you, however, that I had nothing whatsoever to do with the Party, with anti–Semitism, or with the whole National Socialist ideology.[18]

Compare this with Harlan's interview with *Der Film* at the time of the film's release, especially this claim that the Nazi helmsman emphatically did *not* bother repeating for Rabbi Prinz: "Around the middle of the film, we show the Purim festival, a victory festival which the Jews celebrate as a festival of revenge on the Goyim, the Christians."[19]

Harlan was acquitted in two trials for inciting hatred and was allowed to direct films again in Germany in the 1950s, though he would never attain his exalted status as the top filmmaker of Nazi Germany. In fact, the great film critic David Thomson noted that Harlan, who started directing in 1935, was only able to attract Goebbels' attention because the country's really talented directors had already fled Germany. Harlan died of pneumonia on the island of Capri on April 13, 1964, having never once apologized for his loyalty to the Third Reich, his helming their most notorious film or his enthusiastic promotion and encouragement of anti–Semitic persecution (shooting *Jew Süss* on location in Poland, he used Jewish extras who were forced to perform in the film by the usual brutal SS men standing just outside of camera range). As a sad postscript, German-Jewish actress Dora Gerson, Harlan's first wife, was murdered in Auschwitz in 1943, with barely an acknowledgment of the deed from her former husband. Suzanne Korber, his daughter with his second wife, actress Hilde Korber (Harlan married three times, always to actresses), converted to Judaism but committed suicide in 1989.

Harlan's wife, Kristina Söderbaum, continued to star in his films, but she too also failed to rise to the former level of stardom that she enjoyed under the Nazis. In fact, in some postwar efforts at reviving her stage career, the former Drowned Corpse of the Reich found herself the target of several flying tomatoes, rotten fruit and a wide variety of leafy vegetables. By

1960, she would run her own modeling and photography agency, with only sporadic appearances in German films. She died in Lower Saxony, Germany, on February 12, 2001.

However, saddest of all was what happened to the tormented actor whose subtle underplaying of the lead role was, if one forgets that it was an anti–Semitic stereotype, a very good performance as the kind of villain one usually finds in costumed melodramas. According to Ferdinand Marian's biographer Friedrich Knilli, the actor never got over his anti–Semitic portrayal of Süss Oppenheimer and he became an alcoholic. Having just been notified that he had been approved to work again by the U.S. War Department's film officer (and Austrian Jew) Eric Pleskow (who would become a producer for U.A.), he was reportedly driving to Allied headquarters in Munich on August 7, 1946, to pick up an application for Denazification procedures. Some say Marian had been celebrating his reinstatement, which included drinking; some say he was sober at the wheel. Nevertheless, Marian lost control of his car and it crashed, killing him instantly. Though ruled an accident, some people, like Friedrich Knilli, believe he purposely crashed his car. Three years later, this tragedy would be compounded when Marian's distraught wife, former actress Maria Byk, was found drowned in her bathtub.

Though there was an attempt to suppress *Jew Süss* by the Allied occupation authorities, the film would continue to surface in subsequent decades. It ultimately turned up in the 1960s in the Arab nations of the Middle East, where inspiring anti–Semitic violence was *not* a problem. It would remain there and be seen by mostly Muslim audiences as a factual portrayal of the Jewish experience (had they been reading Veit Harlan's previous claims of authenticity about the film?). In recent years, however, producers of Holocaust Studies programs transferred the film to DVD, where audiences around the world could view it as a powerful example of ignorance and intolerance.

Meanwhile, shortly after *Jew Süss* was released in Germany, American audiences would see one of their greatest comedians take on the role of one of the world's most evil men. "Dictators free themselves, but they enslave others!"[20]

It is said that Charles Chaplin was working on an idea of doing a parody of Hitler as early as 1937; some say '38, though he was able to finally put the idea before the cameras by 1939. In that time, Hitler and his armies had moved much faster than any filmmaker who had notions of doing any satires of Europe's or Asia's madmen dictators.

The legend, perhaps spread by Chaplin himself, has Hungarian-Jewish producer Alexander Korda suggest to the comedian that he should do a picture where he plays Hitler, but it would be a case of mistaken identity. Certainly, no one disputed that Charles Spencer Chaplin had a controversial history. A frequent lover and leaver of pubescent girls, Chaplin would use his self-congratulatory autobiography to diss his exes, as well as their allegedly money-hungry stage mothers, and never once accept *any* kind of personal responsibility for the obvious pain he caused. But this was Charlie Chaplin, renowned comic genius (which he most certainly was); unfortunately, along with this adulation came a monstrous ego and the boundless sense of personal entitlement that came with it (hey, welcome to Hollywood). Much of this belief that he was the sun around which everyone else revolved would culminate in acts of cruelty and selfishness that fairly shocked even the hedonists of 1930s and 40s Hollywood. Certainly, a good example of this disregard for others was the comedian's notorious penchant for being a credit hog.

In early 1938, Chaplin was working on a script called *White Russians of Shanghai* (in 1967, Chaplin would take this creaky material and film it as *The Countess from Hong-Kong*, with

Führer complex: Charlie Chaplin (forefront) as a comical Hitler figure in *The Great Dictator*. The comic icon would cynically take credit for another writer's idea, and his schizophrenic screenplay would be subjected to the ambiguities of international politics.

cinematic has-been Marlon Brando). While in Pebble Beach, California, where he spent some time ducking a subpoena from Tobis Films for allegedly stealing the assembly-line sequence for *Modern Times*, he met Konrad Bercovici and Melvyn Douglas at a cocktail party on April 1.

After Chaplin expressed disenchantment with the *White Russians* script, Bercovici reportedly asked him, "Why don't you do something for *yourself*?" Certainly asking a selfish egomaniac that question was in itself dangerous, but Bercovici had no inkling just how seriously Chaplin would take his advice.

In a few days, Bercovici had a six-page synopsis which he suggested calling *The Dictators* or *Heil Hitler* or *The Man with the Chaplinesque Moustache*. It was all there: Chaplin as either a barber or a paperhanger (Hitler's earlier profession); Chaplin standing up to storm troopers and being helped by a girl from the village ("maybe she is Jewish and maybe not" ventured Bercovici); Chaplin being thrown into a concentration camp and escaping by wearing an officer's coat; mistaken for his double, Hitler, the barber eventually leads an invading army into Austria; Chaplin has a "ballet dance with the globe"; and his meeting Benito Mussolini as they try to constantly one-up each other. But, Joyce Milton writes in her *Tramp: The Life of Charlie Chaplin*, in one of the more famous scenes, Bercovici was more specific: "One of the big scenes in the [screen]play could be Hitler's speech. Ch could do that in gibberish, the same as the song in *Modern Times* or the opening in *City Lights*."

Having read the treatment overnight, Chaplin was excited by the possibilities of the project, but when he met Bercovici and Douglas at his home the next day, he assumed the role of a Doubting Thomas. He claimed that the United States was not at war with Hitler or Mussolini; Bercovici responded that their names could be changed and that the U.S. couldn't ban satire (he had yet to deal with the stuffy Joseph Breen). Claiming he had to ask a contact in the State Department, Chaplin left the room. In a few minutes, he returned and said that he could not film it, astonishing his guests, who knew that Chaplin usually did not give a hoot what the government thought. Six months later, *Variety* announced that Chaplin was going to film a satire of Hitler and Mussolini titled *The Dictator*.

Quickly discovering this, Bercovici sent Chaplin a registered letter demanding to know what was going on, but received no reply. The writer ran into Chaplin twice at a Hollywood restaurant, but the star reportedly ducked out the back door, a scenario more in line with one of his own comedies. Soon, Chaplin hired young Communist writer Dan James to help him with the script. Needless to say, not only would James never get any credit for his contributions to the script, but Chaplin ultimately paid himself over $340,000 for his work on the film, yet he never paid James more than $80 a week.[21] As they met for their collaboration, James would claim that Chaplin was suddenly inspired by comedy bits and story ideas that were terrific for the screenplay—story ideas and bits that were obviously created by Konrad Bercovici and brilliantly acted out by Chaplin to make them look like they were *his* inspired ideas.

Having close contacts to many Hollywood Communists, it would be alleged by his biographer Joyce Milton that a few of these "friends" would give him "advice" about the direction of the script; an allegation which might explain James' participation. Was Chaplin a Communist? No; if only because the vain comedian could not obey anybody's rules and dictates but his own. Yet the pro-war stance that the Party had in the first half of 1939 was going to hit a roadblock once Hitler and Stalin had their representatives sign a nonaggression pact in August. To top it all off, the pact had "secret protocols" which allowed the two totalitarian nations to carve up Eastern Europe between them. To this day, many believe that World War II started when Germany attacked western Poland, and rarely is it mentioned that this was possible because the Soviets agreed to attack Poland's eastern half two weeks later. In the United States, Communists suddenly had to explain to their members that the Nazis whom they hated for so many years were now not so bad after all.

Thus, Chaplin, who wasn't a Communist, but definitely *was* a Communist sympathizer, ordered James to change certain scenes in the screenplay. And so, the film, which became very popular and a major box-office hit for Chaplin, takes on an odd political schizophrenia. After his Jewish barber returns from the Great War suffering from amnesia, he is unaware that the nation of Tomania (get it?) has been taken over by Adenoid Hynkel and "the Sons and Daughters of the Double-Cross." Attacked by storm troopers, he naturally fights back and, helped by the girl Hannah (Paulette Goddard), the message is clear that the oppressed should fight back against those that oppress them. Yet during a scene where it is decided that one of the villagers should be chosen to assassinate Hynkel (seen by all as a suicide mission), and after a painfully interminable scene in which everyone sneaks a gold coin (something like pulling the short straw to choose the assassin) into the barber's pudding, it is ultimately decided that the people should stay where they are and attend to their own affairs. Well, which is it? Fight back or keep the status quo? Later, when the barber and Hannah avoid the storm troopers' attack by fleeing to the roof, *again*, we are reminded of the need to fight back.

II. Rage (1938–1941)

Suggesting that they leave the country and open a chicken farm, Hannah makes the ironic comment about it being a good time to raise chickens.

The theme of the film flips yet again by the time of Chaplin's controversial six-minute curtain speech, with the barber, now seen as Hynkel, exhorting the Tomanian soldiers to "fight for a free world," apparently the only "fight" that was handy at the moment. And despite the many references to "in the name of democracy," how did Chaplin expect us, the audience, to "fight for a free world" without physically and in any other way possible fighting an enemy of democracy like the Nazis; who, by the way, were still the newborn pals of Chaplin's Soviet friends (who were *also* enemies of democracy)? Conservative newspaper columnist (and future TV entertainment icon) Ed Sullivan would accuse Chaplin of trying to sell Communism to the audience with that final speech.

Certainly, Chaplin should be applauded for openly mentioning two persecuted minorities who were *never* mentioned in an American cinema under the thumb of Joseph Breen ("I should like to help *all* people; Jew, gentile, black man, white..."). Yet Sullivan might not have been too far off the mark. Though the speech calls for, essentially, world peace, how could one take such a sentiment seriously when Nazis were conquering Western Europe and the Soviets were conquering the eastern half? Calls for peace may have sounded nice, but the problem was that the Nazis and the Soviets (as well as Imperial Japan and fascist Italy) *loved* the idea that the rest of the world was at peace and not attacking them as they conquered the world without interference. These totalitarian powers *also* did not want war, they wanted *surrender*.

Meanwhile, as Chaplin portrayed a Jewish barber, *real* Jews were going through their own hell. Besides the persecution and mass murders already starting in Germany and other Nazi-occupied territories, the Jews were also being depicted on German screens as something less than human.

"These sequences and the contrasting Jewish types from all parts of the world providing devastating proof ... that for all his apparent adaptation to countries, languages and ways of life, a Jew is always a Jew." This statement could have come from the private conversations or personal correspondences of anyone in Roosevelt's State or War departments (or, for that matter, anyone in Anthony Eden's Foreign Office), it actually came from a field report filed by agents of Reinhardt Heydrich's SD, the secret intelligence arm of the SS (it is said that Heydrich had files on everyone in the Nazi hierarchy, including his boss Himmler, and even Hitler himself). Goebbels had Heydrich send out his agents to German theaters, especially around Berlin, and act as goose-stepping movie reviewers. The quoted statement is just part of a voluminous file on a so-called documentary "directed" by fanatical Nazi filmmaker Fritz Hippler (who usually shot "approved" newsreels). At the time referred to as *The Wandering Jew* or *The Eternal Jew*, its German name when released was *Der ewige Jude*.

Shot in Nazi-occupied Poland, *The Eternal Jew* levels both barrels on the purported enemies of the so-called Master Race. It begins with a stern off-screen narrator informing us that the film we are about to see "shows us the Jews as they really are, behind the mask of the civilized European." Calling the Jewish people "civilized" is the greatest compliment the filmmakers offer; it is all downhill from there.

We see close-ups of Jews, some religious, some secular, with comical music played on the soundtrack as the narrator calls attention to their non–Aryan features. Shot in the Jewish ghettos of Poland (ghettos which the Poles themselves had driven the Jews into long before

Nazi and Soviet armies marched into the country), we are given a kind of Aryan grand tour of the *Untermensch*. According to the narrator (as the cameras focuses on the Jewish residents), their faces are "grotesque, comical," and later on, as the camera pans over a lineup of Jewish men, goofy, comical music is again played so that German audiences can freely laugh at them. However, no sooner does the Jew become a comical figure not to be taken seriously than sinister music is played on the soundtrack and the Jew's alleged fondness for money is mentioned. Soon, we are told that, within an hour of the German occupation, the Jews "resumed their money dealings." Indeed, the words "money," "business," and "merchandise" seem to be the three most used words when describing the Jews in this film. We are, however, also informed that "The things that are valued by the creative Aryan peoples have been reduced by the Jew to the level of a mere piece of merchandise, which he buys and sells but he cannot produce himself."

And if that is not enough to convince us, our friendly narrator tells us that "The Jews are a race without farmers and without manual laborers, a race of parasites." Like the later film-within-a-film shot in occupied Poland that was discovered in recent years, *A Film Unfinished*, this so-called documentary pushes supposedly well-dressed and thriving Jews before the cameras to give the German audience the impression that these "parasitic" people are profiting off the war while the gentiles suffer. The narrator contrasts the Jew of the pushcart with the Aryan of the fields and farmlands. The Aryan, we are told, "enjoys working with his hands"; of course, we assume he had to when he built Auschwitz. And we are told that, as far as the Jewish people are concerned, "Their homelessness is of their own choosing and is in accordance with their whole history!" Suddenly the Jews' flight from pogroms and persecution becomes a personal choice.

Comparing some people to rats and parasites was one thing, but by the end, the film's racist doctrines extend to insulting other persecuted peoples as well. Showing a clip of a black female singer, the shouting narrator claims that, thanks to the Jews, the arts have become "niggerized and bastardized!" Then there is the list of the escapees, those Jewish or half-Jewish artists who were smart enough to break out of the madhouse and get to America. Here is where some of the *real* spite of the Nazi filmmakers is revealed as they heap scorn on the artists who fled the New Order to become success stories in America. While showing clips of these artists, the narrator screams out phrases like "The Jew Lubitsch!" or something like that, with the celebrity's last name always having the words *The Jew* screamed in front of it. We see "The Jew Chaplin!" with the narrator neglecting to inform us that the comedian was raised as an Anglican. We are shown the big underworld trial scene that climaxes *M* (obviously without Erich Pommer's permission) while the narrator screams, "The Jew Lorre!" again neglecting to say that the actor was *half*-Jewish. Still, Lorre's sympathetic portrayal of the child-murderer is seen as typical of Jewish ethics; besides saying that Jews side with murderers and degenerates, the way Hippler presents the scene basically implied that Lorre really *is* like the murderer he portrayed. This was a little Nazi spite here: Lorre had previously turned down countless requests from Goebbels to return to Germany and play murderers for the new Nazified film industry. Soon, the actor would give a little payback of his own while working in Hollywood, happily playing Nazi villains in films like *All Through the Night* and *The Cross of Lorraine* and making anti–Nazi films all through the war.

In one of the more disgusting scenes, Hippler has a Hasidic Jew cut the throat of a cow on camera, an act which is supposed to show how cruel they are when they slaughter livestock;

II. Rage (1938–1941)

however, this act should channel our rage towards the director and the gun-toting Nazis off-camera forcing the Hasidic man to kill the animal. After this and other inflammatory, yet cartoonish scenes, with each trying to top the previous in mindless delirium and sophomoric accusations, we are exposed to another example of ritual cruelty: Hitler addressing the Reichstag in 1939. On the January 30 anniversary of the Nazi takeover, the Führer warned that any attempt by "international finance Jewry" to push people into another world war, will result in the "destruction of the Jewish race in Europe," a declaration that's met with thunderous applause from the packed chamber. Unfortunately, this speech was never at any time taken seriously by either the American or British governments.

As the Jews of Europe would soon tragically discover, Hitler's dire prediction of their fate was the only truly honest moment in the entire hour and three minute running time of the truly execrable *The Eternal Jew*. "Invasion is to be undertaken only if no other way is left to bring terms to Britain…"[22]—Diary, General Franz Halder, Chief of Staff, German Army, July 22, 1940. Despite the Nazis' willingness to attack Britain, it probably would've surprised some folks to know that Hitler was actually entertaining the thought of a diplomatic solution, even after Britain and France declared war against him. With Poland conquered by both the Nazi and Soviet armies, and with the fall of France assured, Hitler and his staff now felt that Britain was a reluctant belligerent who no longer had any reason to still be at war with Germany. On the other side of the coin was Britain's legendary stubbornness, even in the midst of their defeat at Dunkirk; an act which some saw as Anglo resolve to fight on to the bitter end. As American journalist Virginia Cowles wrote in *Looking for Trouble*: "I was more than impressed, I was flabbergasted. I not only understood the maxim (that England never knows when she is beaten); I understood why Britain never *had* been beaten." Ms. Cowles seems to overlook a little skirmish called the American Revolution, but why interfere with myth-making rhetoric?

Nevertheless, on June 23, 1940, shortly after the fall of France, Dr. Joseph Goebbels told his staff that England was on its last legs. Seeking the removal of Churchill's government, the propaganda minister chortled, "A compromise government will be formed. We are very close to the end of the war."[23] Not only did Goebbels underestimate the English people, as well as the RAF, he totally underestimated the bulldog-faced man who ran the country.

Winston Churchill was one of the greatest figures of the 20th century; a tenacious fighter with stubborn resistance in his genes (after all, his mother came from Brooklyn). Predictably, he and his government disdainfully refused to answer Germany's communications calling for Britain's immediate surrender.

Disappointed by Britain's refusal to have Nazi armies march in and take over as they had done in so many other places, and prodded by Anglophobes like Foreign Minister Joachim von Ribbentrop, Hitler was finally giving some thought to authorizing Operation Sea Lion (the invasion of England), which had actually been planned months before England's refusal to capitulate. In the wake of the nation's defeat at Dunkirk, the British public felt that the invasion of their island was a foregone conclusion, but for once Hitler paid attention to the warnings of his generals and hesitated. England's traditional pea-soup weather in which rain and fog seemed to go hand-in-hand to foul up the aims of even the most determined of would-be conquerors put a kibosh on any attempts at using the same *Blitzkrieg* methods that had worked so well in smaller, weaker and far sunnier nations. This, coupled with the fact that Britain was an island whose waters were patrolled by one of the greatest navies in the world, made even the German navy, no slouch itself in the war department, take a second look at attempting an invasion of the British coast. Even with German subs and shipping launched from newly captured ports in northern France, the odds of a successful amphibious assault were with the defenders.

By July 7, however, with the sounds of silence greeting every dispatch calling for England's surrender, an angry Hitler abandoned his attempts at a diplomatic solution (of course, for the Nazis, repeated calls for another nation's surrender were considered "a diplomatic solution") and told Count Galeazzo Ciano, the Italian foreign minister, that he was prepared to "unleash" a storm of wrath and steel upon the British.[24] With invasion an iffy proposition at best, and an amphibious assault prohibitive (a decision that reportedly angered Admiral Erich Raeder, who was more than willing to trump the *Wehrmacht* and *Luftwaffe* and use his navy to blockade British shipping), Hitler and Göring instead prepared the *Luftwaffe* for repeated air assaults on England's factories and heavy war industries. However, frustrated by the RAF's deadly toll on German planes, and after postponing Operation Sea Lion from September 3 to September 21, Hitler finally postponed the invasion indefinitely on September 17. By the 20th, Göring's *Luftwaffe* would switch from daytime air attacks to nighttime sorties; within a year, their targets would expand from war-producing factories to civilian population centers in London, Surrey and all over England's southern coastline.

Yet Hitler's use of the *Luftwaffe* to "unleash a storm of wrath and steel" upon England was but one way the Nazis hoped to one-up the British Empire. With Goebbels and his propaganda ministry at the helm, Germany's Nazified film industry was going to unleash their own "storm of wrath and steel" onto the nation's cinemas…

In September 1940, as the RAF and Fighter Command's ground crews were putting up stiff resistance to *Luftwaffe* bombing raids, plans were put in motion to deal England a devastating blow; the only hitch was, it would be on German movie screens.

Despite insisting that German filmmakers keep their budgets down, Goebbels authorized an expenditure of a whopping 5.5 million Reichsmarks for a new anti–British production that the propaganda minister felt was "important to the State."[25] Others, particularly British military commanders who saw the film after the war, had another opinion, and "hardly cricket" was not one of them.

Ohm Krüger starred Emil Jannings, the Swiss actor-turned-Hollywood-Oscar-winner-turned-Nazi-film-star/propagandist. An international stage and screen star whose presence almost always blew away his less grounded co-stars (with the exception of Marlene Dietrich), Jannings worked in several Nazi propaganda productions, some of which contained antiforeign or anti–Semitic elements sprinkled about the usually over-the-top historical pageantry. Still, his work in these films usually involved portraying some giants of German history; added to these characterizations were his sizable ego and larger-than-life personality. In fact, despite his annoying off-screen arrogance and vanity, there was no mistaking Jannings' on-screen charisma; a quality that would have been suppressed in a Hollywood that valued youth and beauty, with the middle-aged, corpulent actor a shoo-in for wise, curmudgeonly grandfather parts instead of starring roles.

Having played Kaiser Friedrich Wilhelm I and Dr. Robert Koch, with a portrayal of Bismarck in his future, Jannings became the Reich's most dynamic portrayer and embodiment of the *Führerprinzip* (the Führer principle), in which the actor would play stubbornly self-righteous leaders who *always* knew what was best for everyone, just like a certain strutting little man with a funny mustache. In the fall of 1941, Goebbels had Tobis Films assign the actor the part of Paul Krüger, the feisty president of the Transvaal Free State in Dutch-populated South Africa. Known as "Uncle" ("Ohm" in German) Krüger, he became just one of the many players in England's colonial power-grab during the Boer War. As directed by pro–Nazi fanatic Hans Steinhoff, *Ohm Krüger* twists the history of the Boer War, but not much, to portray a greedy and exploitative England that merely takes whatever it wants, even if it rightfully belongs to someone else. However, though the film was clearly Nazi propaganda, British colonialism itself was no fabrication.

The movie begins with excitement at a Swiss hotel around 1900 when it is discovered that Paul Krüger (Emil Jannings), former president of Transvaal Free State, is staying there. All the journalists want to talk to him; however, only his doctor and his cute nurse are allowed to be with him. Now going blind and sensitive to light, the old man tells them his story. Before you can say "Queen Victoria is an old drunk," the film whisks us back to Transvaal Free State where Krüger is their president, presiding over his nation much as a father raises his children. He is wise, gruff, curmudgeonly, but tough and forceful when the need arises.

However, lurking in the shadows like evil, stiff-upper-lipped phantoms, are the British, who desire the land of the Boers. We see British politician, mining entrepreneur, colonialist and all-around rat's ass Cecil Rhodes (Ferdinand Marian) lovingly gaze at a globe and express his desire to capture Africa's gold for England. Though this propaganda piece would concentrate on South Africa's oppressed Aryan population, in real life, Rhodes was also known for trying to push black tribes off their ancestral lands, an important detail missing in this Nazi epic.

It is certainly interesting to see Marian, a few months after finishing up his part in the inflammatory *Jew Süss*, playing the part of Rhodes with the same oily demeanor and low-key purring of his lines that he used when trying to rape Kristina Söderbaum. Unlike the anti–Semitic stereotypes of *Jew Süss*, however, *this* time the villainy within Marian's role is based on history. The real Cecil Rhodes had been appointed by the British government as prime minister for the Cape Colony in 1890. However, Rhodes' jurisdiction did not extend to the Transvaal region. Hoping to rectify this, and use his political clout to grab the area's mineral deposits and veritable riches in diamonds, he got the full support of Secretary of State Joseph Chamberlain to use British troops for an incursion into the Transvaal. Unlike his namesake of the future, however, the only "peace in our time" *this* Chamberlain was interested in was the peace of the grave.

Launching the infamous Jameson Raid (named for British colonial statesman Leander Jameson) with a regiment consisting of company policemen (or rather thugs) employed by Rhodes' and partner Alfred Belt's British South Africa Company, the raiders underestimated the resolve of Kruger's irregular Transvaal militiamen, who soundly routed the colonialist scabs. The resulting failure to grab land for the British resulted in Rhodes' sacking as prime minister for the Colony, though he would remain a powerful force in British military-industrial circles and continue to use his clout to destroy the region's natives, both black and white, and capture it for England. In the film, we see Rhodes with his wife, Flora, as he boasts of his plans to conquer the Boers. In their real-life relationship, Rhodes would declare to his wife that he was too busy to be a good husband. This has caused many historians to suspect that Rhodes was gay, though no concrete proof of this was ever discovered.

In the film, while seeking to conquer the goldfields of the Transvaal, Rhodes has Jameson arm the black tribes to attack the Boers; this will trigger British intervention and, of course, a takeover of the goldfields. In the next scene, which is both controversial and inflammatory, we see a pair of elderly British missionaries piously singing hymns as they hand over loaded rifles to black tribesmen (whom we assume are the Zulus who were also a big part of the Boer War). In this film we see actual black actors playing the tribesmen. This paradox of furthering Aryan superiority while using black people to promote it was just another descent into weirdness for the Nazi controlled German film industry. More than an attack on England, the scene is both racist and anti–Christian as it shows ministers of the church arming black people for the implied purpose of murdering their white neighbors.

In the presidential chamber, we see Krüger's staff catch Jameson, who's been arming the tribesmen, and promptly put him in handcuffs ("How can you deliver such weapons into the hands of the blacks?" one of Krüger's ministers demands to know). Soon, Krüger arrives and has the prisoner released, but with a warning for Rhodes and his English bosses not to mess with the Boers. A brutal realist, Krüger knows never to trust an imperialist England and to always have his people armed and vigilant. Soon, however, his son Jan (Werner Hinz) arrives, having just spent some time in, of course, England. Having become an Anglophile, Jan is horrified at his father's militancy, and cannot possibly believe that the British would ever, *ever* take over someone else's land! Outraged by his son's naïveté ("The British Empire rules in the name of progress. Whoever belongs to it lives in peace and prosperity."), Krüger sees Jan as a traitor to his own people.

When the tribesmen continue to attack Boers, Krüger personally goes into the village to see his former friend, Chief Lobenguela (African actor Louis Brody, who had been in Germany since the silents). Lobenguela tells Krüger that he is no longer a Christian, but "an Englishman." Again, the Nazis use the mirror image of projecting their own distortions and abuses onto their enemies. In the film, it is implied that you cannot be both Christian and British. In reality, the Nazis kept drumming into their citizens that they couldn't be both German and Christian; to them, Hitler will always trump God. However, since Krüger is again a strongman character who closely follows the Nazis' way of Aryan superiority and the *Führerprinzip*, he can easily twist Lobenguela around his pudgy finger and get him to renounce the English to the rest of the tribe in half a second. This scene, steeped in Nazi racism, implies the supposedly child-like nature of the black African tribes, with the benign but forceful Krüger able to quickly get the chief to change his mind through his own special brand of tough love.

Grabbing the lapel of Lobenguela's vest, Krüger calls him a "black wretch" and demands that he give them all the guns the British have given him ("And then we can be friends again," Krüger promises). Another present the British have given Lobenguela is a huge picture of Queen Victoria, whom the chief calls "White Mother." Again, Krüger's treatment of Lobenguela is not that accorded a chief, and certainly not an equal, but a disobedient servant, and a not-too-bright one at that. All through the scene, Krüger is physically aggressive and bossy, grabbing the chief and demanding answers from him as if he has a right to; strong-arming his way through the hut until he finds the hidden guns behind a sheet, and then demanding every one of them without so much as offering anything in return. Unfortunately, Krüger's treatment of Lobenguela in this film was no different from the insulting condescension the British themselves had displayed to African natives for decades.

In the next scene, we see Chamberlain addressing a wheelchair-bound Queen Victoria (Hedwig Wangel). Seeing her reluctance to have England take over the land of the Transvaal "dirt farmers," the imperialist Chamberlain reminds her that "Destiny has called upon England to take on the education of the small and underdeveloped nations." Soon, Her Majesty changes her mind about a military incursion when the minister tells her of gold on the Boers' land, and that the report came from Cecil Rhodes. Commenting on Rhodes' bad reputation, Chamberlain sagely replies, "The men who made England great have always had a bad reputation." Then, getting into a coughing fit, the Queen calls for her "medicine," which just happens to be a bottle of booze. Wanting to show England's "good intentions" to the rest of the world, she insists on having Krüger sign a peace treaty, and *then* Chamberlain can have his war with the Boers.

Basically, the scene hits us over the head so much with its anti–British propaganda, viewers will get a headache. It is *extremely* doubtful that even the most disreputable British imperialist ever commented on himself or his own country in such a brutally frank way. Like the Nazis, the British would have thought that what they were doing was good and that no one in the world but themselves had the right to do the things they did. Considering the overbearing and sinister comments from the film's own British characters, the audience almost expects them to twirl their black mustaches and cackle with glee as they relish their evil deeds.

Ultimately, Krüger travels to England and signs a peace treaty with his hated enemies, knowing full well that they will tear up the pact and attack his tiny nation. The screenwriters and director had apparently missed the irony of the Munich Pact, the Nazi-Soviet Pact, and God knows how many other promises Hitler made to weaker nations *not* to attack them.

Hoping to influence Krüger to allow England to annex his country (and take over the gold deposits), Rhodes personally visits the president, a man he actually admires, and offers him a chance for the Boers and Englishmen to live in peace. And, ahem, he also offers him a bribe to grease the wheels. Of course, Krüger goes into a rage, shouting that he knew the treaty was not signed by England in good faith ("It would be the first time in English history!"). Tearing up Rhodes' piece of paper giving England the right to annex the Transvaal, Krüger orders the slimy minister out of his office. If anything, one is impressed, not by Krüger's ironclad principles, bluntly projected to the back rows by Jannings' overacting, but by Marian's subtle performance as Rhodes. Supposedly the bad guy, Rhodes is played as a refined and sensible charmer, a smiling and sincere snake who happens to slither into Krüger's war-torn South African paradise. Marian almost makes you actually *like* the man, certainly far more than the real-life colonialist land-grabber who wanted to make all of Africa into an extension of England.

Finally, Krüger orders a mobilization for war. When Jan finds out about this, unlike other young men, he refuses to fight England, calling his father's warlike attitude "madness." Angrily, Krüger throws his treacherous son out of his office. Soon, war occurs, and though one almost expects Harpo Marx to ride through the warring countryside like Paul Revere in *Duck Soup*, here, the comical scene is taken quite seriously. If anything, Steinhoff *does* film the battle scenes very well, using practically every one of the Reichsmarks Goebbels authorized for the production (much of which probably had to go to Jannings' salary). Ultimately, the Boers triumph, just as they did in real life.

However, the decision is soon made in the English corridors of power to replace their losing commander with General Horatio Herbert Kitchener (Franz Schafheitlin). Heaping scorn on "certain militaristic principles" and "humanitarian sentimentality," Kitchener calls for the burning of the Boers' farms and crops, as well as the immediate imprisonment of their women and children in concentration camps. Now, *Ohm Krüger* enters into its most controversial sequences. As Kitchener coldly delivers these chilling lines, one is reminded, not of an imperialist British general planning the systematic liquidation of his nation's enemies, but a speech made by Heinrich Himmler, as he informs his underlings what has to be done with the Jews and other "inferiors." Yet for all the Nazi propaganda blather about what monsters the British were, what is even more chilling is to find out that most of it, especially with reference to England's use of concentration camps to destroy their Boer enemies, turned out to be absolutely true.

Long before Nazism was born, the British had basically invented the concentration camp. Devoid of gas chambers, canisters of Zyklon B or crematoriums, these camps held thousands of Boer women and children; and, due to British callousness, these camps were saturated with disease, bad sanitation, practically no food, overcrowding, no medicine or medical facilities; beatings were sometimes given to keep order. All in all, over 26,370 women and children, many of them infants of only a few months old, died as Great Britain attempted to "civilize" the continent. Some authors would later take the pro–Nazi filmmakers to task for the hypocrisy of their accusing Britain of having concentration camps while the Germans ignored their own Auschwitzes and Treblinkas spread all over Europe. These film historians were absolutely right to point out the double-standard, but there was no denying the truth about British barbarism on lands that clearly belonged to other peoples.

Soon, Kitchener's Nazi-like dictates are put into effect, and British troops engulf the Transvaal, going house-to-house to kidnap women and children and burn their homes. At home with his wife, Petra (Gisela Uhlen), Jan goes into rhapsodic praise for the British and harbors the fervent hope that his land will be part of "the English family of nations." When an English sergeant shows up *that very second* and demands entry, Jan gladly opens the door, believing that, since he's not a soldier, he has nothing to fear. The sergeant, big and ugly and sneering all the while, accepts their offer of wine. But when he demands whiskey and Jan leaves the room to get it, the sergeant attempts to rape Jan's wife ("Your husband brought this on. He is a friend of England!"). Running into the room, Jan breaks the bottle over the non-com's skull (the shot is done with Paul Krüger's portrait blatantly seen on the wall in the background), a blow that kills the sergeant. After Boer guerrillas chase away the Brits, their commander, General De Wit (called the "Black Christian," despite his being as white as everyone else) is happy that the now-patriotic Jan wants to fight with them against his former friends.

Soon, women and children, including Jan's wife and their friends, are herded like cattle into a concentration camp run by a fat Englishman with a bulldog. Film historians of the period have written that the camp commandant is (as written by the scenarists) Winston Churchill himself. Certainly the figure, though definitely meant to *suggest* the image of Winston Churchill (despite his reference to fighting in India and Sudan, as Churchill had done), the character was obviously not him. The future British prime minister would have been around 26, thin, and with a head full of hair, not the corpulent, jowly, man with thinning hair as seen in the film. Besides, during the second Boer War, Churchill was a war correspondent with the *Morning Post* and was later imprisoned; however, he soon made a successful escape from an Afrikaner P.O.W. camp in Pretoria, reportedly traveling hundreds of miles cross-country to get back to the British lines.

In the camps, the British soldiers barely feed the "Boer wenches" and give them poor medical facilities, allowing them and their little children to die of starvation and disease. Meanwhile, Krüger, who is going blind, travels all over Europe trying to get help to stop

II. Rage (1938–1941)

England's slaughter of the Boers, but gets only sympathy for his pleas (even in Germany!). After finding his home burned to the ground, Jan comes upon the concentration camp holding his friends and just happens to meet Petra there as they sentimentally reach out and touch each other through the barbed wire. But they are discovered and Jan is captured. Just before he's hanged, he curses England with his dying breath, but when his wife echoes his cry, she's quickly shot dead. The killing causes a rebellion among the women and soon the guards open up with rifles and mow them all down. Steinhoff's camera pulls back and shows the horrifying tableau of dead women and crying infants strewn all over the hillside as a hanged man is clearly seen in the background. Tragically, similar scenes were then being reenacted in real-life, with Jews as the main targets, all over the conquered Eastern territories. Ironically, this scene was shot on the outskirts of Berlin, just a few miles from the actual Sachsenhausen concentration camp where over 100,000 prisoners perished.

In the present day, Krüger predicts that there will be a revolt against "English tyranny" and that a "greater nation" will knock it down.

Released on April 4, 1941, the film was a box-office smash in merry old *Deutschland*, or at least that's what Heydrich's SD reported to Goebbels' Propaganda Ministry on May 12:

> The characterization of Ohm Krüger is unanimously regarded as a really masterly piece of acting. On numerous occasions audiences from all sections of the population have expressed the view that the film provides the first convincing demonstration that it is cinematic artistry of the highest order which heightens a film's effectiveness as propaganda.[26]

Though the British would have their own opinions on the film's artistry, not to mention Jannings' "masterly" acting, the SD also expressed some serious reservations about the film. Typically, the SS' intelligence arm still had to deliver their usual master-race nitpicking:

> Knowledgeable audiences and people with experience of Africa have moreover raised the question whether it was ill-advised to make heroes of the Boers in this way, since along with their good features as a race they also display some very pronounced negative factors, and in terms of character, economics and politics they have by no means always played a positive role. The character of this mixed race is ambivalent, and in view of Greater Germany's colonial mission after the final victory they cannot be put forward as a Germanic ideal.[27]

In another bit of twisted irony concerning *Ohm Krüger*, the SD called the shooting of the Boer women "a particularly impressive highlight of the film."[28] Then, clearly *not* making the connection between this scene and their own involvement in atrocities, they added: "In the realism of this scene, the movie has reached the limits of what is bearable."[29]

It is said that Emil Jannings himself brought up the idea with Goebbels of doing a film on Paul Krüger, with himself in the title role, as early as late 1939 (as World War II was starting, *this* was where Jannings' priorities were). Always appreciating the prestige Jannings' portrayals, over-the-top or not, could lend to the new Nazi cinema, Goebbels pressured the studios to give the actor more creative input, including writing, directing and producing (as most German film artists knew quite well anyway, when Jannings was on the set, *he*, not the director or producer, was in charge). In 1938, Jannings became the chairman of the board of Tobis Films (the producer of *Ohm Krüger*) which gave the actor "overall artistic control" over the studio's films.

Backing up this new influence, Jannings wrote the foreword to a reissue of the real Paul Krüger's journals; indeed, Goebbels would authorize the printing of no less than *four* books on Krüger to coincide with the film's release. Introducing Krüger's diary, Jannings blatantly compared the fight against the British in the Boer War to the fight against them in the present day. He wrote that Krüger began "a struggle that will be completed in our own day. Paul Krüger ... has made the world conscious of the fact that national freedom, prosperity and happiness are being threatened by a pernicious disease: British imperialism."[30]

However, the actor and co-opter of the Nazi regime would be singing a different tune after Germany's defeat. Grilled by Allied military officers, including, of course, the British, Jannings claimed that he had rejected "all tendentious and political films, especially the film *Ohm Krüger*, which I refused to play, doing everything to sabotage its realization."[31]

This flies in the face of some incriminating bits of evidence, chief among them being the diaries of the man with whom Jannings had collaborated so closely on the hated production: "He works as though possessed on his Boer film. I am seeing the rushes. They suggest it will become a very great success."[32]

This was Goebbels' diary entry written sometime in December 1940. And so, as he has done to so many others after his death, Joseph Goebbels' own diaries once again ended up indicting a close collaborator in the eyes of Germany's Allied conquerors long after his own suicide. Topping this entry, upon the film's April 4, 1941, release, Goebbels wrote: "Jannings outdoes himself. An anti–England film as one can only hope for."[33]

Unfortunately for Emil Jannings, especially after angry British occupation officers viewed his work on the film, his fate was sealed. Jannings was officially blackballed from performing in Germany; and with a pro–Nazi reputation on his resume, his finding theatrical employment outside the torn country was doomed to failure.

Emil Jannings died of liver cancer in Salzburg, Austria, on January 2, 1950. Unlike the characters he portrayed on stage and film, he died, not in glory or for love or while making some supreme sacrifice for a higher principle, but while he was alone, bitter and in disgrace. Being the first male actor to win the Oscar, his thousands of stage and screen performances in both Hollywood and Weimar Germany would now forever be colored by a legacy that tainted him as a major salesman for National Socialism and the savagery that came in its wake. On November 12, 2004, it was revealed that his hometown of Rorschach, Switzerland, had issued him a special star, similar to the ones on the Hollywood Walk of Fame. However, hours before the ceremony was to take place, controversy over his collaboration with the Nazis reached the media and his star was removed a few days later.

As for *Ohm Krüger*, which was guaranteed *not* to be shown anywhere, and certainly not on American or British television screens for at least another half a century, the film found a new shelf life in the U.S.S.R. Just as they would with the anti–British *Titanic* (made by the Nazis in 1943), the Soviets released *Ohm Krüger* to Russian audiences at the dawn of the Cold War in 1948.

Ohm Krüger was not the only propaganda film coming out of *Deutschland* at the time. Six months after the release of *Ohm Krüger*, Goebbels' Nazified film industry gave German audiences *Heimkehr* (*Homecoming*), a film depicting the so-called harsh treatment of Germans living in Poland, thus justifying the German invasion two years before. We see innocent Germans persecuted by big, thuggish Poles, and even see Germans thrown into concentration camps, though without the gas chambers and crematoriums the Nazis themselves had yet to perfect. Though this film is the typical Nazi projection of their own hatred onto their enemies, there are scenes that ironically bring up, not mere Nazi propaganda, but the Poles' own very real anti–Semitism. In a scene where a young German girl is insulted and has her pendant ripped from her neck by a brutish Pole, we are instead reminded of the persecution of Polish Jews by their Christian countrymen long before the Nazis marched across their border.

Meanwhile, on the other side of the world, loud, strident voices were being heard all over the United States, voices that warned against any American intervention in Europe's wars. One of these voices was that of a famous American hero who mixed his sincere desire for peace with words and doctrines that chillingly sounded like those of America's enemies: "The three most important groups who have been pressing this country towards war are the British, the Jews and the Roosevelt administration." So declared hero aviator Charles A. Lindbergh to a crowd of 8,000 midwesterners at the Des Moines Coliseum on September 11, 1941. Less than three months before the attack on Pearl Harbor, and 70 years before the World Trade Center attack on another September 11, Lindbergh was addressing a rally of the America First Committee—an isolationist, and it would be strongly suspected, pro-fascist group that fought strenuously to keep America out of World War II. Consisting on one hand of sincere antiwar patriots and on the other those who, whether secretly or more openly, were admirers of Hitler's Germany, the one unifying thread to these factions seemed to be a deep suspicion of foreigners and an almost pathological hatred of Jews.

This would be proven immediately after Lindbergh's pronouncement when all 8,000 or so Iowans attending the rally rose to their feet and cheered him till they were hoarse. Though he would later deny that he was anti–Semitic or anti–British ("Both races I admire," he would claim in the same Des Moines speech), Lindbergh's speeches undeniably carried the stigma of hatred and exclusion practically every time he opened his mouth. Claiming that a Jewish media conspiracy was behind the "saber-rattling" in the interventionist movement, the non–Jewish editor of the media-trade journal *Editor & Publisher*, Arthur Robb, quickly pointed out that out of 1,700 owner/publishers in America, only 15—or fewer than 1 percent—were Jewish. Despite this fact, Lindbergh stubbornly continued to stick to his anti–Semitic guns. An entry in his journal on May 1, 1941, could have been mistaken for a page from Goebbels' diary: "Most of the Jewish interests in this country are behind war, and they control a huge part of our press and radio and most of our motion pictures."[34]

Echoing this bigotry, his spouse Anne Morrow Lindbergh wrote in her own journal: "He was naming the groups that were pro-war. No one minds his naming the British or the Administration. But to name 'Jew' is un–American—even if it is done without hate or even criticism. Why?"[35]

The excuses people like the Lindberghs frequently used, that they were not against the Jews, they were just against what they *do*, has long been the excuse Jew-haters use to justify their anti–Semitism. Predictably, when called on their bigotry, they argue that they are just being "honest." In the 1930s and into the new decade, it was no surprise that the results of the Nazis' successes were a catalyst in the rise of anti–Semitism (just as the military and political successes of Islamic terrorism have resulted in the spread of global anti–Semitism today). In America alone, many isolationists took a sharp look at how the democracies had appeased Nazi aggression and many saw it as a validation of their own bigoted opinions. But it was one thing for a lone American bigot to badmouth Jews in private, it was quite another for a man who was recognized as an American hero to speak before thousands and falsely accuse them of possessing so much power that it was harming the nation. In essence, Lindbergh became another Father Coughlin, though without the priest's collar or the religious standing. How did this man, the hero who flew to Paris in a rickety old plane in 1927, and the father who lost his kidnapped son to a murderer in 1934, evolve into a major American spokesman and apologist for fascism in the pre-war period?

One would have to go back to at least the mid–1930s, before the Nazis expressed their designs for world conquest. At the time Lindbergh became a close friend to French eugenicist Dr. Alexis Carrel, a scientist who dedicated himself to the theory of breeding superior beings. Hard to believe from our perspective of a more "enlightened" 21st century, but Dr. Carrel was hardly alone in his opinions on what constituted a "perfect" human being. The United States Supreme Court had already upheld sterilization of the "socially unfit" or so-called "mental defectives" in the case of *Buck vs. Bell* in 1927 (however, the state of Indiana had been using sterilization procedures as far back as 1907).

In a majority opinion that sounded chillingly like something written by Dr. Josef Mengele rather than an American jurist, Supreme Court Justice Oliver Wendell Holmes wrote: "It is better for all the world, if instead of waiting to execute degenerate offspring for crime or to let them starve for their imbecility, society can prevent those who are manifestly unfit from continuing their kind.... Three generations of imbeciles is enough."[36]

Margaret Sanger, the founder of Planned Parenthood, who was later revealed to be a racist and anti–Semite, wrote in *The Eugenic Value of Birth Control Propaganda* in October 1921:

> As an advocate for birth control I wish ... to point out the unbalance between the birth rate of the "unfit" and the "fit," admittedly the greatest present menace to civilization can never be rectified by the inauguration of a cradle competition between the two classes. In this matter, the example of the inferior classes, the fertility of the feeble-minded, the mentally defective, the poverty-stricken classes, should not be held up for emulation.[37]

Claiming that immigration would pollute "the stamina of the race," Sanger, along with other eugenicists, lobbied hard for the passage of the Immigration Act of 1924. The nation experienced a high turnout of some 435,000 immigrants in this country in the years before; thanks to the passage of the Act, the number would drop by a stunning 95 percent. Indeed, by the 1930s, Sanger, Carrel and scores of American eugenicists made no secret of their admiration for the Nazi plan for breeding superior beings. All through the 1930s, American eugenicists kept up a busy correspondence with Nazi scientists; they exchanged ideas, commented on each other's progress, and even visited each others' facilities, all with the total approval and encouragement of Adolf Hitler himself. On top of this collaboration, American industries contributed greatly to funding the Nazi research program into creating "superior races," with the Rockefeller Foundation and the Carnegie Institute being just two of the *many* major contributors to the program.

Like all the other eugenicists, Carrel fervently believed in the breeding of the "racially superior." Already a science buff, Lindbergh was eager to meet Dr. Carrel; the aviator had already heard of his theories about racial eugenics and wholeheartedly approved. In time, the two men would even develop a mechanical heart. However, it was obvious that the invention was meant to benefit "superior" beings only.

According to the excellent *The American Axis: Henry Ford, Charles Lindbergh and the Rise of the Third Reich* (99), Max Wallace wrote:

> [Now] under the increasing influence of his mentor, Lindbergh appeared to be embracing the newly discovered pseudo-science that Carrel espoused, and the righteous dogmatism behind it. "It should now be

II. Rage (1938–1941)

branded on our consciousness that unless science is controlled by a greater moral force, it will become the Antichrist prophesized by early Christians."[38]

Continuing on this track, years later, Lindbergh would write "We must help the strong; only the elite make the progress of the masses possible." By the late 1930s, "Lindy" would openly express the fear that a white Christian Europe would be swallowed up by the "Asiatic" east. In a controversial article in *Readers' Digest* in 1939, months before Nazi tanks rolled into Poland, he expounded more fully on his theory: "We can have peace and security only so long as we band together to preserve that most priceless possession, our inheritance of European blood; only so long as we guard ourselves against attack by foreign armies and dilution by foreign races."

In his diaries, however, Lindbergh makes no bones about what particular "foreign race" he's referring to: "We must limit to a reasonable amount the Jewish influence.... Whenever the Jewish percentage of [the] total population becomes too high, a reaction seems to invariably occur."[39] The "reaction" Lindbergh refers to might have been yet another in a series of "regrets" where he was dismayed by Nazi violence against Jews, such as his reaction to *Kristallnacht*. "I do not understand these riots on the part of the Germans," he wrote in his diary. "It seems so contrary to their sense of order and intelligence" (note that Lindbergh used the word *riots* not pogroms)." However, the aviator also insisted that "They [the Germans] undoubtedly had a difficult Jewish problem...."[40]

Predictably the aviator developed a long-lasting friendship with fascist-leaning industrialist Henry Ford. When quizzed by the special agent-in-charge of the FBI's Detroit field office on just what he and Lindbergh discussed when the aviator dropped by his plant, Ford answered, "When Charles comes out here, we only discuss the Jews."[41]

The inevitable meeting between Lindbergh and the like-minded men who were his ideological soul mates finally came to pass when U.S. military attaché to Germany, Colonel Truman Smith (already well-known in American diplomatic circles as an anti–Semite) extended an invitation to Lindbergh on behalf of Hermann Göring on May 25, 1936, to inspect the facilities of Germany's new air force (the *Luftwaffe*). Though there are those who say that it was our own government who initiated this meeting so that Lindbergh could inspect German aircraft and report his findings back to our own defense establishment, it was an all too predictable certainty that the Nazis would exploit the visit for their own propaganda ends.

It was also obvious what the results of Lindy's "inspection" would be: Göring and his Air Ministry made an elaborate show of German air superiority and technical advancement of fighter planes by showing him older models that were inferior to what Britain and France possessed, while never *once* showing him their more up-to-date fighter aircraft. Indeed, what government, whether fascist, communist or democratic, would reveal their military advancements to a civilian outsider (though commissioned a colonel, Lindbergh was *not* an officer in the regular armed forces who had come up through the ranks or commanded any military personnel), especially one sent to their country by an enemy power, knowing full well that this information would be dutifully reported back? And though it was true that Göring harassed, cajoled and bullied the German aircraft industry to increase both the amount of planes being manufactured and the efficiency of German fighter and bomber aircraft between the years 1936 and 1939, it was almost universally accepted that the Nazi air marshal sold the American a bill of goods, with the upshot being a glowing report on the German air industry to our government, mixed in with dire predictions of disaster should Germany's enemies go to war with them. In fact, at the urging of the anti–Semitic and pro–Nazi American ambassador to London Joseph Kennedy, Lindbergh informed the British that if they or France tried to stop Hitler, they would be committing suicide.

In 1938, while Lindbergh was in the midst of his "inspections," he was invited to a dinner at the American embassy in Berlin by Ambassador Hugh Wilson. Then, as Truman Smith, Hugh Wilson and German aircraft designer Dr. Willy Messerschmitt looked on, Göring suddenly approached Lindbergh and presented him with the Commander Cross of the Order of the German Eagle; the medal, ordered by Adolf Hitler himself, was to honor not only his heroic 1927 flight but his service to aviation. To the end of his days, Lindbergh would remain eternally proud of the award; no Nazi atrocity, whether it was *Kristallnacht*, their conquest of weaker nations, or revelations of the Holocaust, would make him either return the medal or destroy it.

Forever the isolationist, Lindbergh testified before the House Committee on Foreign Affairs on January 23, 1941, in fierce opposition to the Lend-Lease Bill which would have aided the British war effort. In a press conference on April 25, President Franklin D. Roosevelt angrily called Lindbergh a "defeatist and appeaser" and then compared him to U.S. Representative Clement L. Vallandigham of Ohio, the leader of the "Copperhead" movement (the mid–19th century version of the isolationist movement) who opposed the Union's entry into the Civil War. Roosevelt's secretary of the interior, Harold Ickes, with the obvious approval of his boss, went one further, calling Lindbergh America's "Number One Nazi fellow traveler." Believing that his loyalty was being questioned by a president he had nothing but contempt for, a furious Lindbergh resigned his commission as a colonel in the Army Air Corp three days later.

Yet he *still* could not find a reason to send his medal back to the Nazis.

Stubbornly, even vindictively, the angry aviator continued his inflammatory speeches. On April 23, 1941, two days before FDR condemned him as a "Copperhead" and five days before he resigned his commission, Lindbergh addressed a raucous, jam-packed audience of close to 30,000 members of America First at the Manhattan Center on West 34th Street and Eighth Avenue in New York City. To the enthusiastic crowd, he declared:

> France has been defeated; and, despite the propaganda and confusion of recent months, it is now obvious that England is losing the war.
> We have been led towards war by a minority of our people. This minority has power. It had influence. But it does not represent the American people.

It did not take much to figure out just *who* this mysterious and allegedly sinister "minority" was supposed to be, as Jewish groups and civic leaders across the country angrily denounced the former hero the next day.

However, it was not as if Charles Lindbergh was alone in publicly aligning himself with a group whose insistence on not going to war would only benefit the Nazis. At the same America First rally, popular author Kathleen Norris gave a speech criticizing involvement in a future European war. While acknowledging that "a cruel and unbalanced dictator has arisen in Europe to spread panic and assume a temporary puppet government in neighboring states, (Lindbergh would *never* refer to Hitler this way or in any other derogatory manner)," the author added: "(W)e may hope that, within a few years, these despots will disappear, and these peoples will return to their normality and to the sanity we saw in them a short while ago."

Though one can certainly praise Norris for her sincerity, one can also make a good case for her naïveté. The Nazis were *not* setting up "temporary" governments; they had no intention of departing the nations they conquered in anyone's lifetime. Also, despots may "disappear," that is, if a conquered people cares to wait that long (it took over 75 years for the Soviet Union to fall), but it's always been generally accepted that it's a good idea to give them a *good push* on their way out.

Predictably, especially with FDR in charge of the government, activity considered to be treasonous, or at least seen as aiding and abetting a hostile enemy power, was duly scrutinized by our intelligence community. And so, starting in the mid–1930s, the President ordered FBI Director Hoover to monitor the America Firsters and all other isolationist groups (though most so-called experts of the times seemed to think that the Bureau only tailed Communists, in reality, they had *all* suspected fascist or pseudo-fascist organizations under close surveillance as well). Indeed, the FBI compiled a folder on Charles Lindbergh alone that was voluminous, yet these files revealed beyond a shadow of a doubt his close involvement with America's isolationists, as well as his far-too-chummy relationship with leading Nazis. One infamous photograph taken during an America First rally at Madison Square Garden in May 1941 clearly shows Lindbergh, Norris and isolationist senator Burton Wheeler giving a stiff-armed Nazi salute. Lindbergh would later insist that the three were merely waving to supporters, but the "waves" look suspiciously like *sieg heils* even to an impartial observer. Supporting this accusation is the fact that those audience members standing *behind* the three fascist-leaning celebrities were *also* giving Nazi-like salutes. Were these audience members *also* waving to their supporters?

Dutifully, FBI agents attending America First rallies copied dozens of newspaper and magazine articles from every city in which Lindbergh spoke (the Bureau also took note of the appearances of Kathleen Norris and other isolationists at these rallies and copied their speeches as well). According to a confidential FBI memo of December 22, 1941, two weeks after Pearl Harbor, Special Agent D.A. Flinn of the Washington field office apprised Hoover of the arrest and incarceration of Laura Ingalls, author of the rural stories that were, decades later, the basis for the hit television series *Little House on the Prairie*. Though her tales of rural family life were immensely popular, apparently her other activities away from the typewriter belied her homespun image. After searching her luggage (she was about to take a trip to Germany, which had recently declared war on the United States), FBI agents discovered, not only America First literature, but copies of *Mein Kampf* and *The New Order*, complete with Ingalls' own longhand notations approving of certain passages. The agents also found letters addressed to Nazi minister Baron Ulrich von Gienanth, "as well as various propaganda pamphlets that apparently were delivered to the subject by von Gienanth through Julia Kraus as intermediary." Flinn also related that the FBI's special-agent-in-charge McKee, head of the Washington field office, maintained that Ingalls wanted to fly to Germany to "further a peace plan and to advise the German people that the American public was not being told the truth with reference to the war."

The disbanding of America First and all other isolationist groups began in earnest barely after the nation witnessed the sight of sunken ships and incinerated bodies of American sailors at Pearl Harbor. Hitler's declaration of war against the United States three days later put a final nail in the isolationists' coffin. However, one appeaser who never forgot his Nazi friends, or their racist ideology, decided to contribute to the American war effort, but in his own stubborn, iconoclastic way.

In 1942, Charles Lindbergh joined the Army Air Corp as a fighter pilot—against the Japanese...

Besides the usual propagandistic war films, National Socialism made an unusual appearance in MGM's latest melodrama, *Keeper of the Flame*. Released in late 1942, the film, starring Spencer Tracy and Katherine Hepburn and directed by George Cukor, dealt with the death of a Lindbergh-like American hero who turns out be a secret American fascist. "I saw what German women were facing," remarks Hepburn's character, "I saw the enemy." Unfortunately, this comment avoids the detail that German women were certainly no less fascist than their men. The author of the source novel, the Australian writer I.A.R. Wylie, never specified just *who* Forrest was supposed to be based on. The MGM film, with a screenplay by Communist screenwriter Donald Ogden Stewart, slams the rich all-American hero as a wolf-in-sheep's-clothing fascist. In the film, Forrest leads a uniformed youth group, a kind of benign Hitler Youth, if that were possible, called Forward America, a suspicious-sounding title which reminds one of America First. Lowell Mellett of the Bureau of Motion Pictures, the government's wartime censorship organ, was disturbed by the suggestion that the dynamic and wealthy Forrest could be compared to the also dynamic and wealthy FDR. Indeed, was the wealthy and charismatic Robert Forrest based on Charles Lindbergh? Was he based on

All-American fascism: MGM's poster (with Katherine Hepburn and Spencer Tracy) for the film version of I.A.R. Wylie's *Keeper of the Flame*. With a screenplay by Communist screenwriter Donald Ogden Stewart, the film's dead patriot is seen as a wolf-in-sheep's-clothing fascist.

II. Rage (1938–1941)

William Randolph Hearst? Roosevelt? Communist Party boss John Howard Lawson (whose dictatorship of the Party could easily have been compared to Hitlerism)? No one knew for sure, and author Wylie was not saying. Louie Mayer himself stormed out of the film's Hollywood premiere, upset that his studio backed a project that equated wealthy Americans with fascism. Ultimately, the film did not make money, despite its very thought-provoking script and excellent performances by Tracy and Richard Whorf (outstanding in a role far removed from his work at Warners).

However, a year before *Keeper of the Flame* was released into theaters and not making money, Japan had attacked Pearl Harbor on December 7, 1941. Congress had declared war on Japan, which prompted Adolf Hitler to eagerly declare war on the United States a few days later, opening up the prospect of a two-continent war that horrified most of the *Wehrmacht's* staff officers. As far as Hollywood was concerned, never before or since would the film industry focus so much attention on Adolf Hitler and his men as it produced bios, pseudo-bios, wishful fantasies, alternate realities, euphemisms and blatant propaganda pieces on the evils of Nazism. The very fact that the studios never focused on the mass killing of Jews and other victims in Nazi death camps until after the war—that is, until it was *too late*—was even more shocking in an industry presided over by mostly Jewish moguls. The administration of FDR and the Production Code office run by Joseph Breen certainly had no problem with censoring any mention of what would later be named the Holocaust, though the omission would leave a stench of hypocrisy and bitterness for decades to come. But for the next five years, American audiences would view a sanitized version of the Third Reich on screen.

III
INFERNO (1942–1945)
America enters World War II as the combatants attack each other on-screen as well as off

"You are barbarians!"
—Professor Nichols, *Hitler's Children*

By the time of Pearl Harbor, the Nazis were already portrayed as screen villains, but with the declarations of war between Germany and the United States, all bets were off. The Breen office, which was basically populated by bureaucrats who had their own anti–Semitic and racist axes to grind, counseled restraint in the industry's cinematic condemnations of Nazism, even during the war itself. By contrast, the government's Office of War Information and its subagency, the Bureau of Motion Pictures (BMP), run by former FDR media liaison Lowell Mellet, preferred withering blasts at fascism with no ifs, ands or buts. The two bureaucracies gave voice to the message that Nazism was something very bad but still clean enough for all members of the family to see on screen. This policy enabled Hollywood to water down Nazi atrocities that were then occurring off-screen and repackage the agents of National Socialism more along the lines of the traditional screen villain, or better yet, the World War I stereotype of the vicious Hun.

At least while the Breen office was around, this enabled the appearance of Nazi characters in *every* traditional genre. This allowed Hollywood to show Nazi villainy without getting into all that unpleasant superior race stuff that Nazis prized so highly; concentration camps were mentioned, but not shown, certainly not as they really were. The result of all this downplaying of the evils of National Socialism was that Nazi villains could now appear in serials, comedies, musicals and westerns, as well as war and spy pictures. But perhaps strangest of all is how their very presence also affected some horror films.

The Cat People, released by RKO in 1943, is today justifiably regarded as a classic of screen horror, and typical of that classy and sophisticated producer-writer Val Lewton and director Jacques Tourneur (the son of Maurice Tourneur, who at the time was making films for the Nazi-backed Vichy regime). Yet few today know that an early draft of the script for *The Cat People* had a division of Nazi soldiers take over a Serbian village (in the completed film, Simone Simon's cursed heroine is from Serbia). At first, the seemingly gentle villagers offer no resistance to their Nazi conquerors; that is, until night falls and they turn into giant were-cats. With little hesitation, they dispatch their Aryan supermen oppressors, and one little girl who grows up to be Simone's character, escapes to New York where the present version of the film begins. The filmmakers could not have known at the time, however, that the Nazis themselves begat their own monsters whom they would let loose upon the Serbian and Jewish populace: The Ustasha, a paramilitary group of Croatian fascists whose barbarity and homicidal mania actually shocked the SS men who were backing them.

Over at Universal, *Man-Made Monster* (1941) was a good initiation into horror film stardom for the talented Lon Chaney, Jr., but the plot, which had scientist Lionel Atwill turning Chaney into a walking, mindless automaton filled with electricity, also had Atwill's doctor rave about creating a race of supermen controlled by electricity. Here, the screenwriters make a barbed comment about the Nazis' dreams of racial superiority as coming from a mad scientist.

Recently signed with Universal was anti–Nazi German refugee Robert Siodmak (as was his tempestuous brother Curt). Again starring Lon Chaney, Jr., *Son of Dracula* recast the vampire as a pointed euphemism for the spread of fascism. When Chaney's vampire mentions leaving behind a Europe that is barren and dry and his desire to establish himself in a land with a "strong race," it must have been hard for those in the 1943 audience *not* to come to the conclusion that *this* particular Dracula was as interested in destroying America's democracy— known as free will—as he was in obtaining blood. Similarly, Columbia's *Return of the Vampire* had Bela Lugosi as a vampire count who attacked the citizenry of World War I London until he was staked in the heart (since Universal owned *Dracula*, however, instead of a stake, screenwriter Griffin Jay had the vampire put to death with a "spike"). Then it's 1940 and the time of the London blitz; somehow it makes sense that a Nazi bomb unleashes the vampire from his grave and he's back to killing again. The film is well-acted and competently directed (Lew Landers), and the plot makes much of its wartime background, with dialogue about the evils of the "Nazi yoke" on one hand and numerous explanations about vampirism on the other, with audiences quickly seeing a connection between the undead and the Master Race.

Universal released *Invisible Agent* on August 2, 1942, a sci-fi/propaganda effort in which, ironically, Jewish actors play the main fascist characters. Though Jon Hall is the invisible man (a *good-guy* invisible man fighting for his country), he is colorless. With refugee/horror icon Curt Siodmak doing the screenplay, the film is neatly stolen away from the nominal hero by Sir Cedric Hardwicke as ruthless SS commander General Stauffer, Communist actor J. Edward Bromberg as an ambitious underling, and especially Peter Lorre as a sly and pernicious Japanese Baron (with the unfortunate dark-skin pigmentation and oversized teeth of the kind the actor wore as Mr. Moto in his pre-war films). Hall has an interesting speech indicting Nazi evil as Bromberg cowers in his cell, a speech, we remember, written by angry German refugee Siodmak (also in the film, refugee actor Albert Basserman plays an Allied agent who has his fingers broken by Hardwicke's men). However, Siodmak's rage really comes through when, in a typical (and during the war years, *predictable*) double cross, Lorre's Japanese agent gets the best of Hardwicke's Nazi, telling him that "I'll make an honorable man even out of *you*." He then stabs him to death and wipes the blood from his knife onto Stauffer's swastika armband, a gesture of contempt from refugee Lorre as well as Siodmak. Then the Baron commits hara-kiri, with director Edwin Marin pulling his camera back to show a gruesome tableau featuring the corpses of both fascist enemies of America.

Columbia's *Address Unknown* (1944) was not a horror film, yet the stark black and white photography and superb direction by cinematographer William Cameron Menzies turned Kressman Taylor's classic novella (written as letters between a Jewish man in America and his German business partner as Nazism changes the German for the worse) into a disturbing horror story of the kind that was all too real in the Europe of 1944. The Jewish man's daughter (an outstanding performance by the underrated K.T. Stevens) is an actress trying to make it in Germany. Forced to change her name from Eisenstein to Stone, she is outed during a performance of Shakespeare right in front of an audience of murderous Nazi patrons. Menzies and his cinematographer, future director Rudolph Mate, excel in this nightmarish sequence. While explaining her reason for changing her Jewish name, she is drowned out by the anti–Semitic mob, with Mate's camera focusing on the ugly, rage-filled faces of these haters. Notably *not* wearing Nazi uniforms or swastika armbands, the men chase the young woman through the streets of Berlin. Indeed, Menzies and Mate turn the sequence into a living nightmare devoid of political or national allegiances; instead of Nazis chasing down a Jew, these men are like grotesque monsters straight out of a horror film chasing down an innocent victim; terrifying, murderous and seemingly unstoppable, just as the bogey-men of our worst nightmares would be. Later, when the German (Paul Lukas) refuses to give sanctuary to the Jewish girl, she leaves a handprint of her blood on his door, a Biblical allusion to another Jew denied sanctuary; though in this case, the woman's blood will serve to indict the German in the eyes of his Nazi masters.

Released three weeks after *Address Unknown*, *Cobra Woman* returned Robert Siodmak to the world of camp, in a Jon Hall/Maria Montez South Sea island adventure he obviously had contempt for. Still, the anti–Nazi German refugee was able to use the laughable film to highlight, by euphemism, Nazi genocidal doctrine through the figure of Montez's dictatorial island queen. When she enters her palace to begin a ceremonial dance, her subjects raise their arms in unmistakable Hitler-like salutes. While doing her ridiculous dance, she points towards innocent people to be taken away and murdered as sacrifices to the "cobra god." Certainly, those in the know will recognize, despite the exotic set and schlock atmosphere, the Nazi process known as Selection, with victims chosen for immediate extermination while those who survive are worked to death.

Meanwhile, over at RKO, the studio decided to avoid topics like native fascism or genre euphemisms and instead attack the enemy at its source. In fact, one could reasonably say that the studio decided to strangle Nazism in its crib. "'Education for Death' shows how unbridgeable is the gulf between the Nazis and ourselves. Here you see exposed in all of its cruelty and horror the system of perversion with which, since their advent to power, the Nazis have deliberately degraded the minds and morals of the rising generation in Germany."[1]

This summary from Britain's Lord Halifax was taken from a letter written by RKO producer Edward A. Golden, dated May 28, 1942, and sent to Geoffrey Shurlock of the Production Code office. The quote was used to reinforce Golden's claim that the source novel from which his new production was based, was a hard-hitting expose of the Nazis' sterilization program and its methods for indoctrinating the young. *Education for Death* by Michigan-born teacher Gregor Ziemer packed a wallop when it was published in London in 1941. Ziemer had been a teacher in Germany between 1929 and 1939, but, having a ringside seat to the rise of Nazi aggression, the educator fled Germany before the outbreak of war and resettled in the United States.

III. Inferno (1942–1945)

RKO Pictures quickly snapped up the rights to Ziemer's book and assigned Edward A. Golden to produce the film version, with Irving Reis slated to direct. However, Reis would soon argue with Golden and quit the production, with Edward Dmytryk hired to replace him. Unfortunately, with Reis gone, the film version of Ziemer's book, now called *Hitler's Children*, would be robbed of any semblance of class, or for that matter, a mature approach. A Communist who later "squealed" before HUAC, Dmytryk's directorial style always tended towards the violent and sleazy; and his World War II antifascist productions push the envelope towards the grotesque, with the Breen office dictates being the only barrier to restraining Dmytryk's more macabre flourishes (such as the bayoneting of a screaming Chinese infant in *Behind the Rising Sun*). After the death of the Production Code, his direction became misogynistic (*Bluebeard*), gory (*Shalako*), and over-the-top hysterical (*Where Love Has Gone*, *The Carpetbaggers*, etc.).

Our story concerns one Professor Nichols (RKO, and later Warner Bros., contract player Kent Smith), an American teacher in Germany in 1933, kind of like the author of the book that the film is based on. Teaching at the "American colony" in Germany, Nichols exhorts Anna Mueller (Bonita Granville) and other students to question Germany's warlike stance. However, in the regular German school across the way, Dr. Schmidt (Erford Gage) exhorts *his* students to cherish war and give their lives for the Führer. One of his prized students is Karl Brunner (the studio's main cowboy star, Tim Holt), a Hitler Youth who is growing up fast. Since Karl is an American growing up in Germany and Anna is a German from America, the two become attracted to each other. Playing matchmaker, Nichols invites the two to a school picnic; however, when Anna tries to free a boy who's been tied up and gagged, Karl tells her to leave him alone. It seems that the boy is being tested for fitness in the Hitler Youth.

As the years pass and Nazism entrenches itself in the country, Karl becomes a strident SS fanatic and Anna a fervent critic of the New Order. Her opposition soon comes to the attention of Karl's superior, SS Colonel Henkel (an icy Otto Kruger), who has her put into a labor camp; however, making sure that Anna will *never* be in labor is exactly what Henkel and other Hitler Youth officials have in mind for the defiant young woman. Though Nichols tries to get her freed and she and Karl argue about Nazism, Henkel tries to settle the argument by inviting both Nichols and Karl to a sterilization clinic to give them an idea about what will happen to Anna. Nichols is horrified, especially after hearing Henkel proudly claim that Nazi doctors can also control thoughts in certain defiant subjects. Though this sequence is far more restrained (thanks to the Breen office) in its depiction of Nazi medical atrocities, the screenwriter (Emmett Lavery) seemed to forget about our own doctors' use of frontal lobotomies to "calm" certain uncontrollable or rebellious personalities (witness Hollywood's own Frances Farmer).

Trying to warn Anna of what lies in store for her, Karl tries to convince her to have a baby, but the young woman refuses, knowing full well that the baby will not belong to her, but to Hitler. Still, Karl now sees the light and the young couple admit they love each other. Escaping the camp, Anna seeks refuge in a church, but is caught and ordered publicly flogged. Witnessing her torment, Karl suddenly grabs the whip from the SS torturer and whips *him* instead. Now both Karl and Anna are being put on trial, but Karl, slated for death anyway, tells Henkel that he will publicly recant his sudden anti–Nazi stance and praise National Socialism. With an international radio hookup in the courtroom, Karl goes to the microphone; but instead of giving a ringing endorsement of Nazism, the former Hitler Youth proclaims,

Planned parenthood: Unknown Nazi extras pull the reluctant Bonita Granville (center) towards barbaric sterilization procedures in *Hitler's Children*. The film was based on the memoirs of American-born German educator Gregor Ziemer called *Education for Death*.

"Long live the enemies of Nazi Germany!" As the two lovers run to each other, Henkel orders his men to open fire, killing both of them on live radio. Hearing their executions as he boards a plane out of the country, Professor Nichols promises to spread the word about the evils of Nazism to people in America.

Though the film does seem to be right up Dmytryk's alley in its depiction of an extremely unpleasant subject, certainly his rather sadistic handling of one particular scene does stand out. For instance, this is actually the *second* film in a row in which the director has poor Bonita Granville tied to a post by Nazis and mercilessly whipped (the film immediately before this one was *Seven Miles from Alcatraz*). Indeed, one wonders just how much the misogynist director had actually shot, since Joseph Breen ordered some severe trimming to the scene on August 4 before a print of the film was shipped to England: "Reduce to the minimum scene of Anna receiving her lashes and cut sounds of whips." He also insisted that the filmmakers "reduce to the minimum conversation about sterilization of women, and delete scenes of clinic showing operations."[2]

Certainly, Bosley Crowther, in his *New York Times* review of February 25, 1943, did not think much of Dmytryk's direction or his handling of a controversial topic:

III. Inferno (1942–1945)

The SS at work: Bonita Granville (surrounded by unknown extras) as the reluctant beneficiary of Hitler Youth indoctrination in *Hitler's Children*. This is actually the *second* film in a row that sadistic helmsman Edward Dmytryk filmed the actress being tied to a post and whipped by Nazi torturers.

Not only does the plot creak with contrivance but the film, in the telling of its tale, is so rigidly theatrical that it squanders its meager effects. Edward Dmytryk, who directed, set the whole thing in an oratorical style and has given it the quality of a philippic rather than a credible story from life.

By and large, "Hitler's Children" muffs completely a fine opportunity to show the fearful significance of the degradation into which German youth has been drawn. Belatedly and not so effectively, it covers pretty much the same ground as "the Mortal Storm" and "Pastor Hall." But now the interest has shifted more to effect than to cause, and the pertinent question today is how the "children" drugged with Hitler's myths will react to defeat and disillusion and the plans for a future peaceful world.

Nevertheless, because of its rather sleazy and disturbing subject matter (as well as Edward Dmytryk's rather disturbing treatment of it), *Hitler's Children* was a box-office smash for RKO, and on a budget of $205,000, it reportedly earned $3,355,000. The film was also helped by the studio's lurid ad campaign, which featured taglines like "WE KNOW WHAT TO DO WITH WOMEN WHO ARE NOT FIT TO BE NAZI MOTHERS!" and "ALL BABIES BELONG TO THE STATE!" (These original print ads were purposely printed all in caps.) The film became RKO's second biggest hit of 1943 behind *Mr. Lucky* with Cary Grant.

Three months after the release of *Hitler's Children*, a low-budget outfit would attempt to clean up at the box office with its own film with the Führer's name in the title. However, whereas the RKO film dealt with births, this film dealt with taking an enemy's life.

"It is a fact that many American do not know who their enemy is. Recent public opinion polls show that three out of every ten Americans would welcome a negotiated peace with German army leaders." So claims this unsubstantiated allegation from the Office of War Information/Bureau of Motion Pictures to Grinde in a July 25, 1942, letter. The government overseer keeping an eye on Hollywood movies to make sure that the moguls properly contributed to the war effort. Needless to say, such assurances smacked of government censorship. The Breen office also censored films, but the BMP was nothing more than a wartime version of Big Brother, with FDR in control rather than the Production Code Administration.

April 3, 1943, would more likely be remembered as the day anti–Nazi German star Conrad Veidt died of a heart attack on a Hollywood golf course at age 50; but it was also the day that saw the release of a B film whose sentiments the talented Veidt would have wholly approved.

Produced by the independent outfit Charles House Productions on Santa Monica Boulevard, and sold to exhibitors on a States' Rights basis (unlike the majors who had their own nationwide distribution arm of local theaters), *Hitler: Dead or Alive* took a quite different tack on the wishful-thinking fantasy ending of Chaplin's *The Great Dictator*. At the end of that film, and influenced by several of his Communist friends during the time of the Nazi-Soviet Pact, the comedian saw the Hitler figure replaced by his double, who, it was implied, was going to spread peace and brotherhood all over the world. According to Chaplin, this would avoid the necessity of having to fight a war to rid the world of the Führer. In *Hitler: Dead or Alive*, we have the radically different, but far more realistic approach: Not only must Hitler die, but also everyone who assists him in his war of extermination.

The basic premise of this crude and tacky production has an opening scene showing reporters quizzing the patriotic millionaire Samuel Thornton (veteran character man Russell Hicks) who is donating bomber planes to the Army Air Corps. In a flashback, we find that Thornton had advertised to give one million dollars to anyone who can kidnap or kill Adolf Hitler; interestingly, this was supposedly based on a real event in 1939, with another wealthy man offering to do the same thing. In Thornton's case, the motivation is not only patriotism, but revenge: His own professor brother was murdered by the Gestapo. Answering the ad are three gangsters (hitherto referred to by the film's Nazi characters as *"da tree American gangsters!"*). They are the leader, Steve Maschick (Ward Bond), the dumb gangster, "Dutch" Haverman (who else?—Warren Hymer), and the intellectual one, Joe Conway (an unusually bookish Paul Fix). All three actors had seen better days with John Ford, and Bond and Fix would continue working for Ford and with John Wayne, but Hymer's career never got out of the Bs; awaiting him was an early death at 42 in 1948.

Amazingly they have no trouble getting to Germany; after enlisting in the Royal Canadian Air Force, they're sent to England in a bomber, they throw out their captain (who, of course, has a parachute), and force pilot Johnny Stevens (Bruce Edwards) to fly them to Berlin, where they crash-land. Simple. In record time, they're found by the SS (apparently, a kinder, gentler SS) and brought to Dachau (a kinder, gentler Dachau where apparently no one's ever heard of the Final Solution). Though Maschick knows to keep his trap shut, Johnny, young, impetuous fool that he is, condemns their captors and their "dirty Nazi tricks!" After being slapped hard by the commandant, Colonel Hecht (Felix Bascht), he and the others are taken away and, needless to say, have no trouble overpowering their SS guards and stealing their uniforms, all of which happen to fit perfectly. Hearing of the Americans from Hecht,

III. Inferno (1942–1945)

his girlfriend, Elsa (German-Jewish actress and future dialect coach for the Metropolitan Opera, Dorothy Tree) sends a car to help arrange their escape; it seems that the cute *Fräulein* is in reality "Rosebud," the secret leader of the anti–Nazi Resistance. Unfortunately, Haverman is killed during the escape.

Elsa hides the three Americans; and though she agrees with Maschick's mission to kill Hitler, she tries to convince him that the Führer is only the tip of a horrible Nazi iceberg and that the whole system and its enablers must be brought down, not only one man. When Hitler, who is resting at a castle nearby, orders a "blood purge" of villagers if the gangsters are not given up, Maschick is infuriated; he now hates Hitler for personal reasons aside from the reward money. Since Elsa is a dancer, she is called upon to perform for the Führer in the castle's garden. However, she brings along three musicians in her band; these roadies consist of Maschick, Conway and Johnny.

When Hitler (Bobby Watson) arrives, the whole scene stops while he makes a speech to his own men condemning foolish appeasers who were warned years before of his desire for world conquest in *Mein Kampf*. Though he would play Hitler, more or less, for comedy during the war years, Watson would excel in a standout performance a year later in Paramount's somewhat lurid *The Hitler Gang*.

Unfortunately, Hecht quickly recognizes the musicians as "*da tree American gangsters!*" Too late, a gun-toting Maschick grabs Hitler and orders him to have his SS guards drop their weaponry; unfortunately, during the subsequent shootout, Conway is killed. Holding the Führer hostage, Maschick buys time for Elsa and Johnny to escape the country by plane. Also unfortunately, the myth of this B film has it that Germans, including his own men, would never recognize Hitler without his mustache, so Maschick has it cut off. Soon, SS men break in and grab Maschick and others in the Resistance. Brought back into the garden, Maschick witnesses Hecht shoot Hitler (whom he unrealistically does not recognize) as the cowardly Führer flees in panic. With contempt, and in a line obviously backed by both the Breen office and the BMP, Hecht exclaims after the killing, "To think that Germany could produce a piece of filth like you!" To which Maschick replies, "My sentiments exactly!"

First of all, Hitler was *Austrian*; nevertheless, the point is crudely made: Ordinary Germans should take no responsibility for the rise of Hitler, and he is just an aberration who's not symbolic of the "real" Germany. Of course, this reasoning avoids the fact that Germany had a militarist tradition going back centuries, with boys as young as 11 going off to military schools so they could become warriors (as did World War I commander and German president Paul von Hindenburg back in 1847); or that ordinary Germans of the Weimar Republic steadfastly refused to accept their own country's responsibility for the horrors their military committed during World War I; or that after World War II they would *still* refuse to accept responsibility for the atrocities committed by the leaders they supported for twelve long years.

Ultimately, Maschick witnesses the murders of children brought before Hecht's newly improvised firing squad and, learning his lesson too late, declares that the war will not end "until this rotten breed of Nazis is wiped off the face of the earth!" Then he too, as well as Elsa's Resistance friends, is shot dead by Hecht's firing squad. Back in America, Thornton finishes his story, calling Maschick "a great American," and saying, "Our enemies are the warlords and their followers, not just one man or one group. We must shatter the mailed fist forever ... and silence their cry of blood and iron, *with* blood and iron."

In his *New York Times* review of March 31, 1943 (the film was run for some critics before its release on April 3), Bosley Crowther wrote:

> Considering the nature of the production and the creative thought devoted thereto, it is needless to note that the effort meets with eminent success.... And the gangsters, in sacrificial fade-outs, are hailed as towering heroes.
>
> Folks who read the comics should recognize the style—and should be the most (if not the only) appreciative audience for this film.

Unfortunately, one does wonder if the esteemed critic actually saw the film since he also wrote that Hitler is "betrayed by a lady" and that there were *four* American gangsters (Johnny is an American army air corps pilot, not a gangster).

In a letter to the film's director, B maven Nick Grinde, dated July 25, 1942, as the film was being prepared, an unknown writer from BMP's "Motion Picture Analysis Section" went into great detail on what direction the film's story should take: "Not all Germans belong to the Nazi-gangster group. Within Germany right now there are many who are fighting for a democratic victory ... and upon them rests our hope for an eventual enduring peace." Unfortunately, this is the kind of politically convenient thinking that had let too many of the guilty off the hook.

The BMP letter continued: "Most important, the Americans and their wealthy backer must realize that destroying Hitler alone won't finish off the Nazi gang. From the standpoint of the war information program, this is *the* vital message to be gotten across in this film."

Later in the four-page letter, the BMP writer points out a particularly offensive line in the script. On page 37, when Maschick is making a certain point to Johnny, he ends it with "And that is how darkies were born." The BMP writer then insisted that "The government feels that the full cooperation of the 15,000,000 U.S. Negroes are needed for the success of the war effort. This type of casual humor at their expense is very much resented among colored Americans. Wouldn't another line serve the same story purpose?"

All in all, *Hitler: Dead or Alive* was an interesting hybrid; a film that starts out, more or less, as a wacky comedy about how three fantasy gangsters, who have never heard of Vito Genovese or Lucky Luciano, attempt to kill Hitler for money. However, by the end of the film, with children being killed off in "blood purges," the film becomes gruesome melodrama, with Steve Maschick's final cry of vengeance seen less as a BMP-sponsored lesson learned, than a cathartic reaction to Nazi atrocities that Hollywood film characters rarely expressed on-screen.

During those months in the spring of 1943, *two* films would be released that detailed the assassination of a monster—and the horrible aftermath of the deed.

"He made my blood run cold." So said the talented Douglas Sirk about the man he met at a party in Germany sometime in the 1930s. In later years, the man of whom he was speaking would be considered one of the most evil human beings of the 20th century. A few years after this meeting, Sirk would leave Germany, little realizing at the time that he would one day make a film about his erstwhile party guest's assassination. Indeed, there were few people who ever met Reinhard Heydrich who did not in some way feel they were in the presence of a madman.

Born in Halle und der Saale, Prussia, on March 7, 1904, the future Butcher of Prague was the son of composer and opera singer Richard Bruno Heydrich and his Roman Catholic mother, Elizabeth. Having such a music loving father, it was a given that the boy's first name and first-of-two middle names (Reinhard and Tristan) were inspired by characters from Wagnerian operas. There were two more traits young Reinhard inherited early on: one was a talent for playing the violin; another was his parents' rabid anti–Semitism. There are stories of how Reinhard's equally anti–Semitic German classmates would make fun of him for being "Jewish," a false rumor that would pursue him even into the higher echelon of the SS itself. Yet it was his father's stereotypical imitation of the village's few Jews that he came in contact with that caused neighbors and townsfolk to "suspect" that Reinhard came from Jewish ancestry.

By 1930, as the family's fortune was lost during the worldwide Depression, Heydrich abandoned any hopes of a career as a musician and instead decided on a guaranteed paycheck and pension when he joined the German navy. He had already had a taste of quasi-military life when he joined Maercker's Volunteer Rifles, a unit of the fascist paramilitary group, the Freikorps. Anti-Communist, antiunion and rabidly anti–Semitic, the Freikorps terrorized much of Germany and attacked all who they perceived as enemies of militarism all through the Weimar Republic. Little is known about Heydrich's activities with the group during this time, but it was pretty obvious that his relationships within the Freikorps, as well as his anti–Semitic father, might have put him on the road he was to travel; or as he said years later, his membership in the Freikorps was a "political awakening" for him.

Enlisting in the German navy in 1922, Heydrich rose quickly in the fleet, from naval cadet to senior midshipman to ensign, and finally to the rank of sub-lieutenant. Ambitious and well-liked by his superiors and fellow crewmen and officers, Heydrich was also friendly with the captain of his ship which patrolled Germany's northern coast, an intelligent and talented officer named Wilhelm Canaris. Charmed by the young man, Canaris invited him to family gatherings where both Heydrich and the skipper's wife would play the violin. Yet even then, the sharp-witted Canaris saw something in his young friend's personality that never failed to disturb him. Cultured, talented and industrious on one hand, Heydrich also projected another side to him that frankly scared those he came in contact with.

By the end of the decade, it looked like clear sailing ahead for the young naval officer. And so, it was a rude awakening for him when, after announcing his upcoming marriage to the aristocratic Lina von Osten not long after they met at a navy party in December 1930, Heydrich was publicly charged with breach of promise. Cutting a sharply handsome figure in his navy uniform, it was no surprise that Heydrich was a notorious womanizer; apparently he had promised to marry another young woman a good six months *before* he got himself engaged to Lina von Osten. Charged with "conduct unbecoming of an officer and a gentleman," Admiral Erich Raeder dismissed Heydrich from the service. His navy career now broken forever, he still went through with his marriage to von Osten, a woman who had her own plans in mind for her new husband, as well as Germany itself. A Nazi party activist (she had joined them in 1929), von Osten got in touch with SS officer Karl von Eberstein and suggested that he put a bug in the ear of SS chief Heinrich Himmler.

Certainly, if there was anyone in the Nazi hierarchy who could give Reinhard Heydrich a run for his money in the clinical psychopath department, it was the former teacher and chicken farmer Himmler. A bookish, nearsighted, colorless little bureaucrat with a little mustache, he seemed to be the antithesis of the racial purity the tall, blond-haired, strapping Heydrich symbolized. However, the two had three things in common: ruthless ambition, a sincere desire to make Germany the master of its destiny (and in time, the master of Europe); and an insane hatred for anyone who they perceived as standing in the way of their goals.

Though Himmler had actually cancelled the appointment to see Heydrich, Lina allegedly did not tell her fiancée and instead sent him on to SS headquarters in Munich. Since Heydrich had traveled so far to see him, Himmler met the ex-navy man in his office. The legend has it that Himmler gave Heydrich a notepad and several pencils and told him to go in the other room and outline his ideas for an intelligence organization within the SS that would go after enemies of a future regime. Experienced in the navy's chain of command structure (and probably after conversations with Wilhelm Canaris), Heydrich finished up in record time and turned his pop-quiz answers over to Himmler. Duly impressed with Heydrich's ideas of using blackmail, intelligence-gathering, slanderous rumors and brute force against all perceived enemies of the State, Himmler hired the young man on the spot.

As time went on, Heydrich's salary within the party increased, as did his rank. Now a Nazi Pary member (as was his wife and her family), Heydrich had a network of spies and informers already set up within weeks after taking the position. With his men gathering information on everyone considered an enemy of the Party (and the Party *was* the State), Heydrich had thousands of index cards on file at the Munich "Brown House." Impressed with his subordinate's talent for intelligence work, to mark the occasion of Heydrich's marriage to von Osten, Himmler's wedding gift was a promotion to *Obersturmbannführer* (major) of the SS. In a few short years, he would be elevated to the rank of general.

In 1932, Himmler appointed him to the post of chief of the *Sicherheitsdienst*, otherwise known as the SD, the intelligence arm of the SS. By 1933, after Hitler became chancellor, Himmler and Heydrich moved to take full control over the police forces of all 17 German states; a sample of this power grab came in early 1933 when Heydrich, bringing along a crew of SD men in several army trucks, physically took over the police precincts of Munich. In the ensuing years, Heydrich's role in the New Order would expand considerably, with new responsibilities, as well as greater power, his for the taking. Though Göring founded the Gestapo as a Prussian police force in 1933, he transferred his authority over them to Himmler. On April 22, 1934, however, the SS chief appointed Heydrich as head of the Gestapo. On June 17, 1936, Hitler appointed Himmler as chief of all police forces in Germany; but close associate Heydrich was not left out. By the mid–1930s, Heydrich not only commanded the Gestapo and the SD, he was also put in charge of the Order Police, or "Orpo," whose hands would be stained with much blood in the years ahead, as well as Department IV, or "Kripo," the Criminal Police (all these police agencies would be formed into the RSHA, the Reich Security Main Office). These various edicts now put two of the most ruthless men in the country in charge of all police forces and intelligence-gathering agencies in Germany.

In the years ahead, Heydrich would have a major hand in the planning and literal execution of the Night of the Long Knives, the Gleiwicz affair which prompted the invasion of Poland, and *Kristallnacht*. The *Schutzhaft*, otherwise known as "the Gestapo Law," was passed in 1936, giving all police forces under Himmler and Heydrich absolute power to imprison people without any judicial proceedings whatsoever (this extra-legal act was also sardonically known as "protective custody"). Thousands of Jews and others perceived to be enemies of the State were arrested and, if not killed outright (Heydrich's police usually had the right to kill without having to answer to any oversight or board of inquiry), taken away in the middle of the night and thrown into newly-built concentration camps, dozens of which were built around Germany as soon as Hitler took power. After the start of the war, Heydrich formed the *Einsatzgruppen*, the Waffen-SS, and expanded the tasks of the Order Police; all of these military and police squads would become "mobile killing units" who murdered Jews and Slavs in the wake of the German army's invasion of Russia and other nations to the east. On January 20, 1942, he was the primary mover and shaker of the so-called Wannsee Conference, convened in the Berlin suburb of Wannsee, where invited officials from various government departments were wined and dined as they plotted the extermination of the Jews of Europe.

Added to all these endless examples of bottomless evil, Heydrich was also a man who thrilled to new adventures that he could experience firsthand. Physically fit, he was a good fencer, horseman and pilot, endeavoring in his own way to be the physically superior specimen of Aryan health and purity the Nazis had always cherished. Reportedly, he flew combat missions over France, Poland and Russia; though in the latter country he was shot down in August 1941. Found by the occupying Nazi army, he was returned to the Führer for the inevitable scolding. However, the upshot of Heydrich's misadventure on Soviet territory was Hitler's order for him to take over Czechoslovakia (referred to by the Germans as Bohemia and Moravia) as Reich Protector.

The order was not only given to keep Heydrich away from taking his little joy rides over places like Russia and Poland, but to instill a degree of terror and cruelty into the Czech populace. It was a job Heydrich embraced with his usual enthusiasm. "We will Germanize the Czech vermin," he said about his new mission. Replacing the allegedly "soft" Konstantin von Neurath on September 27, 1941, Heydrich set up his headquarters in Prague Castle and lost little time in letting the Czechs know who was their master by ordering the executions of 92 innocent people within three days of his arrival.

Though cruelly arresting hundreds of Czechs and having them tortured and executed for months after his takeover, Heydrich apparently felt that no one in his right mind would try to kill him. Traveling about in an open car in broad daylight with only a driver armed with one Luger pistol, the new Reich Protector felt he had a charmed life. All that would change on May 27, 1942.

Trained by Britain's Special Operations Executive (SOE), Czech patriots Jan Kubiš and Jozef Gabčík headed a special team to infiltrate their home nation and take out Hitler's specially appointed Reich Protector and prove to the world that Nazi mass murderers were not infallible supermen who could survive a well-aimed bullet. Usually ignored by the British government (unlike the Poles, whom the British treated with somewhat more respect), the Czech government-in-exile, headed by Edvard Beneš, desperate for some kind of standing with their snotty hosts that would make them respect their anti–Nazi efforts (and help restore Beneš to power), sold them on the scheme to assassinate Heydrich. Intrigued by the plan (and never once considering the consequences that such an act would bring onto the Czech populace), the British green-lighted the operation. And so, with British weaponry, the two would-be assassins and their team parachuted into Czechoslovakia on December 28, 1941, hiding for some months until it seemed that the time was right for the hit.

In later years, documents would be discovered which revealed that Hitler was going to order Heydrich to be the new military dictator of France, where the thrill-seeking SS commander would have a chance to instill his own special brand of terror onto the French Resistance, as well as increase the number of French Jews for transport to death camps in the east. However, before this happened, Heydrich was to meet Hitler in Berlin and finalize the details of his move to Paris. Fearing they would never get another chance, the Czech commandos realized they now had to work fast.

Headed in the direction of the Troja Bridge, Heydrich's car passed through the Prague suburb of Liben. At a junction which split on one way towards the bridge and the other towards the Dresden-Prague Road, the car slowed down for a sharp turn. As the car turned, Gabčík appeared with a Sten submachine gun, aimed it at Heydrich and pulled the trigger, but the gun jammed (British-made; figures). However, instead of ordering his driver to speed up as a normal person would have done, Heydrich ordered him to *slow down*—apparently so that he could confront his would-be attackers personally. Seeing his co-assassin fumbling with his crack British-made weapon, Kubiš threw a bomb at Heydrich's car (which, as it turned out, was an anti-tank mine) just as it stopped. Right after the explosion, both assassins were stunned to see the Reich Protector, Luger in hand, leap from his car and chase down his assailants. Kubiš was able to escape the pursuing Heydrich and peddle away on his bicycle, but Gabčík was able to wound the driver in the leg. Somewhere in the midst of this short chase, the weakened Heydrich crumpled, grabbing his bleeding hip. Ironically, it would be a Czech woman who would summon help for the fallen Reich Protector and it was a Czech deliveryman who would use his van to deliver him to the nearest Nazi-sanctioned medical facility, which turned out to be the Na Bulovce Hospital. Heydrich had severe injuries to his whole left side, as well as damage to his chest, back and left lung; his left rib was fractured as well. After doctors operated to remove bomb splinters and numerous blood transfusions, it looked like Heydrich was going to pull through.

But then something went wrong (or rather, something went *right*), and the stricken Reich Protector took a turn for the worse. For it seemed that, besides the bomb blast, Heydrich's body had also withstood the full force of the car's backseat cushions, now blown to smithereens, being plunged into the rear of his body during the impact of the explosion. Needless to say, whatever germs or chemical impurities within the car's body itself was now also, thanks to the explosion, transferred into Heydrich's physically pure Aryan system.

Almost literally sweating bullets and fully aware of the consequences if Heydrich failed to rally, the doctors nevertheless were unable to stop the Reich Protector's slow and agonizing death spiral. Visited by Himmler on June 2, it is alleged that Heydrich, in his delirium, actually recited a quote from one of his father's operas: "The world is just a barrel-organ which the Lord God turns Himself / We all have to dance to the tune which is already on the drum."

Certainly, it looked like the place Heydrich would perform this dance was going to be awfully hot. Soon, the former Reich Protector slipped into a coma after Himmler's visit and finally succumbed to his wounds at 4:30 p.m. on June 4.

A huge funeral was held by the occupiers on June 7; it was replicated on a massive scale in Berlin (for propaganda purposes) in the Reich Chancellery two days later, with Himmler reading the eulogy and the Führer himself awarding the corpse all sorts of medals for his service to the Reich. Privately, however, Hitler thought Heydrich's arrogance in riding out in broad daylight in an open car in a nation of enemies "stupid and idiotic."

Betrayed by a comrade, the two assassins were chased down and forced to take refuge in an Orthodox church in Prague. Surrounded by hundreds of SS troops, instead of surrendering, the two men shot themselves. They would not be the only ones to die in the aftermath of Heydrich's assassination. His own SD falsely linked the villages of Lidice and Ležáky to the crime, with the claim that these villages had harbored the assassins for months before their attack on Heydrich. Starting on June 10, six days after Heydrich's death, all male residents

III. Inferno (1942–1945)

of those villages over the age of 16 were shot dead; and all but four of the women of Lidice were sent to the Ravensbrück concentration camp, where most of them died (four of the women were pregnant, but the SS forced them to abort their babies at the same hospital where Heydrich died). The children that were not kidnapped and forced into Hitler's Germanization program were sent to the Chelmno concentration camp where they also died. Both towns were burned to the ground and Lidice's ruins were leveled, as if the town had disappeared off the face of the earth. All in all, over 1,300 people were murdered to avenge the death of a man who had sent thousands more to their deaths, and whose plans for the construction of new concentration camps would doom thousands more. Upon Heydrich's death, the post of "Reich Protector" was filled by Karl Hermann Frank, who, on May 28, would be succeeded by the equally brutal head of the Order Police, Kurt Daluege.

On June 10, 1943, one year to the day of the beginning of the Nazi roundup of the Czechs, MGM released a film directed by Douglas Sirk detailing the assassination of the Nazis' specially appointed "Reich Protector"...

It took a certain amount of guts to release a film about the assassination of Heydrich less than two months after the release of another film about the assassination of Heydrich. Directed by Fritz Lang, *Hangmen Also Die* was bigger, longer and delivered the required anti–Nazi goods. Released on March 23, but "opening wide" on April 15, the film made little money. Lang's own feelings about the film varied. Dismissing the film shortly after its failure, he would later call it the second most important film he directed, and even boasted that it was ahead of its time. Not exactly; the pace is slow and the film's running time is far too long, as if Lang was back in the silent period filming old Germanic legends or tales of over-budget futuristic cities.

Far more interesting were the behind-the-scenes *mishegos* involving Communist screenwriter John Wexley stealing credit for the screenplay from the master plagiarist himself, Bertold Brecht (suggesting there was indeed no honor among Marxists). The production also had to contend with the director's usual sadistic treatment of actors, with his leading lady, poor Anna Lee, being his prime victim. Added to the fact that Lang insisted that all the Czech characters had to have American accents, preferably from the Midwest, the film looked like a truly bizarre version of the aftermath of Heydrich's assassination.

The only time the film differs from the usual anti–Nazi propaganda piece is Lang's fascinating depiction of the Nazi occupiers as jaded bureaucrats sometimes bored by the tasks they must perform. For instance, there is a standout performance from Reinhold Schünzel, the Hamburg-born writer and director of many comedies and musicals shot in Germany from the days of the Weimar Republic and into the Nazi years. Having had a German father and a Jewish mother, he was tolerated by the authorities as a "half–Aryan" until their interference in his projects, coupled with personal anti–Semitic harassment, became too much. In 1937, he and his family, like so many others before them, fled to Hollywood, where he found steady work as a film actor and sometimes director. His performance as a perpetually bored Nazi interrogator gave a spark of life to this dull and contrived film. The other performance which stands out is that of Gene Lockhart as a Quisling. When the Resistance turns the tables on him and he is believed to be a double-agent, this, of course, gives Lockhart a scene where he does his patented specialty, whimpering and pathetically begging for mercy before Gestapo men force him at gunpoint to run away; this gives them an excuse to shoot him in the back and later claim in their official report that they finally got the man who killed

Heydrich. Here, Lang makes a good point about the backstabbing bureaucracy and lying cover-ups that were part and parcel of the Nazi State.

Released by MGM on June 10, *Hitler's Madman* had a far more interesting back story than the Lang film (even with all the *Sturm und Drang* involving Brecht and Wexley), and is, in many ways, actually the better film. For instance, originally, MGM didn't make the film at all. It was, of all things, a PRC production; the same company who gave us *The Mad Monster, Flaming Bullets, Girls in Chains* and *The Devil Bat* (as well as its equally ludicrous sequel, *Devil Bat's Daughter*), though they *did* also give us the underrated *Strangler of the Swamp*, directed by German émigré Frank Wisbar. With the blood of Czech victims barely drying on the plowed-over ground of Lidice, screenwriters Emil Ludwig and Albrecht Joseph copyrighted their screen story, *Victims Victorious*, which, in turn, was based on an *unpublished* story by B screenwriter Bert Lytton, in June 1942 (other sources name Lytton's unpublished *novel* called *Hangman's Village*). The Breen office, being the Breen office, inexplicably banned the project's purported title, *Hitler's Hangman*. PRC, being PRC, simply shortened the title to *The Hangman*. Then the studio had second thoughts (if that was possible). Fully aware that the Lang project was shooting not too far away under the title *Hangmen Also Die*, PRC producer Seymour Nebenzal knew that audiences would easily confuse the two films. If anything, Nebenzal was closely acquainted with his subject matter; in the 1920s and 30s he was the head of Berlin's Nero Films and had guided many productions which pleased Weimar audiences until the Nazi takeover forced the exodus of Jewish filmmakers (he was also the uncle of the brothers Robert and Curt Siodmak). As a major power behind Poverty Row PRC, Nebenzal would be instrumental in utilizing the talents of the seldom-hired German émigrés Edgar Ulmer and Frank Wisbar. With the newly rechristened *Hitler's Madman* (which in Hitler's regime could have been *anyone*!), Nebenzal hired another recent German émigré to Hollywood, Douglas Sirk (he had Americanized his name from the original Dutch Hans Detlaf Sierck).

The complete credits of the film do show an interesting abundance of Jews, many of them German refugees; chief among the screenwriters being the famous Yiddish theater playwright Peretz Hirschbein. Here, the author of classics like *Green Fields* (the film version of which was shot in Long Island by Edgar Ulmer in 1937) puts a somewhat autobiographical spin onto the victims of Nazi terror in *Hitler's Madman*. Born in 1880 in Kleszczele, Poland (now part of Russia), Hirschbein was *very* familiar with Polish and Russian anti–Semitism; banned by the Breen office from mentioning anti–Jewish persecution, Hirschbein and his co-scenarists are instead forced to turn the presumably Christian villagers of Lidice into the standard cliché-ridden victims of oppression that Joseph Breen insisted be nonethnic enough for American families to see.

Our story begins with the voice of screenwriter/actor Carey Wilson (voiceover narration was the mainstay of his on-screen work) reciting a line from Edna St. Vincent Millay's poem, "The Murder of Lidice." Reportedly after commissioning Millay to write the poem, the U.S. government made sure that it would be recited on national radio programs in the wake of the massacre.

In the employ of the British, Czech patriot Karel Vavra (Alan Curtis) easily parachutes into his homeland, and with pinpoint accuracy, lands within a kilometer or two of his home village of Lidice. Right away, audiences will know as far as casting goes what to expect when they see the handsome Chicago born native landing on PRC's European set. Compounding the All-American miscasting of villagers in *Hangmen Also Die*, the Czech village of *Hitler's*

III. Inferno (1942–1945)

Madman would be, for the most part, populated by familiar character actors more at home in California's San Fernando Valley than Prague. Vavra is soon reunited with his love, Jarmila (the beautiful future Broadway star, New York–born Patricia Morison); as well as her father, Jan Hanka (New Yorker and PRC regular Ralph Morgan), who disagrees with Karel's insistence that the villagers rise up and fight their occupiers. He also meets the constantly imbibing reprobate Nepomuk (from Northern California, a surprisingly effective Edgar Kennedy), who sees nothing wrong with cadging a drink or two from the Nazis while retaining his good relations with his fellow villagers.

The film barely begins before the occupiers grab a resistance fighter from his family in the middle of the night (his compassionate wife, Maria, is played by Elizabeth Russell, taking a breather from Val Lewton horror films at RKO). As the unofficial head of the village, Hanka goes with Maria to see Mayor Bauer (Ludwig Stössel), to beg mercy for the prisoner. But Bauer is the very definition of the term Quisling. Though Czech (and played by an Austrian-Hungarian actor), Bauer sees the Germans as the Second Coming and is constantly singing their praises. When the two Czechs arrive in their threadbare clothes to beg for leniency, director Sirk has Bauer presiding over a feast, with a table full of food and other delicacies the poor, oppressed Czechs could only dream of. In fact, Bauer is so pro–German, he and his wife have allowed their two sons to fight for the Fatherland on the Eastern Front. Provided with first-rate meals in starving Nazi occupied Europe, it is just one of the perks the Reich grants to its privileged bootlickers.

A word about the actress who portrays Frau Bauer, Johanna Hofer. A veteran performer from the Weimar era, Hofer was trained by Max Reinhardt. Already having appeared in many films, she would marry actor Fritz Kortner and, when the Nazis came to power, like so many others, the couple fled to Hollywood. Kortner would give a memorable performance as Gregor Strasser in Paramount's *The Hitler Gang* around the same time his wife did the Sirk film. In 1951, Hofer would play the emotionally dependent Frau Hermann in Peter Lorre's euphemistic indictment of pro–Nazi Germans in *Der Verlorene* (*The Lost One*). In *Hitler's Madman*, Hofer's Reinhardt training is put to good use by Sirk; though her scenes are short, she makes an unusually strong impression as the doting *Hausfrau* who inevitably turns against her husband and his Nazi mania.

When Karel attempts to organize the villagers, as led by the live-and-let-live Hanka, they reject his militancy in the hope that the Nazis will roll back their brutality. Then, after close to a half hour of romantic clinches of Karel and Jarmilla and other staid village scenes, like a ray of black light, Reinhard Heydrich and his SS posse ride into the scene. As played by John Carradine, the film is suddenly pulled up several notches and everyone's attention is riveted. A good actor who can be subtle when he respected the material, Carradine was also a notorious scene-stealer whose presence usually raised the value of substandard material to heights of high camp. An actor who easily bounced back and forth between A films and low-budget trash without ruining his career in any way, Carradine could play the silent but scary Nazi assassin in Fritz Lang's *Man Hunt* over at Fox, yet also play the mad Nazi scientist using zombies to fight for the Reich in Monogram's laughable *Revenge of the Zombies* with equal skill. Covered with a pointy nose appliance to suggest Heydrich's nose (according to at least one movie magazine of the era, it was created by Carradine himself), the gaunt actor, outfitted in a black SS uniform and waving a riding prop, easily steals the film from the persecuted villagers, whom, after all, we were supposed to admire.

Hangin' with the Resistance: Czech partisans Alan Curtis and Patricia Morison have to deal with John Carradine's overacting in this publicity shot from *Hitler's Madman*. Depicting the assassination of SS chief Reinhard Heydrich and its aftermath, this controversial film switched studios, replaced much of its cast, and even provoked the Production Code office with its depiction of Nazi depravities.

Rudely crashing a university philosophy class, Heydrich, accompanied by his right-hand man, Muller (played by B western and serial veteran John Merton) and a platoon of SS troops strong-arm the hapless professor (veteran actor Tully Marshall) and "take over" the lesson. Seating himself in the professor's chair, Heydrich, theatrically propping his boots on the educator's desk, archly condemns "the intellect," and praises all actions "backed by force." Then

III. Inferno (1942–1945)   93

he calls for male volunteers for the Russian front while also offering the class's many female students the chance of "entertaining our brave German soldiers" who are battling the Red Army. Needless to say, among both groups, he gets no takers. Soon, Heydrich, straddling a turned-around chair in a bogus hospital, ogles a lineup of female captives, including the up-and-coming starlets Ava Gardner and Frances Rafferty. When Clara Janek (Texas-born Jorja Curtright) refuses to submit to the Nazi doctor's plans to sterilize her, she leaps out of the building's window. Though violating Production Code Administration rules on showing suicides, Breen was placated by Sirk's cutaway to the horrified reactions of the girls as Clara leaps from the window. Not missing a black-humored beat, Carradine's Heydrich remarks, "You see, Muller? Another victim of the ze intellect!" It is probably a testament to an actor's likability in that Carradine's German accent is terrible, yet he makes the Nazi butcher so entertaining and over-the-top that you *still* accept him in the part.

However, Heydrich's next outrage crosses the line into religious bigotry (not anti–Semitism, but the kind Joseph Breen was comfortable in showing: anti–Catholic bigotry). Heydrich and Muller stop a Catholic procession, led by Father Cemlanek (played by German-born Jew Al Shean, half of the vaudeville comedy team of Gallagher and Shean). Trying to provoke the prelate, Heydrich slaps him and then wipes the dust from his boots with an altar cloth. "The Holy Cross!" cries the priest before he rushes forward and is blown away by Muller. Satisfied that he has proven that the meek emphatically do *not* inherit the earth, Heydrich crows triumphantly, "So I couldn't provoke him, eh?" Not shown in this film, of course, was the fact that the Vatican had signed a Concordat with Hitler and Mussolini, or that the Church, with the glaring exception of many individual courageous priests, backed Europe's fascist regimes, including that of nonbelligerent Francisco Franco.

After witnessing this outrage, Hanka is thrown into Karel's camp, and soon the two of them plot to take out the overacting Reich Protector once and for all. They are indirectly assisted by, of all people, Frau Magda, the wife of the ass-kissing Mayor Bauer. After getting a letter informing them that both their sons were killed on the Russian front, Magda is bitter when her husband merely accepts it and says that they died proudly for the Führer. Visiting Hanka, she lets loose the fact that Heydrich travels a certain country road at certain times of the day, information she overheard her husband say. Using this inside info, Hanka and Karel soon shoot and blow up Heydrich as he passes by in his touring car.

Now on his death bed, Heydrich is visited by Himmler (Howard Freeman, the pompous Bund leader of Fox's *Margin for Error*). It goes without saying that Freeman looks *nothing* like Himmler; no little Hitler mustache and he's got maybe fifty extra pounds on him. Unfortunately, despite his cynicism on the deathbed, the script has the dying SS commander unrealistically damning Hitler and Nazism and predicting the Allies' eventual victory, something the eternally loyal Heydrich, no matter how many doses of morphine he was hopped up with, would never have uttered. However, Himmler *does* listen to Heydrich's regret that he could not murder every Czech he could get his hands on. First to be arrested is the kowtowing pro–Nazi Mayor Bauer, who is taken away by two Gestapo men (one of which is anti–Nazi German actor Peter Van Eyck, who was also in *Address Unknown*).

And so, practically everyone in the cast is rounded up and shot to death, a scene that is still harrowing to this day. However, Karel, after gunning down two Nazi soldiers who had shot Jarmilla, is able to escape and continue the fight.

Again, though Sirk stops short of the wry, black-humored view of the Nazi bureaucracy that Lang instills in *Hangmen Also Die*, during the climactic roundup and executions, he is able to suggest, even under the restraints of the Production Code, the tragic dimensions of the real life massacre (especially upsetting is seeing the village's screaming children taken away). Then, moments before the firing squad opens up, the cynical Nepomek is the first one to passionately start singing the Czech national anthem (though Kennedy himself is dubbed by an actual singer), with the verses taken up by the formerly appeasing Hanka and the others. After the bullets strike them, Nepomek is the last one standing before he finally falls.

Produced by Seymour Nebenzel's Angelus Productions, the film was budgeted at $280,000, with $212,000 of it put up by anti–Nazi Swiss businessman Dr. Erwin O. Brettauer (described in the TCM website of the film as "German refugee Irving D. Berttauer"),[3] as well as businessman Peter R. Van Dulnen, the Bank of America and other investors. Ironically, the first choice for the role of Heydrich was real-life Czech actor Francis Lederer. A fervent anti–Nazi who already gave a fine performance as the gullible Nazi bundist in *Confessions of a Nazi Spy* (and he would make a truly memorable Count in *The Return of Dracula* many years later), Lederer's participation would have put a stamp of poetic justice on the project by having a Czech play his nation's worst enemy. Having performed in Weimar-era films (he was the leading man in G.W. Pabst's *Pandora's Box*), Lederer witnessed firsthand the Nazi takeover of the German film industry.

With the surefire commitment Lederer would have given to the part, it is unknown just why Nebenzal instead went with the New York–born Carradine for the role of Heydrich, except perhaps for some extra box-office value since the latter actor was more famous playing villains (Lederer would reprise his role of Count Dracula in a memorable episode of *Night Gallery* in 1971, where his vampire count and other monsters put an end to invading Nazis, whose commander is played by anti–Nazi veteran actor Helmut Dantine). In another piece of ironic casting, the tragic Frances Farmer was set to be cast as the doomed Jarmilla; that is, until her firing from a Monogram B for slugging a hairdresser, and her eventual blackballing from films.

Production started just months after Heydrich's assassination, with Sirk getting his first shots in on October 27, 1942. The cast was the same with a few glaring exceptions. For instance, as originally shot by Sirk, *Hitler's Madman* had character actor Hobart Cavanaugh as Himmler. According to his IMDB profile, Cavanaugh excelled at playing "downtrodden or henpecked little men,"[4] not exactly the performer you'd use to portray Hitler's Deputy *Reichsführer SS*. However, perhaps seeing this role as a way to break his own typecasting, Cavanaugh reportedly did an excellent job as Himmler. Still, fate had another plan in mind for Cavanaugh, as well as the film which would have ushered in a whole new career for him as a character actor. With *Hitler's Madman* slated for release by Poverty Row PRC, Nebenzal was shocked that Louie Mayer's MGM actually expressed interest in distributing it. Also admiring the consummate skill put into the production by Douglas Sirk and the generally good performances by the cast, Republic Pictures *also* expressed interest in releasing the film. On a promise to reshoot some scenes, add others, and generally tighten up the narrative, Nebenzal chose to go with more prestigious MGM, a decision which infuriated Herbert Yates at Republic enough for him to file suit against the larger studio. However, Mayer's people quickly saw Cavanaugh as a weak link in the film; again, renowned for performing in comedies, the little bald actor would now have all his good work cut out of *Hitler's Madman* and rudely thrown on the cutting room floor.

The film also had some other off-screen shenanigans to deal with concerning not only

III. Inferno (1942–1945)

the script, but its execution. In a letter to Seymour Nebenzal, dated October 10, 1942, Father John Devlin of West Hollywood's St. Victor's Church complained about the role of the Saint who recites Millay's poem at the beginning of the film. Having been given the script to read beforehand, the clergyman wrote, "To be perfectly frank with you, it has a phony quality." He even suggested that a recitation of The Lord is my Shepherd be changed to another prayer.[5] Not only did Nebenzal inform Joseph Breen two days later that Father Devlin read the script and "has no objections," but the producer defiantly went ahead and kept the voice of the "Saint" in the picture. Indeed, the voiceover actually recites the poem while the camera is focused on the statue of St. Sebastian (in this October 12 letter, Nebenzal also apprises the priest of the picture's imminent release by *Republic Pictures*[6]).

However, the religious preoccupations did not end there (this was, after all the Breen office). In a letter from October 19, 1942, Joseph Breen warned Nebenzal that "The business of the priest making the sign of the cross will probably be deleted by the British Board of Film Censors."[7] He also maintained that British censors usually delete the words "Our Father" from Hollywood films, and that they would do so at several points in the *Hangman* script.

Sirk was to show some restraint in his direction when Heydrich says the line, "A pretty girl like you can serve so much better entertaining our courageous German soldiers with her feminine charms...." Also on Breen's chopping block was a character in the script who didn't survive an early draft of the screenplay:

> Pages 78 and 79: The greatest care should be exercised in the playing of the scenes between Heydrich and his mistress, Brigitte. In this connection, we request, in Scene 213, that the business of the girl snuggling against Heydrich and his pulling closer be eliminated. At most, this illicit affair should be suggested, rather than emphasized.[8]

This was just the beginning of the changes the censors demanded of MGM. In fact, thanks to Breen office interference, the sterilization scene had itself been removed by Sirk and Nebenzal while the film was still at PRC. However, by the time MGM purchased the film, the whole sequence was put back in, including Clara Janek's fateful leap from a window. The whole episode quickly revived the controversy about the scene's sleaze and bad taste, as well as having the stigma of a character committing suicide, a Breen office no-no.

With the film now in MGM hands, an angry Joseph Breen wrote to Louis B. Mayer on March 3, 1943:

> We regret to report to you that it is our considered and unanimous judgment that all of the action beginning on page 24 and continuing through to page 26, dealing with Heydrich's interest in procuring Czech girls for the German army on the Russian front, together with showing the room where they are examined by physicians for this assignment, is completely and entirely unacceptable under the provisions of the Production Code. At the time the script was prepared by Angelus Pictures, we went over this point with them, saying that, at most, there could be but the vaguest suggestion of the fate of the girls. The present dramatization, therefore, brings up again this particular business which had been reported to them as unacceptable.
> We regret further to state that the glorified suicide of Clara, on page 26, is also unacceptable.[9]

In an April 14 memo summarizing the controversy, the Breen office's C.R. Metzger reiterated MGM's re-inserting the scenes of "the selection and procurement of these [Czech] girls by Heydrich," which Breen forced Angelus Productions and PRC to remove, as well as they're having "re-inserted the glorified suicide of one of the girls, Clara, which we likewise disapproved."[10]

However, Metzger also reported that, upon his receiving the March 3 letter, MGM producer Al Block called him and stated that

[T]he producers assigned to this story at Metro had seen the clinical sequence of the picture, HITLER'S CHILDREN [RKO], and were determined to include a similar sequence in their re-editing of THE HANGMAN. Mr. [Geoffrey] Shurlock, who had reviewed HITLER'S CHILDREN, called attention to the fact that the clinical sequence in that picture dealt with the sterilization of girls believed unacceptable as mothers of the future German race. The present clinical sequences of THE HANGMAN seemed to suggest only an examination for possible venereal disease, and whether these Czech girls would be acceptable as prostitutes for the German soldiers.

This time, MGM's logic was flawless, as they strongly insisted that if the Breen office could pass a sleazy Nazi sterilization sequence in RKO's *Hitler's Children*, then why couldn't MGM show an equally sleazy Heydrich ogling girls in a sterilization lab before sending them to the Russian front to serve as (in the words of the Breen office) "entertainers" for German soldiers? The ploy worked; grumbling, the Breen office allowed the sequence to stay in the film.

Not wanting to confuse audiences with a title that sounded too close to Fritz Lang's *Hangman Also Die*, Mayer ordered a change in title, but instead of *Hitler's Hangman* (the replacement for the original title, *The Hangman*), the studio got far away from anything with "hangman" in it and now called the film *Hitler's Madman*. Yet when one views the film's opening credits, one can easily see PRC's cheapjack artwork in the background which consists of bad drawings of nooses!

And so, the changes continued. Working fast, in a span of eight days in March 1943, Sirk reshot all the Himmler scenes with actor Howard Freeman, who looked a lot less like Himmler than Cavanaugh did. Then, at the insistence of Louie Mayer who wanted to promote his up-and-coming starlets, close-ups of Ava Gardner and Frances Rafferty, as two of the women Heydrich ogles during the sterilization scene, were inserted into the film (notice that when Clara jumps out of the window, neither Gardner nor Rafferty are seen in the medium-shot of the girls when they give horrified reactions to her suicide). In fact, handling the scene as tastefully as possible (if indeed such a sequence could be handled with any kind of taste), Sirk shot Clara's obvious "glorified suicide" by having her dare Muller to shoot her and then, after the director cut to a horrified shot of the girls and one shot of the disappointed Nazi surgeon, he cut back to the window frame, with Clara no longer standing in it. We could safely assume that if she did not jump, she just quietly flew away.

Not stopping there, Sirk also shot new Heydrich scenes, with Carradine now called back to reprise his role of the fallen Nazi butcher for a cool $2,500. No wonder he looked like he was having fun with the part! Plainly seeing this aspect of his performance on screen, the nation's critics gave polite praise to the film itself, as well as the other performers, but went wild over Carradine's memorable take on the late SS *Obergruppenführer*. Carradine's "makeup is excellent and his performance is good enough for you to hate the sight of him," said the *New York Daily News*.

Echoing this praise, in the *New York Times*, while admitting that the film delivered the required "anti–Nazi bill of particulars," critic "T.S." wrote on August 28, 1943: "[But] the fact remains that as a film, "Hitler's Madman" is tritely constructed and badly played, with the exception of John Carradine who lends some cold reality to the central role of Heydrich."

"Trite" could not be said of the film's director, or the career he would make for himself in the years to come. Yet after sixteen years in Hollywood and his elevation to major filmmaker at Universal-International, Sirk would once again return to the world of National Socialist savagery in a film based on the work of Erich Maria Remarque.

III. Inferno (1942–1945)

In the meantime, exactly three months after the release of the Sirk film, and long before it would grow into a major film company, Universal would release a B melodrama that suggested that the Adolf Hitler the world was seeing in newsreels and public events, was, in fact, not really Hitler at all...

September 11, 1943, was perhaps not as momentous a day as another September 11 decades later, but significant nevertheless. Two days before, Mussolini's fascist government had been overthrown, but on the 11th, German troops occupied Rome, Naples and all of Northern Italy, forcing its king and prime minister to flee towards the Allied lines. September 11, 1943, was also the day that saw the release of Universal's newest B contribution to the war effort, a what-if, wishful-thinking fantasy about the alleged death of the man who ordered his troops to reoccupy Italy and keep the formerly fascist state in the Axis.

Reportedly based on an idea by studio contract director Joe May and German refugee actor Fritz Kortner (soon to be a memorable Gregor Strasser in Paramount's *The Hitler Gang*), with a screenplay by Kortner, *The Strange Death of Adolf Hitler* was indeed an odd film coming out of *any* studio during the war. With strong similarities to the low-budget *Hitler: Dead or Alive* and its doppelganger subplot, the Universal film detailed what happens to a good husband and father and his basically decent family and how this family is destroyed, not only by the Hitler regime, but by the husband's unfortunate "talent" for sounding exactly like the Führer.

Our story begins when a minor local Viennese official, Franz Huber (Viennese-born refugee actor Ludwig Donath) is doing his patented Hitler imitation before his weasely co-worker Graub (a permanent fixture to European-set World War II films: Ludwig Stössel), a spot-on impression that drives the little Viennese paper-pusher to tears. After Graub informs higher-ups in the Nazi-occupied government of Huber's uncanny impression, he is arrested by the Gestapo. Interrogated by Major Mampe (Rudolph Anders; hurray!) and other Gestapo men, all of whom were cast, not because of their flawless German accents, which were terrible, but because they were all tall, rangy and scary-looking (indeed, opposite a native German like Anders, these Gestapo sound like beer truck drivers from Milwaukee). Pleading his innocence, Huber is promised his release, but typically, like any other so-called promise made by Nazis, it is a lie and Huber is soon knocked out and smuggled to a secret hospital where Nazi surgeons perform plastic surgery on him. Afterwards, the poor man awakens to find that the doctors had given him *der Führer's face*! Mampe and the others order him to cooperate—otherwise, he and his family will suffer.

The Gestapo then politely inform Huber's distraught wife, Anna (Jewish Communist performer Gale Sondergaard) that her husband was executed as a traitor. Formerly ostracized by their schoolmates, the two Huber children soon become Hitler Youth members (the group is run by veteran German actor Kurt Kreuger). After Anna's neighbor Frau Reitler (former cabaret performer and German-Jewish actress Trude Berliner) is raped by German soldiers on furlough and attempts suicide (but she fails thanks to the Breen office), another soldier tries to do the same thing to Anna, but she wounds the would-be rapist. Tried in court, she is sternly informed by the judge that it is her patriotic duty to be raped by Germany's brave soldiers home from the front. Family friend and Swiss diplomat Marbach (Universal contract player George Dolenz) comes to her defense by claiming that he and Anna are engaged. Their marriage protects Anna from any further visits by Hitler's crack troops. Unfortunately, Anna's children are now full-fledged Aryan zombies; and in a chilling scene, as Anna puts the kids

You look kind of familiar: Ludwig Donath (left) as the Hitler look-alike and George Dolenz as his friend in Universal's *The Strange Death of Adolf Hitler*, a sometimes disturbing B film that would be one of the first to show Hitler with a doppelganger.

to bed with prayers for the Lord to protect them, the two little darlings raise their arms in a Hitler salute and give Thanks to the Führer.

Meanwhile, Huber is used by his Gestapo handlers as a decoy, making speeches all over the country while the real one is far away. One night, Huber visits his family, but misses Anna. Instead, he meets her new husband and confesses his real identity; Marbach, already in contact with pro–Resistance city official Bauer (the screenwriter himself, Fritz Kortner), has a plan to assassinate the real Hitler and then, after reuniting Huber with his wife, hopes to smuggle the family to Switzerland and safety (good thing they were not Jewish bank depositors, the outcome might have been far different).

In a park where Huber, as Hitler, is making a speech, the bitter Anna tries to get close to him so she can put a bullet in him for his part in her husband's death and the loss of her children to National Socialism. Seeing her in the crowd, he orders his guards to bring her to him at the nearby hotel where he figures to reveal to her who he really is. But once Anna is brought before him, his wife produces a gun and shoots him dead; his Gestapo bodyguards then open fire and kill her. Their two children will be raised by "the State," forever trapped in a living death of Nazi hatred and intolerance. Morback and Bauer agree that National Socialism will never die unless *all* of Hitler's men die as well.

In this interesting parable written by an actor from a totalitarian state who did not have the usual sunny Hollywood point of view, *The Strange Death of Adolf Hitler* may reveal the evils of the Third Reich (though other works have been far more effective), but the film is also rather depressing. Here we have a man blessed (or rather *cursed*) with a certain talent, and it is because of that talent that his life will be ruined and finally destroyed. His wife, also a good person, will have, first her husband, then her children, taken away from her and destroyed by the Nazi regime. At the end of the film, she too will die for trying to kill an enemy of humanity, with the stench of a nitpicking Breen office dictate demanding her "punishment" for taking the law into her own hands (even if she tried to kill Hitler!).

The project was started at Universal by Kortner and director Joe May, with the helmsman looking to make a big budget film out of the property. However, his strained relations with the studio, including his fondness for long, money-draining shooting days, mixed with his own arrogant personality, caused the studio to force his resignation. His replacement was James Hogan, a B director at Paramount and Columbia who helmed their Bulldog Drummond and Ellery Queen series, respectively. For material like this, which could use a director of real imagination and skill, we get a low-budget quickie just good enough to get by as a second feature and nothing more. Hogan himself died of a heart attack at 53 shortly after filming Universal's rather underrated *The Mad Ghoul*.

In the meantime, over in merry old *Deutschland*, the Nazi film industry was going to use the worst maritime disaster up to that time as a euphemism for unrestrained British greed...

For those who thought that the British *A Night to Remember* or *Titanic* with Barbara Stanwyck and Clifton Webb, or even James Cameron's highly overrated *Titanic* were the, more or less, definitive film versions of the tragedy, they would probably be surprised to know that the Nazis had also made their own film version; though since it was made by the Nazis, they exploited the tragedy with the usual hateful propaganda points.

Commissioned by Dr. Joseph Goebbels as a slam at British greed, the film not only portrays John Jacob Astor and his fellow corporate big shots as symbols of British greed, but it also alters history by giving the doomed ocean liner a *German* first mate. The film's plot basically has the evil John Jacob Astor (Karl Schonbrok) and other White Star Line stockbrokers hoping to make a financial killing by having the *Titanic* sail from England to New York in record time. The captain and crew, under orders from the duplicitous stockholder, obey him blindly; the only fly in the ointment is First Officer Peterson (Hans Nielson), a man of integrity who turns out to be the lone voice warning the captain, Lord Astor and anyone who will listen, that the *Titanic*'s engines cannot take the strain. Also, sailing through icy waters at high speed (supposedly 27 knots, though the real Titanic could not go more than 23) puts the ship in danger of hitting an iceberg—but such things couldn't possibly happen, could they?

The film has the usual inaccuracies of any film supposedly based on history commissioned by Joseph Goebbels. The first officer was *not* German; Lady Astor was not around the same age as her husband, she was all of 18 years old *and* pregnant; the hold of the ship which kept poor Italian and Jewish immigrants now has poor *German* immigrants; and Lord Astor was *not* the cowardly villain the film portrays.

During the film voyage, Peterson, the lone voice of sanity in the wilderness, meets the Countess Olinsky (the tragic Sybille Schmitz). Originally written as a Danish aristocrat, Goebbels himself had the role rewritten as a Russian aristocrat; in this way, especially when she receives a telegram informing her that her brother has been arrested and her wealth confiscated by the new regime, the propaganda minister now made her a member of the Czar's circle, meaning that she was an enemy of the Bolshevik regime, the same system of government Germany was warring with at the time. At first, looking down at her because of her wealth, Peterson changes his tune and falls for her (and she for him) when she tells him that all her wealth is gone and that she is now just as good as he is. In fact, when the ship starts to sink, she abandons her previous haughty ways and pitches in to help put women and children passengers in lifeboats; as she does this, she even has Peterson's officer's coat draped on her shoulders, as if the righteous German's integrity has literally rubbed off on her. At the end of the film, Peterson and his new ex-countess babe are at a British Board of Inquiry to bear witness to Astor's crimes, but the court completely absolves him of responsibility, prompting the German narrator to say that the sinking was the responsibility of greedy Englishmen seeking profit.

Despite the propaganda, the film is actually well done, and Peterson is a very likable hero; the audience is actually happy he survives and ends up with a woman of equal integrity at the end. One almost feels like applauding when he rescues a crying little girl trapped in a stateroom as the boat starts to fill with water. However, despite its excellent execution, far more fascinating is what was happening *off*-screen.

Titanic was directed by Herbert Selpin, a constant collaborator of popular German film star Hans Albers. Certainly, no study of the Nazi film period would be complete without a brief mention of its biggest matinee idol. A veteran of the First World War and a star during the Nazi regime, Albers actually detested Goebbels and the rest of his Nazi bosses. And though he would do his share of anti–British and anti–Semitic propaganda during their reign, he would also infuriate Goebbels by remaining faithful to his Jewish wife, Hansi Burg, who was safe in London at the time. After the war, the popular Albers had no trouble returning to the screen as a star; and after Hansi returned to Germany, he lived happily with his Jewish sweetheart until his death at 68 in 1960.

As for Albers' favorite director, his fate would be far different. While working on *Titanic*, Selpin was unfortunately saddled with screenwriter Walter Zerlett-Olfenius, a friend and frequent collaborator, but a fanatical Nazi. The scenarist was chiefly responsible for many of the anti–Semitic and anti–British slurs and derogatory characterizations in several films directed by Selpin and starring Hans Albers, including the well done but inflammatory *Carl Peters* (in this highly inaccurate biopic, the filmmakers turned the cruel imperialist into an icon of German expansionism and his brutal policies in Africa into acts of heroism). On *Titanic*, the tempestuous Zerlett-Olfenius did double duty, not only as Selpin's screenwriter, but also as his assistant director.

According to IMDB, Goebbels gave *Titanic* (1943) a budget of 4 million Reichsmarks (the equivalent of $180,000,000 in 2012); no expense was too great. Apparently this included using actual German navy personnel for the shooting. Taken off Nazi destroyers and U-boats, these men were tasked to be extras at the Gdynia shipyards in Poland, with Zerlett-Olfenius put in charge of the second unit and getting their scenes on celluloid. Traveling to Gdynia with his own crew, Selpin was horrified to find that Zerlett-Olfenius had shot nothing. With cost overruns hitting the roof, the helmsman demanded to know why nothing had been done with the navy extras. In response, the A.D. replied that the sailors and officers were only interested in romancing (or something far sleazier) the actresses cast in the film. The A.D. also claimed that the navy men were heroes, supermen even, they were winners of the *Ritterkreuz* (German navy decoration), and as far as the fanatical Zerlett-Olfenius was concerned, they could do anything (or in this case, *anyone*) they damn well pleased. Already turning to alcohol from the pressures Goebbels inflicted on him, Selpin exploded. The two friends shouted at each other, with Selpin finally cursing out the winners of the *Ritterkreuz*—and all they stood for—to the strident screenwriter.

The matter went all the way up to Goebbels' office. In a tumultuous meeting between the propaganda minister and all the concerned parties, the stubborn Selpin refused to take back what he had said about the German navy men. This was indeed pushing the envelope, since attacking Nazi military personnel, either physically or verbally, especially slandering them in public, was punishable by death. Furious, Goebbels ordered the director taken away by the SS. The morning of August 1, 1942, it was reported that Selpin had committed suicide in his cell by hanging himself with his own suspenders. Of course, *no one believed that!* Nevertheless, director Werner Klinger was assigned to finish Selpin's work on the film. Goebbels issued an order that anyone refusing to speak to Zerlett-Olfenius, whom most film professionals now *hated*, would answer to the propaganda minister personally.

As it turned out, Selpin's work was so good, that by the time of its purported release in Germany in mid–1943, Goebbels banned the film, this expensive, *expensive* film, for the unstated, but obvious reason that its scenes showing the passengers' horror and panic at the ship's sinking were uncomfortably close to the average German's reaction to daily Allied bombings.

Goebbels instead ordered its premiere in Prague on September 24, and it also opened in Paris on November 10, where it reportedly was a great success. German audiences, however, would not see the film until many years after the war. When Allied authorities tried to release it in West Germany, British occupation officials bitterly complained of its anti–British bias and had it banned for years. However, like the anti–British *Ohm Kruger*, Communist governments had a great need for anti-capitalist and anti–British propaganda pieces like *Titanic*. And so, with a little rewriting and a *lot* of redubbing on the soundtrack, the film was released in East Berlin on April 8, 1950. In 1953, 20th Century–Fox liberally used scenes snatched from the Nazi-era *Titanic* for their own version of the tragedy; needless to say, the studio did not bother to give the original filmmakers, who had worked for a defeated enemy, any credit.

As for the sultry Sybille Schmitz, a fate not too far removed from that of Herbert Selpin was awaiting her in the years to come. The dark-haired actress, a former star of *Vampyr*, *F.P.1 Doesn't Answer* and *Fährmann Maria*, would survive the Allies' Denazification years, as well as a divorce at the end of the war after five years of marriage. However, Sybille lacked the usual blonde, blue-eyed Aryan appearance supposedly demanded by German audiences. And so, though still starring in German films, due to her Jewish looks (and reportedly close ties to the Jewish community), her career declined. Finally, the talented actress committed suicide by overdosing on barbiturates, at the age of 45, on April 13, 1955.

But back in Hollywood, far away from SS assassinations and self-important propaganda ministers, Nazism continued to be big box office.

"They're [Hitler and his men] a bunch of degenerate gangsters!" So said Paramount production chief B.G. "Buddy" De Sylva in a meeting with Production Code head Joseph I. Breen in the fall of 1943. Their discussion was about the studio's latest foray into wartime propaganda.

By May 6, 1944, the Allies had set a target date for Operation Overlord for June 5 (weather delays would cause them to postpone the invasion to the next day). As they were planning their invasion of Western Europe and several months after De Sylva's meeting with Breen, Paramount released *The Hitler Gang*, a film which detailed the rise of the movement the Allies were now fighting.

At rise, World War I Corporal Adolf Hitler (Bobby Watson, not long after his performance as the Führer in the semi-comic *Hitler: Dead or Alive*) has just been wounded; doctors, however, quickly diagnose his "wound" as psychosomatic, with a further prognosis of neurosis and paranoia. When the Corporal overhears a plot by soldiers to start a coup, Hitler informs his superior, Captain Ernst Röhm (Communist actor Roman Bohnen); from then on, Corporal Hitler becomes a paid informant. With Germany in postwar economic chaos, thanks to Rohm, Hitler joins the German Workers' Party, later to become the National Socialist German Workers' Party. There he meets Rudolph Hess (Victor Varconi), Heinrich Himmler (Luis Van Rooten), Hermann Göring (Alex Pope), Gregor Strasser (actor/scenarist Fritz Kortner), Alfred Rosenberg (Tonio Selwart) and later Dr. Joseph Goebbels (the propaganda minister's definitive portrayer, Martin Kosleck). Rohm and other party bosses quickly recognize Hitler's talent for making speeches and promote him to be their figurehead, with the future Führer thence quickly taking control of the party. When it is decided that they need a scapegoat to blame Germany's problems on (the Catholic Church is turned down; they decide it is too big to attack), Himmler suggests the Jews, with Hitler quickly talking himself into a lather over their supposed power.

To protect Hitler from being attacked while making speeches at beer halls, not only does Röhm lend him the use of his own gang of thugs, the SA, but ex-hero pilot Göring brings along his own bully-boys called the Gestapo. Jews and others who dare shout down Hitler are taken away and beaten up; with no barriers to his speeches, Hitler influences thousands. In 1923, he wins the backing of former World War I commander Erich von Ludendorff (anti–Nazi refugee and filmmaker Reinhold Schünzel) and he leads a *putsch* in Munich. This first grab for power is a failure and he and his men end up in prison. Hitler however has something on the men who jailed him and he is given a light sentence and privileges, including permission to write his autobiography, *Mein Kampf*. An astrologist (perennial Three Stooges nemesis Phillip Van Zandt) counsels Hitler to use the next few years to bide his time and consolidate his power. The future Führer agrees.

Once released, Hitler promises everything to every one of his constituents, allowing him to attain the backing of wealthy industrialists and causing the working class to join the Party by the thousands. During these early years, Hitler stays with his sister; there he develops incestuous feelings for his niece, Geli (Poldi Dur). In a well done understated scene, Hitler loosens his tie and enters her room, where it is implied he rapes the girl. Later, the Party orders the SS to murder her and fake her suicide.

Soon, elected chancellor, Hitler is second in power only to President Paul von Hindenburg (a non-comic Sig Rumann). When the former hero general dies and the Reichstag is mysteriously burned ("They can't say it's a lie ... *if it happens!*" says Goebbels chillingly), Hitler and his men institute a state of emergency and take control of the country. Sensing that Röhm and his men plan a takeover, Hitler, backed by the army and Himmler's SS, personally leads the Night of the Long Knives, murdering his old friend and thousands of SA men. In these scenes, with Rohm and his men caught in nightshirts and not-fully-dressed,

III. Inferno (1942–1945)

the screenwriters cunningly imply the homosexual undercurrent of Röhm's SA. Insisting that the purge is a good thing for Germany, Goebbels tells Hitler that the nation must be cleansed of "these *degenerates*!" In the coming years, Hitler grows in power and the Nazis take over most of Europe, but the end implies a reckoning from a united front of determined Allied nations.

As directed by talented contract helmsman, John Farrow, *The Hitler Gang* packs a wallop; populated by non-stars and familiar character actors cast more because they resembled the Nazis they are portraying than their box-office clout, the film retains an impressive documentary feel. Now given large roles, these character actors give it their all and succeed admirably. Most impressive is Bobby Watson as Hitler, indeed a long way off from the feature-length Hitler parodies made by Hal Roach (like *The Devil with Hitler*) only months before the Farrow film. Still, one cannot help but wonder how the performances would have played out had Paramount utilized some of the actors they originally had in mind for the various major roles: Claude Rains as Hitler, with Alexander Knox and even Orson Welles also considered for the role; German refugee Albert Basserman as President Paul von Hindenburg; and Porter Hall as Heinrich Himmler. But the most interesting idea would have been to cast German actor (and then Warner contract player) Kurt Kreuger as Heydrich.[11] Perhaps seeing far too many Nazi officials in the film, and with the SD leader's assassination occurring shortly before the film started production, it was decided to remove Heydrich from the script. Nevertheless, both De Sylva and Farrow fought the studio to cast "unknowns," with the director shooting the film in the style of a newsreel ("a brand new technique," according to Lon Jones of the *Sydney Morning Herald* on June 8, 1944).

However, though mostly accurate (former *teacher*, not chauffer, Heinrich Himmler was inspired by his reading of *Mein Kampf, then* he met Hitler), the film suffers from the screenwriters' insistence that Hitler was propped up by his "gang" more than the fact that he himself was their guiding force. The screenwriters, Frances Goodrich and Albert Hackett (with contributions by future director Kurt Neumann), implies that Goebbels, Göring and company could toss Hitler aside with no problem, but in the meantime, as the Reich Marshal states, "We still need him."

In a letter to Paramount executive Luigi Luraschi, dated October 25, 1942, as the film was being prepared, Albert Deane of the Production Code Administration's Foreign Department wrote: "If one could view this script in the abstract, without knowing anything of history, he would certainly nominate Adolf Hitler as a 'fall guy'—which is the last thing that we would want to have in a picture planned so definitely and positively as an indictment."[12]

However, by the following summer and further changes in the script, this erroneous characterization would pale besides more controversial aspects. On August 10, 1943, Breen himself would list several incidents in the script and he insisted on their removal before his office approved of the film. Such as: Removing "the definite suggestion of sex perversion in the characterization of [Ernst] Rohm"; change the characterization of [Julius] Streicher as a sex criminal"; and the removal of any "suggestion of Hitler's impotency" as well as "the suggestion of incestuous love for the girl, Geli."[13] On September 1, Breen referred to a certain speech calling Hitler "the Jesus Christ as well as the Holy Ghost of the Fatherland" blasphemous.[14]

However, the two biggest thorns in the self-important censor's side were the many, *many* scenes of what Breen called "sex perversion":

Scene A-12: All the business in connection with Rohm and the photographs of athletes in various classical poses, must be deleted.
Scene A-27 and A-28: All the business of "the good-looking young boy" and Rohm's attention to him must be entirely deleted.[15]

Breen's concern about "sex perversion" also extended to the usually brown-nosing Hess, including an insistence that he *not* drape his arm over Hitler's shoulder. Then, in Scene A-45, Breen insisted on cutting Rosenberg's line "He was sent to jail for enticing little girls to…" and on page 77, the censor found a scene that would not be acceptable if there is "the possibility of an illicit sex affair between Hitler and his niece, or alleged niece."[16] Also removed from the film, though certainly implied by John Farrow, was Göring's addiction to morphine (which the future head of the *Luftwaffe* attained after he was seriously wounded during the Munich putsch).

The Hitler Gang certainly would have been far more violent had Breen allowed original scenes in the script that showed "naked men lying on benches. In the action of the man tarred and hung, with a torch applied to his body, this is sure to be deleted." In a scene opposite a German pastor, Hitler should not refer to Jesus Christ as a "Jewish tramp," though Breen seemed to have no problem with the phrase "Jewish fanatic."[17] In the completed film, Hitler shocks the clergyman by declaring "I am greater than Christ! And he was a *Jew* at that!" Ultimately, the Breen office even cut a scene suggested by Paramount's New York office to reveal Goebbels' real-life penchant for skirt-chasing ("not a motion picture actress" insisted studio executive Bernard Goodwin in a December 15, 1943, memo to Luraschi), which has him giving a young woman his address after one of his speeches.[18]

Unfortunately, after the film's premiere in Boston, certain members of the audience decided to broadcast their own Hitler-like feelings. In a special-delivery letter to the film's producer, Joe Sistrum, dated August 14, 1944, Jack Karp of Paramount's New York office (Karp would later run the studio by the 1960s) wrote: "Outside of the isolated incident at opening day, HITLER GANG in Boston when a few people applauded anti–Semitic utterance by Hitler in picture, we know of no noticeable favorable reaction to anti–Semitic portions in any theater where picture has played so far or any demonstration by audiences at those portions."[19]

In his *New York Times* review of May 8, 1944, "P.P.K.," Bosley Crowther practically repeated Albert Deane's complaint about Hitler being a tool of his comrades: "The man whom we have been led to look upon as an instigator of mass murder and a terrifying megalomaniac adds up here to little more than a confused, contemptible person who had an evil greatness thrust upon him by history and sinister counsel."

Soon, the anti–Nazi propaganda of *The Hitler Gang*, which showed Germany in the past, would be small potatoes compared with the world-shaking events that were rapidly unfolding between the film's release and the spring of 1945. D–Day, the Battle of the Bulge, the Red Army's advance, all of these added up to a turning point in the life of Nazi Germany. For Hitler and his "gang," the war was lost, though many Germans were slow to accept the fact, their Führer being the worst of the fantasists. Yet even as the Nazi elite and their armies were going down the drain, other events were taking place behind closed doors.

On March 8, 1945, in a small "safe house" in Lucerne, Switzerland, amidst a roaring fireplace and plenty of schnapps, Allen Dulles, assistant director of the OSS was having a warm, friendly chat with Waffen SS General Karl Wolff. In a meeting set up through the intervention of the Vatican, at the behest of the pro-fascist Pope Pius XII, Dulles was to negotiate a surrender, through Wolff, of all SS forces in Northern Italy. And despite Dulles' already growing reputation in intelligence and diplomatic circles as somewhat of a rule-breaking loose cannon, the negotiations *were* made with the full knowledge of the Roosevelt administration. However, the president wanted Dulles to issue a take-it-or-leave-it offer of unconditional surrender; Dulles, on the other hand, liked Himmler's former chief of staff immediately and tried to broker a peace that would have allowed the SS murderer to escape punishment scot-free; Wolff had even been given the impression that he'd be part of a post–Hitler government.

For years, Karl Wolff had been Heinrich Himmler's right-hand man, and it was an inescapable fact that he was chiefly responsible for shipping thousands of Jews to Treblinka, and then procuring trains from a desperate *Wehrmcht* (who needed them to ship military supplies to the front) so that even *more* Jews could be sent to their deaths. Certainly, it would have been hard for any normal human being to ignore Wolff's evil nature when he admitted that he felt a "special joy now that five thousand members of the Chosen People are going to Treblinka every day." However, no one ever claimed that the future head of the CIA was what many people would call "normal," certainly not by any conventional standards of right and wrong.

Dulles and others in the intelligence community were fully aware of the mass murders of Jews being perpetrated by the Nazis. Yet anything that called for a rescue of any sort was the furthest thing on the intelligence chief's mind. In the powerful *The Nazis Next Door: How America Became a Safe Haven for Hitler's Men*, author Eric Lichtblau gives a full account of Dulles' "concern":

> In Switzerland, he [Dulles] was getting regular reports of the Nazis' widespread massacres of Jews and European civilians, but his secret cables back to Washington included remarkably little on the topic. If reports of Jewish towns being evacuated and "liquidated" were mentioned at all in his cables, Dulles would pass them along to Washington either without comment or an air of resignation. In 1943, his boss in Washington asked Dulles about a report that the Nazis had hauled four thousand children, some as young as two years old, in boxcars from Paris to "unknown destinations. Dulles responded that such reports "exist in all countries under German domination," but unless the United States was going to undertake a massive refugee program, "I do not see much that can be done in regard to this type of situation."[20]

Considering this rather casual attitude towards genocide, it would not be a surprise that Dulles, once he became the director of the newly formed CIA, would go to the wall to block any indictments against Karl Wolff and other high-ranking SS officers for crimes against humanity. In fact, immediately after the war, and with Dulles' enthusiastic support, the American intelligence community would soon strike a devil's bargain with the same men who would have so much blood on their hands.

However, on March 2, 1945, six days before Allen Dulles met a mass murderer in a comfortable Swiss chalet, Warner Brothers released a film that showed a once-proud hotel as a microcosm for the destruction of a nation.

> Have you not read the Bible, Martin Richter? God would have forgiven Gomorrah if He could have found ten good men there. *Ten*, only ten. But He did not find them and He destroyed Gomorrah. There are not ten good Germans left and He shall destroy Germany. We shall be wiped off the face of the earth... [Professor Johannes Koenig (*Hotel Berlin*)].

Jewish author Vicki Baum was born Hedwig Baum in Vienna, Austria-Hungary on January 24, 1888. In the days when women were supposed to take a backseat to the men in their lives, Vicki Baum was an oddity. Raised in a hub of culture like turn-of-the-century Vienna, she learned to play the harp when she was very young. After graduating from the Vienna Conservatory, she played in an orchestra in equally cultured and enlightened Berlin for three years at a time when the lion's share of musicians were all men. As a journalist and later as the author of more than fifty novels, she used her background hobnobbing among the intellectuals of Western Europe to dig beneath their cultured shells and probe the tangled frustrations underneath. Through it all, she never forgot her pride as a woman and her heritage as a Jew in a pervasively anti–Semitic Austrian/German culture (according to IMDB, she once said "To be a Jew is a destiny"). Still living and writing in Weimar Berlin, and pushing forty, she fairly shocked her friends when she took up boxing, going to the same gym where another empowered female artist, Marlene Dietrich, would get to practice her own roundhouses and right crosses. Having published her first novel at 31 in 1919 (*Early Shadow*), Vicki was a prolific writer all through the 1920s, but hit her stride at the end of the decade, ironically at a time when a nightmare was lurking in the shadows waiting to engulf Germany. *Menchen im Hotel* (*Grand Hotel*) sold millions of copies and was published in dozens of languages, making Baum one of the first authors, male or female, to be called "bestselling authors." After a failed marriage in 1910 (two years), Vicki struck gold when she married her childhood friend and co-worker during her orchestra days, conductor Richard Lert, on August 29, 1930; a marriage that produced two children and lasted until her own death in 1960.

Consistently producing bestselling novels into the early 1930s, her work was suddenly halted in early 1933 and she would not get back to writing for three years. With the rise of Adolf Hitler as Chancellor on January 30, Vicki and her family saw the writing on the wall, and it said "No Jews Allowed." And so, despite her having served in a capacity as a nurse during the First World War, she was condemned as a "Jew writer" and her work was banned; her 1932 novel, *Leben ohne Geheimnis*, would be published, not in Germany, but in the United States and England as *Falling Star* in 1934. With MGM offering to buy the rights to her *Menchen im Hotel*, Vicki and her husband and children packed their bags and moved to the United States, settling down in Southern California. On May 10, 1933, as the Baum/Lert family fled their home in Germany, the Gestapo, Hitler Youth members and students from some of the nation's finest universities, burned hundreds of thousands of books considered "un–German" in huge bonfires, not only in Nuremberg, but around the country. One of the more famous authors whose works were consigned to the flames was those of the Austrian-Jewish Vicki Baum.

By the early 1940s, with another full-blown world war engulfing the globe, Baum harked back to the dynamics of her pre-war 1937 novel, *Hotel Shanghai*, to chronicle a few weeks in the life of a Berlin hotel under constant Allied attack. Serialized in *Collier's* from November 4 to December 6, 1943, *Hotel Berlin* (sometimes called *Hotel Berlin '43*; sometimes called *Here Stood a Hotel*) was eventually published in the United States by Doubleday in the spring of 1944 and, predictably, like many of Baum's other works, sold well. Seeing world history moving faster by the week, Jack Warner quickly bought the rights to the book and ordered the film version to be shot as fast as possible to take advantage of a predicted Allied conquest of Germany. Under the direction of Warner contract helmsman Peter Godfrey, the production was slated to be shot between November 15, 1944, and January 15 of the following year, a generous allotment of time for a film produced by the notoriously cheap Jack Warner.

The story begins in a Berlin withstanding constant Allied bombing. Director Peter Godfrey and screenwriters Jo Pagani and communist writer (and later member of the so-called

III. Inferno (1942–1945)

Hollywood Ten) Alvah Bessie begin the film with a bang. A friend of the famous Resistance fighter Martin Richter is in the hotel when a platoon of Gestapo rudely enters the lobby looking for *someone*; and from their demeanor, we can tell that it is not for a friendly chat. In this audacious opening scene, Godfrey is still able to have the Nazis, despite their imminent defeat, inspire fear in audiences by giving the Gestapo men a tight close-up shot from below as they march into the hotel lobby bearing truncheons, a shot emphasizing their status as a potent force still to be reckoned with in a dying Germany.

After beating up the man and taking him away, an air raid siren sounds and we get a close look at the various characters populating this German "Grand Hotel." There is the sardonic little hotel manager Kleibert (the Austrian-Hungarian Steven Geray); the stiff-necked General von Dahnwitz (Toronto-born Raymond Massey); the world-weary Baron von Stetten (the usually excellent, and British-born, Henry Daniell); the arrogant Major Plottke (played by that prolific portrayer of Nazi characters, Alan Hale); the cynical, world-weary scientist, Dr. Johannes Koenig (and never-without-a-cigarette, Peter Lorre); the cruel Colonel Joachim Helm (the screenwriters dispensed with actual German military rank like *Obersturmbannführer* and just used standard American ranks—and played by the British-born George Coulouris); and the hotel's promiscuous "hostess," Tillie Weiler (the top-billed, but underrated, Faye Emerson).

All in all, the casting is strictly along Warner Brothers stock company lines; and though most of the actors playing Germans are from anywhere *but* Germany, all are good actors and, in the days when accurate accents were not a requirement to play a foreign-born character on-screen, all of them still do a good job. The only sour note is Alan Hale; usually cast as the hero's best friend, the actor looks uncomfortable as a Nazi officer.

As the film progresses, we see that General von Dahnwitz was one of the officers implicated in the plot to kill Hitler (there were reportedly *many* attempts to kill Hitler, but the one everyone knows about is the July 20 plot headed by Colonel von Stauffenberg). His close friend is the wily Baron von Stetten, whom we see meeting with another Nazi official as they are already planning an escape to America where they will start a Fourth Reich.

Tillie is friendly with Plottke, and it is implied that they were lovers, though the pompous officer acts like the affair never happened. One must give some credit to actress Faye Emerson (*and* author Vicki Baum) for etching a memorable character; topped with what looks like a slutty blond wig and wearing a moldy business suit, calling all her male friends "Schnooki" and always looking for a good pair of shoes, the actress stands out among a plethora of ruthless Nazis and equally ruthless Resistance fighters masquerading as hotel personnel. However, Emerson was given top billing not because of her talent but because the pro–FDR Jack Warner was doing the president a favor. Calling in his marker, Roosevelt might have cajoled Warner into giving the actress, newly married to his son, top billing over the more deserving Massey, Andrea King and Helmut Dantine.

Meanwhile, hiding out in the hotel's elevator shaft (just as in the book, the main elevator is out of commission) is Resistance fighter Martin Richter (anti–Nazi Austrian-Hungarian actor Helmut Dantine). Just arriving at the hotel is Major Kauders (the *only* German performer among the featured roles, Kurt Kreuger), a wounded pilot looking for some excitement during his 24-hour leave. It seems that the hero officer and Tillie know each other (apparently our gal Tillie knows *a lot* of men, wink-wink). Also showing up is the beautiful and dazzling actress Lisa Dorn (played by the beautiful and dazzling actress Andrea King). It seems that

Lisa is just another of those actors who sold their souls to Joseph Goebbels and the new Nazified film industry; though not exactly on the level of an Emil Jannings, Veit Harlan or Kristina Soderberg, Dorn has moved about freely among the Nazi elite, and is currently having an affair with General von Dahnwitz. However, in Bessie and Pagano's screenplay, her loyalties will constantly be in question throughout the film, with the two screenwriters totally ignoring Vicki Baum's more sympathetic portrayal of the German actress in the novel.

Up in Dahnwitz' suite, the Baron tells the general that all those implicated in the plot to kill Hitler have been "accounted for" but him; "accounted for" meaning the officers were murdered in various violent ways (or, according to Baum in her novel, another "heart attack" or "accident"). Interesting dialogue ensues in this scene, much of it from Baum's book, with the Baron saying that "Maybe history will justify you," while the general replies that "History won't take notice of a coup that didn't come off." Of course, though this is a very truthful statement (how many failed coups against dictators are taught in the world's classrooms?), time has treated Colonel von Stauffenberg quite well. Though very few know by name the many righteous Germans who tried to bump off Hitler (not to mention the names of the Colonel's co-conspirators in the July 20 plot), von Stauffenberg himself is seen today as a hero, with all sorts of honors and tributes paid to the courageous officer all over present-day Germany. Still, the upshot of the meeting between the two old friends is never in doubt: The Baron informs Dahnwitz that he must kill himself or the Gestapo is going to come by and do the job for him—that is, after the usual long and painful torture session before his predictably long and painful death (in reality, Stauffenberg was shot by firing squad and many of his co-conspirators were hanged with piano wire).

Meanwhile, Major Kauders is up in Tillie's room and the two are smooching on her bed. However, obeying Production Code rules—even in Nazi Germany—Tillie's feet are still on the floor. When Kauders finds a hidden picture of a handsome, dark-haired man, the officer rather tactlessly says that "He looks like a Jew!" Indeed, just what is Tillie's relationship to the man in the photograph?

Soon, with the help of the mostly anti–Nazi wait staff (including the German-born Frank Reicher as headwaiter Fritz), Richter is given a waiter's uniform and assigned to room service. However, while in Lisa Dorn's room, the actress takes note of his nervousness when two SS men arrive looking for Martin Richter. In an early production memo, an unknown Warner executive criticizes this sequence: "Page 57: I think it is wrong to make the SS men out as fools. I like the stealing of the soap, but not the foolish inhaling of perfume."[21] Instead, Godfrey had one of the SS men just smell the soap before he pocketed it.

Pretending to leave, Richter overhears Lisa calling Commissioner Helm to set up a meeting in the cocktail lounge. Here, Godfrey gracefully switches the scene to Helm's office and the next peg of the plot. After telling his aide Heinrich (underrated Warner contract player of German ancestry Peter Whitney) to pick up Fritz and "ask" him about Richter, the officer interrogates Plottke about his crooked dealings. It seems that the American-accented Nazi has been converting his money, German money, into "foreign securities," a practice Helm tells us, "hundreds" of the Nazi elite have been doing but is now illegal. In the novel, Baum has Plottke and dozens of Nazis investing stolen loot in Swiss banks, which makes *far* more sense than Bessie and Pagano's version of Nazi corruption, and turned out to be historically true.

When Richter makes another visit to Lisa's suite just as Dahnwitz rings her doorbell,

Aryans in trouble: Nazi general Raymond Massey and German actress Andrea King in the film version of Vicki Baum's *Hotel Berlin*. Jack L. Warner tried to rush the film into release to take advantage of Germany's imminent collapse, but the Production Code office insisted on cutting some controversial scenes.

the actress tells the resistance fighter to hide in her bedroom. Not knowing that his pilot has been arrested, Dahnwitz invites Lisa to escape a crumbling Germany with him, but the actress vindictively tells him that if he tries to escape, he'll be caught. Andrea King delivers the line with just the right amount of defiance and meanness, the line implying that Lisa is more pro–Nazi than Richter suspects. In the novel, Dahnwitz is far more violent and emotional in his appeals, but Lisa's refusal to go with him shows that she has some independence, not that she is pro–Nazi. After Dahnwitz leaves, Richter bonds with Lisa and, remembering her kindness, offers to get her out of Germany, an offer she enthusiastically accepts.

Then, after he goes out onto the window ledge, Richter is able to enter the room of Professor Koenig, who is now drunk and dressed shabbily—but it hasn't dampened his grim view of life in the Fatherland. It is now that the film abruptly screeches to a halt and lets Peter Lorre own the scene lock, stock and barrel, as he gives trenchant commentary to everyone in the audience on the state of *his* Germany. In fact, Lorre's words and his delivery of them are so powerful, they might have been coming from the actor himself, a half–Jewish performer who had found his fame in Germany 13 years before *Hotel Berlin* was shot, and then suddenly had to take his family and flee for his life from everything he had known before. And though Lorre the improvisational actor gives Koenig a couple of bitter laughs between razor-sharp observations and aborted attempts to lie down while insisting that Richter just go away, his mood swings do not lessen the impact of his words. In a performance of sudden highs and lows, of keyed-up energy mixed with attempts to calm down, Lorre's characterization, more than anything else in the film, points up the fact that Germany had sold its soul to a gang of psychopaths all for the sake of a fantasy of greatness.

Especially telling is Koenig's line about how "we Germans" can now, "in our gas chambers in Birkenau alone, exterminate six thousand people in twenty-four hours." For the Breen office, as well as the studio moguls and the Allied governments, the Holocaust was something they tried to pretend did not exist. For Professor Koenig to even mention this in a major film was a rare occurrence in a Hollywood movie produced by self-hating Jews and under the watchful eye of an anti–Semitic censorship office. Yet there it was for all the world to see; not only the horrible use of "science" in mass murder, but, as Koenig adds, "we have achieved a complete utilization of the corpses." Again, the end result of a living people, particularly Jews (though Koenig never once mentions them), and the implication of the Nazis turning even their dead bodies into something "usable" (with their skin being made into soap and lampshades), must have been a shock to an audience weaned on silly musicals and wartime films which never *once* mentioned genocide, much less persecution of the Jews. For director Peter Godfrey alone, it was a long way from pap like *Christmas in Connecticut* or *That Hagen Girl*.

One can certainly credit Helmut Dantine—playing Richter—for basically hanging back and letting Lorre steal the scene, the actor realizing full well that what his character had to say was important. Then Lorre tops even this with his classic "ten good Germans" speech (accompanied by his mock search around his sloppy room for those "ten good Germans"). The scene finally ends when Richter reminds Koenig of a young boy who was beaten to death at Dachau, uttering the professor's name before he died. Emotionally beating Richter's chest, Koenig finally collapses in tears and begs his forgiveness. It is a perfect end to the scene, and one of Lorre's best in his entire career.

Looking around Lisa's room with the maid, Tillie finds Richter's waiter's coat and then informs Helm, but the Gestapo chief gives her nothing in return. However, when Frau Sarah Baruch (German refugee actress Helene Thinnig) visits the hotel, Tillie turns down a good time with Kauders to see the old woman. It seems that Frau Sarah is the mother of Max, the young man in Tillie's photo. Like his mom, Max is a Jew (or at least that's the implication). Here, we find out that, long before she was the "hostess" of the Hotel Berlin, Tillie was Max's secretary in the department store he once owned, and that the two wanted to marry until Max was taken away to a "labor camp." Besides begging for medicine for her sick husband, Frau Sarah also announces that Max is alive, having been freed by the Resistance and that he still loves Tillie. Appalled that the man she loves will not accept her since she's been (again, implied) sleeping with Nazis like Kauders and Plottke, Tillie hopes to at least protect Max's mother from harm.

Up in Lisa's room, Richter is now adorned in a swiped Nazi officer's uniform which happens to fit perfectly (the Resistance apparently had wonderful tailors). However, a suspicious

III. Inferno (1942–1945)

Helm, acting on Tillie's tip, visits the room and, Luger in hand, catches Richter. Of course, the Resistance fighter is able to knock the gun out of his hand, a fight ensues and the Gestapo chief is beaten unconscious. Then Richter throws Helm's body down the empty elevator shaft to the bottom, killing the officer. In the novel, the sequence reinforces the steel inherent in Lisa's character, the toughness beneath the exterior of the pampered actress, and Lisa herself mentions how the episode bonds her further to Richter.

Trying Lisa one more time, Dahnwitz is again rejected, and then, after giving Stetten his medals, the general finally shoots himself. Soon, Allied bombers attack and everyone in the hotel again has to go to the underground air raid shelter. During the confusion, Lisa is able to get Kauders to escort Richter out of the hotel, after which he escapes. However, in the shelter, Plottke recognizes Frau Sarah and angrily demands of her, "How dare you leave your district! Where is your star?"

Here, Bessie and Pagano make one hell of a mistake, implying that there were still Jews left in Berlin in 1945 who could simply appear in public by just wearing a Yellow Star. However, in the novel, Vicki Baum clarifies this, and mentions that, out of the few Jews left in Berlin, they're all in hiding. Mrs. Baruch is able to, more or less, go about freely because Baum has Tillie thank God that the old woman "looks like an Aryan." Unfortunately, Vicki Baum, like so many others, was unaware that every Jew who was transported to the east, as Nazi officials put it, *was not* coming back. Therefore, the author falls back on the standard Nazi law (and the policy of many anti–Semitic Europeans long before the Nazis came to power) of restricting Jews to their "district" (meaning *ghetto*), by the wearing of a yellow Star of David. Certainly, after 1942, and the transport of millions of Jews to concentration camps, no Jew in their right minds would openly wear the star.

As Frau Sarah takes out her "star," Tillie angrily knocks it aside and, in front of everyone in the shelter, publically indicts Plottke. It seems that the pompous officer was once a stock clerk who stole goods from the department store once owned by Max. As Tillie states, when Plottke's "gang" came to power, he had them make him the owner of the store and then sent Max to a concentration camp; then he had Tillie paraded down a street with a sign around her neck saying "I love a Jew." (In the novel, her sign says: "*I slept with a Jew.*") It's a good scene, if somewhat unrealistic (shouting at a Nazi officer in public would have gotten Tillie a quick bop in the head with a truncheon, for starters), and though her performance was not as good as Lorre's, Faye Emerson still gives it her all. Her Tillie, though corrupted, is immensely likable, and it's good to see her proclaim her love for a Jew while at the same time indicting the Nazi who made them all suffer so much. Calling for her arrest, Plottke is instead taken away by Gestapo men who have found Helm's body; it is a good bet that he won't survive their grilling.

At dinner with Lisa, now it is the Baron's turn to offer Dorne a safe trip out of Germany. Quickly (and inexplicably) turning the key on Richter, Lisa promises to lead Stetten and the Gestapo to all the Resistance, a conversation overheard by a Resistance member posing as a waiter (the wait staff of the hotel gets so involved in Resistance activities one wonders when they ever have time to serve food).

At Resistance headquarters, the inhabitants include a now-safe Frau Sarah and Tillie, who is forgiven her sins and will soon be reunited with her Max, if only off-screen. We also see a neat and sober Professor Koenig, who, in a blatant move by Jack Warner, ass-kisses FDR by quoting one of his speeches; in this case, the one about forgiving the same German people who had so enthusiastically supported the Nazis for so long. There are several tall, hulking American fliers just passing through; and finally we see an embittered, and possibly brokenhearted, Richter. It also seems that the Resistance, headed by Walter Balmer (and played by American-born German character actor, Wolfgang Zilzer) have kidnapped the treacherous Lisa and locked her in the basement. It is at this point that Richter, gun in hand and despite Lisa's vows of eternal devotion (Andrea King in ham overdrive here), shoots her. After the murder, Balmer tells Richter that "Nazis never change." Then, titles come up on the screen quoting Roosevelt, Churchill and Stalin about forgiving the German people. This quote completely goes against the previous scene of murderous payback, as well as Balmer's remark that Nazis "never change," leaving us with a very confused message.

Certainly, Stalin had no illusions about forgiving the German people, despite this lying end-quote, since he had ordered the Red Army to rape Berlin's women and murder scores of the city's residents.

Typically, however, the Breen office dampened Warner's rush to release the film to take advantage of timely events by making their usual nitpicking objections. Top of the list were complaints about both Dahnwitz' suicide ("it is most important that it not in any way be glorified or justified, but played as practically an execution ordered by the Gestapo"[22]); and the inescapable conclusion that the sleeping medicine Frau Baruch wants her husband to take (in the book, he's dying of *cancer*) will help him sleep *permanently* ("The justification of mercy killing contained in the episode between Tillie and Mrs. Baruch is entirely unacceptable..."[23]). Of course, the solution for Dahnwitz was for Helm and Stetten to turn the screws on him a little more (Vicki Baum basically has Helm tell Dahnwitz to hurry up and die already); and Frau Baruch never clearly states just *why* her husband is in pain and needs to sleep, the implication being that Mr. Baruch would be just fine with a supply of Ambiens.

But clearly, the Breen office's biggest headache was the irrepressible Tillie. "Tillie should not be identified as the hotel prostitute,"[24] Breen wrote to Jack Warner in a letter dated August 29, 1944. In a previous letter from April 12, Breen had already warned that "there should be no suggestion that Tillie and Kauders are going to her room for immoral purposes." Even Tillie's room itself was suspect: "(It) should be shown as a sitting room and not as a bedroom, on account of the intimate action that takes place."[25] In a letter from November 6, Breen suggested that the screenwriters "insert a line of dialogue definitely establishing that Tillie is an entertainer in the bar or the hotel...."[26] In his reply later that day, producer Louis Edelman wrote Breen that "We are referring to Tillie in the early part of the story as the official hostess of the hotel."[27] However, Edelman might have got the idea from Vicki Baum herself, who, on page 204 of *Hotel Berlin '43*, has the embarrassed Tillie lie to Frau Baruch that she is "sort of a social hostess in this hotel."

"Social hostess" or not, certainly the billing of the two female leads was switched prior to filming. Faye Emerson had married the president's son, Elliot Roosevelt, during the shoot, causing Jack Warner to reduce the top-billed Andrea King and elevate Emerson in her place, a fact that could not have made King very happy. One undated press release reported that both ladies were coached on their German accents by actress and cabaret artist Trude Berliner (she played the victim of Nazi rape in *The Strange Death of Adolf Hitler*).

Still, the part of Lisa Dorn, star of the German stage and screen, was not originally set for Andrea King, and it was even said that Warners was willing to go as high as borrowing Hedy Lamarr from MGM to fill the role. However, in a letter to Jack Warner, dated October

III. Inferno (1942–1945)

14, 1944, executive Steve Trilling wrote: "Re: 'Lisa'—Hedy Lamarr is out of the question.— and Signe Hasso seems to be our best bet ... unless you have any objections, am going to go through the process of seeing if Metro is interested in loaning her to us."[28]

Ultimately, instead of borrowing a performer from another studio, Warner opted to go for his cheaper contract players (though the talented Swedish actress Signe Hasso would have been a fascinating choice). Taking note of this, Bosley Crowther wrote in his *New York Times* review of March 3, 1945: "Double-crossing is much in fashion and villainy stalks the hotel—a form of human endeavor at which the Warner stock players are most adept." However, the critic turned more serious when he complained that

> ... we have a picture in which "good Germans" are distinguished from "bad"—a dramatically convenient distinction which is politically questionable. True, the Warners have protected their thesis with a good-will epilogue, quoting the words of President Roosevelt, Prime Minister Churchill and Premier Stalin. But the question remains: what's the idea of giving any Germans our solicitude?

And though the *Hollywood Reporter* seriously erred in its review of March 2 when it proclaimed that "Alan Hale, in a small part is, as always, exceptionally good," they also wrote that "Faye Emerson, as the young hotel hostess, does the best job of her career and now seems to warrant the star billing that Warners had promised her." True, Emerson *was* good, but the actress had contempt for her "star billing," Jack Warner, and eventually movies in general. After just three more films at Warners, the actress left the studio and soon successfully pioneered the talk-show format on early television, becoming one of the first female hosts of the medium.

As for Vicki Baum, who would continue to write more books until her death in Hollywood on August 29, 1960, at age 72, the author used Lisa Dorn's escape from the Hotel Berlin and her rendezvous with Martin Richter as a euphemism for not only an Allied victory, but the rebirth of a new democratic Germany: "Somewhere in the destruction of this night was the hope for better days. Somewhere in this burning Sodom and Gomorrah lived the Ten Righteous Men for whose sake God would forgive all the wicked. 'I'm coming, Martin. Please wait for me,' said Lisa Dorn."[29]

IV
FINAL SOLUTIONS
(1946–1954)

Postwar Hollywood and Washington continue to ignore the Holocaust even as Nazi war criminals are hunted down on-screen

> "An intelligence officer should be free to talk to the Devil himself..."
> —Allen Dulles, Director of the Central Intelligence Agency

On May 8, 1945, the Supreme Allied Commander, General Dwight D. Eisenhower declared "Mission accomplished" in Europe. In three more months, Imperial Japan would also be brought to heel. Revealed to the world for the first time through Allied newsreel footage was not only the physical wreckage of a defeated Germany, but the horrors committed during the past four years in Hitler's concentration camps. With justifiable anger, the Americans and British military occupation authorities forced most German adults to view this raw, unedited footage; with horror, these former members of the "Master Race" now saw just what they had been ignoring for so many years. In a frighteningly short amount of time, however, after all the horror, guilt and revulsion disappeared, reverting to type, Germans acted as if they had nothing to be ashamed of; some of them even nostalgically wished for the days of Nazi power to return. This would be demonstrated in their stubborn resistance to indicting the Nazi war criminals in their midst and, in literally thousands of cases, allowing them, as former members of the military, to live comfortably and even collect pensions.

The Allies, the victors who triumphed over the Nazi evil, had their own dirty little skeletons to hide. Starting as soon as the last of the enemy was vanquished, America's intelligence community grabbed up every high-level Nazi officer, engineer and scientist they could, far too many of them being the same members of the SS who had so enthusiastically murdered millions of Jews, Slavs, homosexuals, Gypsies and others for the previous four years, and instead of arresting them, put them on the government's payroll. SS doctors would also reap the benefits of the CIA's and FBI's mercy, with these agencies clandestinely recruiting those who had conducted brutal experiments on concentration camp inmates, as well as engineers who had forced prisoners to work on building rockets and other weaponry in slave-labor factories. The Cold War had begun, and now the American government aggressively moved to

IV. Final Solutions (1946–1954)

thwart the Soviets' global ambitions by enlisting "talent" from Nazi Germany's former military-industrial complex.

In the nation's cinemas are heard the vows of screen heroes chasing Nazi war criminals that the world will never forget their crimes and that such men would be pursued to the ends of the earth. In reality, however, the CIA and others in the U.S. defense establishment actively blocked all efforts to deport the Nazi murderers in our midst and quashed any indictments (as they did when the French tried to get hold of the Butcher of Lyon, Klaus Barbie) which would have surely called for their executions. SS men, Nazi scientists, munitions manufacturers, aerospace personnel, and others guilty of war crimes were transported to America along with their families; those who had participated in genocide were given jobs in counterintelligence; Nazi scientists who had cruelly ran slave-labor factories were sent to American air bases to contribute to our space program. Men like Wernher von Braun, who ran factories where concentration camp prisoners had to work brutally long hours, would be openly lionized by media giants like Walt Disney and hailed as heroes who promoted the advancement of science. More than 10,000 Nazi officials made it to these shores and were generously supported by our government, living the American dream while supposedly gathering intelligence on the Soviets. Ultimately, however, the Nazis recruited by the CIA quickly took the Americans' money and patronage and in return gave their American hosts faulty intelligence; in far too many cases, their own arrogance and boasting blew their cover.

Not that the rest of the Allies were any better. The British, the French (the pursuers of Barbie), and especially the *Soviets,* despite their loudly proclaimed hatred of fascism and their repeated reminders of all the suffering the Russian people went through during the war, *also* grabbed up all the Nazi officers they found in their own zones and enlisted them, as we had, as intelligence agents, scientists, engineers and munitions experts. The Arab nations, not wanting to lose out on obtaining skilled officers who also happened to hate Jews, protected many of these murderers, and even used them to help train their armies and police forces; they also used Nazi scientists and engineers to develop weapons that would target Israel (Frederick Forsyth's novel, *The Odessa File,* was based on fact, with Egyptian dictator Gamel Nasser enlisting ex–Nazi scientists to develop rockets with atomic warheads). Latin American dictators *also* utilized the services of former SS members to train their military.

Needless to say, none of these examples of international chicanery ever appeared in the postwar films made by any of the above nations, particularly Hollywood, who probably would not have made a film of our government's protection of Nazi war criminals even if they *did* know about it.

In the newsreels, we were to see the more famous Nazi leaders in the docks of a Nuremberg courtroom, not the low-level murderers who ran concentration camps, being fed and provided for by our government. Also invisible to the American movie-going public was the vast financial and political support made by American industrial giants who contributed to the Nazi war machine (as did other corporations all over Europe). If Krupp, I.G. Farben (the makers of Zyklon B) and Dresdner Bank AG were heavy contributors to the SS extermination program, American companies like Ford, General Motors, IBM, Chase, the Carnegie and Rockefeller Foundations and far too many others kept Nazi armies and slave-labor factories running even after Hitler declared war on America. Henry Ford (whose anti–Semitism was legendary) had his plants in Germany fall into receivership as enemy property; yet the firm, with SS backing, freely used slave labor all through the war.

In the meantime, as the films of Hollywood and the international community promised eternal vigilance and a relentless pursuit of those who murdered millions, off-screen, the Eichmanns, Mengeles, Barbies and Wernher von Brauns of the world were living high on the hog, protected by friendly governments as they thumbed their noses at their pursuers.

At the end of Universal's 1948 *Rogues' Regiment*, as the film's Nazi war criminal Martin Bruner (an obvious stand-in for Martin Boorman, and played by Stephen McNally) is about to be hanged for his crimes, the film's narrator proclaims: "And the last steps of Martin Bruner upon that scaffold are a warning to the world that such men must not march again!" "Such men" didn't have to march again. The Nazis' former enemies were already paying their travel expenses.

Again, as in almost every major historic event that was even the least bit controversial (in this case, the end of the war and revelations of the Holocaust), Hollywood withdrew. There would be literally dozens of films featuring characters either returning from the war, or characters who, years later, would mention that they had fought it. However, with piteously few exceptions, Hollywood stayed *far* away from showing any realistic pursuit of Nazi war criminals or any recitations of their crimes, with the possible exception of the sometimes hokey *Rogues' Regiment* and *Tangiers*. Dick Powell would play Nazi-hunting army veterans in both RKO's *Cornered* and U-I's *Rogues' Regiment* (three years later). In Universal's *Tangiers* (1946), Maria Montez, of all people, wanted revenge against the Nazi who murdered her parents. *This* was Hollywood's standard answer to chasing down Nazi war criminals; not once was a *Jewish* protagonist ever allowed to seek vengeance on the murderers of his people, but Maria Montez!

Finally released to the general public on September 2, 1946, after several limited showings through the years, *Strange Holiday* was an oddity featuring Hollywood actors, yet made during the war years for the workers at GM plants. The film starred Claude Rains as a family man who goes on vacation, and when he returns, finds that his country has been taken over by fascists. Though the word "Nazi" is never once mentioned, in a montage showing the whispering campaign spreading hatred against Christians and Jews, a swastika appears, suddenly giving these nameless fascists a more recognizable identity. Later, when Rains is interrogated by one of these Nazis (not in an SS uniform, but in a suit), it is the ubiquitous Martin Kosleck. At one point, going into a passionate speech on a New American Order, he cries, "This is *our* America!" Then, clearly embarrassed by his own tirade, he lamely says, "Sorry, I got carried away." Coming from the definitive portrayer of Joseph Goebbels, it's the best thing in the film.

However, the most famous film dealing with the pursuit of Nazi war criminals was Orson Welles' *The Stranger*. Well made and well acted by all, with the glaring exception of a hammy Loretta Young, the film tells the story of a wanted Nazi who committed genocide hiding out in a small New England town and becoming a college professor. Opposite Edward G. Robinson as a "war crimes investigator," Welles still injects black humor references on his unrepentant war criminal. When he forgets something, a colleague calls him the "absent-minded professor," a comment pointing up the fact that Welles' Franz Kindler wants everyone, including himself, to forget his Nazi past. Another scene has an impatient Kindler using a pad and pencil in a phone booth and idly drawing a swastika, then marking over the page so no one sees it. Still, one does wonder why Kindler should fear pursuit, when in reality the CIA or the Odessa group would have protected him for life.

IV. Final Solutions (1946–1954)

Nazi hunter: Dick Powell as an American army investigator who tracks a Martin Bormann–like SS officer into the Foreign Legion in this publicity shot from *Rogues' Regiment*. Meanwhile, off-screen, Nazi murderers were escaping Allied justice by the thousands—thanks to the Allies!

Things would be a little more direct in films made behind the newly erected Iron Curtain. *Council of the Gods*, filmed in Communist East Germany, was actually a well-made indictment of I.G. Farben and other industrialists for contributing not only to the Nazi war machine, but to the methods of extermination used in the Holocaust (it would appear the Communists mentioned the Holocaust *only* when they could attack fascism or capitalism, not to sympathize with persecuted minorities). However, the most over-the-top postwar indictment of fascism and capitalism was made by the Soviet Union in 1949. A total whitewash of Red Army atrocities and a big, wet kiss to the cult of personality of Josef Stalin, *The Fall of Berlin* has never been seen by American audiences outside of DVDs sold by outfits specializing in wartime propaganda films; this is a shame; it may be a long film, but it's a hoot.

Though well directed, the film seems to have stolen a lot of the corny dialogue and situations from Lillian Hellman's *The North Star* made by Goldwyn in 1943. With a script that was rumored to have been rewritten by Stalin himself, needless to say, *The Fall of Berlin* heaped praise on the "great leader and teacher" and essentially portrayed him as Jesus with a bristly mustache. Throughout the film, various characters, even when they are on the battlefield, are wondering what *Stalin* would do in a certain situation. In scenes when Stalin meets with FDR and Churchill, the dying president looks helpless and feeble and the British prime minister is inexplicably wearing a military uniform, as if this implied a warlike nature on the part of the man wearing it (Stalin wore a uniform also). Needless to say, these scenes show Stalin as

War crimes and misdemeanors: A publicity shot of Edward G. Robinson, Loretta Young and director/star Orson Welles as war crimes investigator, innocent bride and ex–Nazi murderer, respectively, in Welles' *The Stranger*. The genius director turned his Nazi officer into another in a string of portrayals of fallen giants.

not only wise, resourceful and innovative, but cooperative as well. We do not hear about his real-life stubbornness, selfishness and outright hostility to his supposed allies all through the war; his massacres of Polish officers in the Katyn forest; his order to hold the Red Army on one side of the Vistula River as the Nazis massacred Resistance fighters during the Warsaw Uprising; his refusal to attack the Japanese until *after* Hiroshima; his grudging acceptance of

IV. Final Solutions (1946–1954)

capitalist help in arms and matériel while never *once* thanking us for it; his continued extermination of his own people because they were "tainted" by being exposed to persons from outside the Soviet Union.

The scenes showing Hitler are even more bizarre. In one scene, Hitler not only thanks several industrialists, including Americans (an obvious attack on capitalists, the same folks who were sending weapons to the Red Army and saving their butts), the Führer even thanks the Pope, kiddingly declaring that the Pontiff would look great in a Nazi uniform!

At the climax, the Red Army storms Berlin and fights a room-by-room battle for the Reichstag. The scene is well filmed, but the whole sequence neglects to show the Red Army murdering thousands of Berliners, including children, and the rapes of hundreds of women, with direct orders from Stalin himself to commit these atrocities. When Churchill confronted him about it, the 'Great Leader and Teacher' just said, "Let the boys have their fun!" Certainly, the Red Army's rampage made a mockery of General Eisenhower's decision (fully backed by pro–Soviets in the late FDR's administration) to "let the Russians have Berlin."

At the end of the film, the Soviet flag is planted on the roof of the Reichstag. In reality, however, the flag was put up there *twice*: once at night when the Red Army actually took the building, and a second time when Soviet photographers could capture the scene the next day in broad daylight. In the film, Stalin arrives by plane to Berlin (perhaps an acknowledgment that he had seen *Triumph of the Will*?), and is welcomed by cheering crowds of happy Berliners who were *not* shot, mutilated, raped, burned out, or driven from their homes by the Red Army. The heroine even gets a chance (during a cutaway) to kiss Stalin as the crowd practically goes into orgasms cheering the man (who in fact *never* flew to Berlin after it was captured). Needless to say, no one outside the U.S.S.R. was going to take this film seriously, even, apparently, Eastern Bloc nations. It was released *only* in the Soviet Union on January 21, 1950.

On March 3, 1953, the 73-year old Josef Stalin would choke to death on his own bile in the privacy of his study, his aides too scared of entering his room to see if anything was wrong (or perhaps they *wanted* it that way while a poison was doing its job?). His death saved the lives of millions of Russian Jews who were to be murdered in a "second Holocaust," the first step being the nationwide pogrom known as the "Doctors' Plot."

Meanwhile, back in Hollywood, in another bizarre doppelganger motif concerning the Führer, an actor was going to use his talents for mimicry to change world history.

"One of the ways in which the George Washington of Germany definitely excelled was in persuading millions of people that that was what he was."—Joachim Remak, *The Nazi Years: A Documentary History*. This reference to Adolf Hitler as the "George Washington of Germany" was made by Liberal member of Parliament and former British prime minister David Lloyd George after a meeting with the Führer in the fall of 1936, a mere four years before Nazi warplanes started dropping bombs on England.

Politically inept though the comment may be (and Lloyd George's seems to have been typical of early British responses concerning Nazism), it pointed to an interesting talent that Hitler, like a great many dictators, had in their relations to the democracies in their formative years; namely, that they had an amazing ability to fool everyone they came in contact with, except the really sharp ones. Stalin *also* had this talent for fooling millions of people into thinking there was nothing but peace in his heart, at least in the beginning, despite the Party-sponsored famines and the show trials. Certainly, a dictator's ability to lead millions of his people to worship him for so many years revealed a charisma, a talent for public speaking and powers of persuasion, as well as a hypnotic force of will, that would cause the masses to swallow practically anything he had to say. In other words, a successful dictator had to be a damn good actor.

Certainly, the Hollywood movies' take on Hitler, more than any other real-life dictator, sometimes imposed on him a doppelganger; someone who looked and dressed like him, but was far more benign. Chaplin could play a lookalike Jewish barber who, as the Hitler figure, called for peace at the end of *The Great Dictator*; Gestapo men could substitute a Hitler double as a convenient decoy for the Führer in *The Strange Death of Adolf Hitler*; a small-part actor could dress up like Hitler and ensure the escape of his troupe in *To Be or Not to Be*; we are told that Hitler has doubles everywhere in *Hitler: Dead or Alive*, but somehow his own men fail to recognize him without his mustache; Moe Howard could do a hilarious impression of the Führer in several wartime Three Stooges comedies; and even Danny Kaye can do a Hitler impression in *On the Double*. Yet somehow through all the farces and far-fetched melodramas, especially *The Great Dictator* and *The Strange Death of Adolf Hitler*, there is the wistful fantasy of having someone who is a good person, but looks and dresses like Hitler, who is able to use the limitless power of a dictator to save the world.

Released by Columbia on August 13, 1951, *The Magic Face* uses the doppelganger motif seen in so many Hitler films and takes the above wishful thinking fantasy to the nth degree.

At the opening it is Germany after the war; journalist William Shirer, of all people, appears in the first few minutes of this B film to tell us about the inexplicable poor decisions and blunders made by Hitler that contributed to the collapse of the Nazi war machine. He tells us of an interesting story told him by a mysterious woman five years ago that might explain just why Hitler acted the way he did.

A curtain rises on Germany's greatest actor (a title which must have infuriated egomaniacal rivals Werner Krauss and Emil Jannings), world-famous impersonator Janus the Great, aka Rudi Janus (played by Luther Adler in a rare starring role). Janus does flawless impressions of Haile Selassie, Benito Mussolini, and needless to say, the Führer himself, a talent that does *not* thrill the various SS men in the audience. It is 1938 in Austria, shortly after the *Anschluss* (director Frank Tuttle shot the film on location in Vienna, using the city's actors for supporting roles); and Janus is married to his grasping, social-climbing wife, Vera (Patricia Knight), a woman who thinks nothing of rubbing shoulders with Nazi bigwigs as her husband seethes with jealousy. One night his flawless impression of the Führer is interrupted by the arrival of the real thing (Luther Adler, *also* as Hitler). Invited to a nightclub afterwards, Vera is dazzled by Hitler and quickly accepts, but her husband refuses. At the club, a jealous Janus arrives and sees his wife with the Führer, but he's arrested by SS guards and thrown in prison. Months pass; it is 1939 and World War II has started. In jail, the actor witnesses the beatings of a husband and wife by an SS major; when he is forced to give information, the husband commits suicide in front of Janus. This causes the actor to vow to put an end to Hitler's reign once and for all.

When a drunken SS officer insists that Janus entertain at a party, Janus uses the opportunity to disguise himself as the officer. The actor is a hit at the party, and is so convincing as the officer that he's able to use the disguise to walk out of prison. Afterwards, the actor calls up the officer and threatens to expose how he got out of jail unless the SS man has him (Janus) declared dead. In record time, Janus is able to get a job as Hitler's butler; he finds

IV. Final Solutions (1946–1954)

Bunker mentality: Patricia Knight and Luther Adler in *The Magic Face*. With a prologue featuring future groundbreaking historian William Shirer, this B film again used a Hitler doppelganger in an unbelievable tale depicting an actor substituting himself for the Führer.

that Vera is now the Führer's mistress. One day, when the SS is not looking, the actor is able to poison Hitler and shave off his mustache (shades of *Hitler: Dead or Alive*). Claiming that the dead man is Janus himself making an assassination attempt (*again*, without his mustache, Hitler is not recognized by his own men), the faux Hitler is able to hook up with Vera (who *also* fails to notice his fake mustache) and settle into his new role as World Pariah. In the years to come, Janus-as-Hitler makes one military blunder after another, both indirectly destroying Nazi armies and aiding the Allies in the process.

Finally, he and Vera are in the bunker when, as the damaged lights flicker in their room, Janus takes off his makeup and reveals himself. Panicked, Vera escapes the bunker and goes out into the bombed streets. The last we see of Janus, he is mounting the stairs and heading for the surface as bombs continue to fall outside. We never see either him or Vera get killed, but after the scene shifts back to Shirer in the present-day, he tell us that they never found Janus' body. And remember, Shirer got his wild story from a woman who survived the war, possibly Vera, who knows the truth about Janus and Hitler (though one wonders how she knew about Hitler being poisoned, etc., since Janus never *explained* anything to her; he just shaved off his mustache).

Farfetched even for a Hollywood B, the film implies that, instead of naked greed, a lust for world conquest, copious amounts of drugs, a misguided devotion to crackpot astrological projections, and a pathetic disregard for the advice of his generals, Hitler lost the war because an anti–Nazi actor played him! Certainly, if Janus *really* wanted to thwart the Nazis' plans, why didn't he use his new powers as Hitler to order a stop to the Holocaust? Typically, Columbia avoids any mention of it, or for that matter, the persecution of Jews or anyone else. Or, if indeed Janus is playing Hitler to make blunders to help the Allies, why did he strengthen Nazi resistance during the Battle of the Bulge? Apparently, the well-respected William L. Shirer, who was paid by the producers for his appearance in this B version of alternate history, had no answers. A decade later, Shirer would write the phenomenally bestselling *The Rise and Fall of the Third Reich*, a yardstick for World War II historians to follow and a major contributor to a revival of interest in all things Nazi in the early 1960s. Predictably, during his many interviews with the media about his classic tome, the esteemed author-correspondent did *not* mention his involvement with *The Magic Face*.

Echoing the film's ridiculously fantastic concept (unbelievably promoted by a future groundbreaking historian), Bosley Crowther, in his *New York Times* review of October 1, 1951, noted that

> the cock-and-bull story that unfold smacks of nothing more firmly reliable than the vaporing of a scriptwriter's brain. And, as a piece of free-flight romancing, it ranks somewhere between "The Count of Monte Cristo" and "Hitler—the Beast of Berlin."
> More than the story is fantastic. The way that it is played, under Frank Tuttle's unrestrained direction, is beyond fairly rational belief. Luther Adler, who portrays both the actor and the unlamented boss of the Third Reich, throws himself into this nonsense with the affected seriousness of a small-time vaudeville "ham"....

It is true that Adler, rarely given a starring role in films, seized the opportunity to play it for all it was worth. Unfortunately, at the time, the actor was gaining weight and his Führer is a little *too* pudgy to fit into his Nazi uniform. However, this didn't stop 20th Century–Fox from casting him for a two-minute bit as the Führer in a *much* better film, *The Desert Fox*, starring James Mason as a British-accented Field Marshal Rommel.

Perhaps the last comment on this oddball film came from Bosley Crowther, at the end of his review of *The Magic Face*: "Says Mr. Shirer, in conclusion, 'an amazing story, almost beyond belief—and yet it is difficult not to believe it.' That's what you think, Mr. S!"

Meanwhile, in merry old *Deutschland*, a cinematic icon was returning to Germany for the first time since becoming a star in Hollywood. Internationally famous for portraying homicidal maniacs, he was going to star in and direct a film where he plays a killer in a land that had so recently cherished its killers.

"During the war, it was horrible. Horrible because you felt a face-maker from Hollywood was so useless. Now it is different. Now you want to let them know they are not forgotten."— Peter Lorre in 1949, shortly after a tour of veterans' hospitals in Northern California and the Pacific Northwest. After the war ended, and unlike many a Hollywood celebrity (excluding Marlene Dietrich that is), Peter Lorre visited Germany to get a firsthand look at the land where he had first gotten his fame—and been chased out as a Jewish pariah. The nation that had supported a dictator and had been responsible for so much suffering, including the genocide of a people, now lay in bombed-out ruins. Sometimes joining Jeanette McDonald and her entourage, or going off alone with his actress wife Kaaren Verne (his co-star in Warners' *All Through the Night* in 1941) and their daughter, Lorre toured army hospitals all over Germany's western sector, cheering many a wounded or maimed soldier with his wisecracks and wry observations ("I don't sing or dance," deadpanned Lorre when asked by a reporter whether he had an act[1]).

In an interview with the newly liberated, non-fascist *Der Spiegel*, Lorre said: "In the United States, there are 150 of the most modern military hospitals for the war wounded, with all the amenities. But without the essential, what the human being needs, contact with the outside world. This is supposed to be done by actors.... Can you imagine how much that helps! And that's why I'm also in Germany."[2]

He posed for pictures with bedridden soldiers, displaced civilians, maimed and scarred children, victims of bombings and victims of starvation and rampant disease; though most of the time, he just made himself available when no camera was in sight, cheering them on if it was possible to, cracking the gentle smile only his close friends saw and movie audiences and the Hollywood press would never see, making their days (sometimes their last) brighter if only for a few moments. For the most part, established Hollywood stayed far away from such misery; there wasn't a buck in it. Lorre himself took note of the nonappearances by Hollywood heavyweights, as well as the all too shallow denizens of the film industry he associated with back in California. When asked if he missed the life he left behind in Hollywood, he responded that he missed his horses and dogs, but not the people, a remark those same Hollywood power-brokers were not happy about. And so, after delivering a fantastic performance as a wily French detective in Universal-International's remake of *Algiers*, this time called *Casbah*, Lorre found himself cast as two-bit sleazeballs in minor productions like *Quicksand* and the British *Double Confession*.

Though badly treated in Hollywood (the future looked bleak; with nothing but random TV appearances and pathetic supporting roles in camp horror and sci-fis all through the '50s and early '60s), Lorre had also become a forgotten man in Germany as well. For close to a decade and a half, Joseph Goebbels had kept Peter Lorre's image off German screens, along with other performers of Jewish blood. To the propaganda minister, Lorre was not only a Jewish actor, but a Jewish actor who was famous for playing psychopaths and criminals. According to new Nazi edicts issued by the propaganda ministry, there was no crime in the New Germany; this left the usually typecast Lorre a nonentity in the land where he had first attained stardom.

Typecast by Hollywood as a villain, this was certainly *not* the image of the man who gave both his time and of himself to cheer the denizens of America's and Germany's war hospitals. In fact, happily losing himself among those broken in body as he himself seemed to be broken in spirit, Lorre justifiably felt a sense of accomplishment no appearance in any Hollywood B film could ever replace. Denying that he was in Germany to make a film, he insisted to reporters that he was there to visit old friends and to dedicate himself to helping those victims of a war that turned Germany into "a land of ruins peopled by ghosts, without government, order or purpose, without industry, communications or the proper means of existence."

Germany was indeed a land of ghosts, Nazi ghosts as well as those of their many victims. The Germans who had ignored the persecution of the Jews were now reaping what they had sown, and in spades. The formerly mighty Third Reich had become a land where fifty thousand children, orphaned by the war, ran wild in the streets as they sought both food and shelter; indeed, food was scarce and the homeless stood for hours on end in long lines to get something akin to morsels of bread; dysentery, typhoid fever, diphtheria, syphilis, gonorrhea, contaminated water, raw sewage and other pestilence were everyday friends in what had formerly been the New Order. Crime was rampant, with robberies, assaults, both sexual and otherwise, common occurrences; black markets and random murders became so prevalent, that occupation troops could not handle the volume. Lorre was one of the few in Hollywood to see it all, and it made a lasting impression on his psyche as nothing else ever did.

In March 1949, after reporter Don Kirkley of the *Baltimore Sun* asked Lorre what he would say to a producer who wanted to do a picture "regardless of box office value, and regardless of the current taboos and censorship rules" and he was given the free choice of subject matter and character, what story and role would he choose? Lorre's answer was indeed startling for an actor who was even then fighting Hollywood typecasting. "The role he chose," Kirkley wrote, "was that of a 'lust murderer.'"[3]

In a meeting with screenwriter Benno Vigny, Lorre thought of doing a melodrama, supposedly based on a story by Guy de Maupassant, about a man who, according to Vigny, "revenges himself of the betrayal by his fiancée and later is reminded of this experience by all the women he meets."[4] The title of the script was to be called *Das Untier* (*The Monster*) and was going to have Lorre play, like the child murderer in *M*, a killer who could not control the forces that drove him to murder; this motif also suggested de Maupassant's classic short story, *The Horla*. However, things took a positive turn creatively when screenwriter Egon Jacobson dropped in on Lorre and Vigny and showed them a clipping of that day's newspaper. It was the story of a 43-year-old doctor, a "Carl N." who threw himself in front of a train near the refugee camp where he had been working. His young female medical assistant was found "fatally wounded in the stomach." They had both been living in the camp with forged documents. Investigating the matter further, Jacobson discovered that "Carl N." was actually a Hamburg physician named Carl (sometimes listed as "Karl") Rothe. Reportedly, a delighted Lorre interrupted Jacobson to declare, "This will be my new film!"

The script went through many, *many* drafts, and though officially credited to "a novel by Peter Lorre," the very lack of said novel having ever seen the light of day, as well as the input and imagination of three other screenwriters (Axel Eggebrecht, Nazi-era film director Helmut Kautner, and Benno Vigny, not to mention Jacobson's investigations) made the project a true team effort. Even then, as a director, Lorre, the experienced improvisation actor from the Berlin stage, used his talent for spontaneity to replace already scripted dialogue with noirish visuals and only the barest amount of dialogue for character development. Heatedly denying to journalists that he had returned to Germany to remake *M* ("I had promised myself never again to produce a film like *M* or a sex murder"[5]), Lorre instead claimed that "I changed my mind because of this remarkable eyewitness report from Egon (Jacobson) about a figure that touched me so strongly that I wanted to make this film.... If my film helps to lighten the conscience of only a single man, then it will not be made for nothing."[6] In fact, the "figure" touched Lorre *so* deeply that he refused to change his real name for the film; his doctor/murderer would also be named Karl Rothe. Soon, in the hands of the actor and his collaborators, Lorre's driven psychopath would be viewed as a microcosm for all those Nazis who killed without guilt, as well as those Germans who allowed it to happen.

It was a long road to the film that was eventually titled *Der Verlorene* (*The Lost One*), with the actor becoming screenwriter, director, producer, star and editor. Not that *Der Verlorene* was totally financed by Lorre. It was produced by Arnold Pressburger (no relation to Michael's Powell's frequent collaborator, Emeric Pressburger), a veteran who had produced and financed films in Hollywood, England, France, Germany and his native Austria-Hungary. Obtaining the use of studios in Hamburg, Pressburger was able to grease the wheels with both German film professionals as well as occupation authorities to bring Lorre's vision of national guilt and bitter remembrance to life.

The story begins years after the end of the war in Hamburg (where much of the film was shot). Appearing in the frame as if by accident, is Dr. Karl Neumeister (German for "new master," and played by the director/star), an always hunched-over little figure without a hat on a cold day and with his hands forever thrust into the pockets of his overcoat. As he approaches the refugee camp where he works, a huge locomotive train, its smokestack belching, passes before he and another man can cross the tracks. In fact, this train will act as a kind of chugging Greek chorus, making unexpected appearances at certain moments throughout the film, usually when Rothe is deeply troubled. The refugee camp itself had once been a former concentration camp for Ukrainians and Russians at Heidenau, several miles southwest of Hamburg. This certainly explains the close proximity of the train, a little detail that couldn't have escaped Lorre's attention.

We see that Dr. Neumeister is kindly and helpful to his refugee patients, although the few people we see treated here could not come close to the multitudes of lost and starving humanity that really packed these places (the present author's own parents had been there). We also see that Neumeister has a love of the sauce, and we're not talking Tabasco, as he freely offers everyone, refugees included, a little *schnapps* along with medical advice. However, Neumeister is no cheerful country doctor; from Lorre's first scene, we see a cool, reserved, taciturn man, undemonstrative, expressionless, and endlessly dour. He also smokes cigarettes—*endlessly*. (Even in his lab, he is *never* without a cigarette in his mouth, a rather careless act for a noted scientist working among chemicals!)

During this refugee camp idyll, a figure from the doctor's recent past appears: his former friend, assistant and Gestapo informant-slash-fink, Hösch (Karl John). Stunned by his appearance, Neumeister gets in his huge overcoat and leaves the camp, his lonely figure a perfect counterpoint to the endlessly gray sky hovering over a broken postwar Germany, a land where a bright sun will decidedly *not* make one single appearance throughout this entire film. He hardly notices the approaching train; when it passes, with hardly a change in his dour expression, he finds himself walking down the tracks behind it, as if the locomotive had already laid out the course of direction his life will now take.

Back at the camp, Hösch, who now goes by the name of "Novak," explains to his former boss, whose real name is Karl *Rothe*, that he seeks from Rothe "a permanent and dependable settlement," whatever that means. Though there is certainly an implication that both he and Rothe, if their identities were revealed, would be in deep trouble with Allied occupation authorities for past support of the Nazi regime. Indeed, admitting to being "on the run," Hösch says he only wants the right papers to guarantee his freedom of movement, a request the former frenemy claims the doctor owes him ("After all, I helped you once"). However, Rothe does not consider Hösch's past deeds as actual "help." In fact, he sees his former labrat pal as one of three people who forever destroyed his life.

Promising to pay back his "debts," Rothe soon produces Hösch's old gun and then they both flashback to December 8, 1943. In fact, Lorre will have Rothe go back and forth in time and be more articulate in these bridging scenes than the doctor is in the entire film; Hösch's appearance has definitely loosened his tongue, and Lorre seems almost cheerful as if this reprobate's reappearance in his life has lifted a heavy burden from him as well as force him to relive memories of lingering pain and torment.

Rothe is a research scientist, and it is implied that he is working for the government. This is established by the appearance of Colonel Winkler (Helmuth Rudolph), who has been referred to by different sources as either an officer with the *Abwehr*, Germany's military intelligence service, or a member of the Gestapo. Nevertheless, Winkler has been summoned by Hösch to turn the key on the doctor's lovely assistant/fiancée, Inge. It seems that the Abwehr has discovered a leak at the facility, and it's not in a Bunsen burner. German agents have discovered that research information Rothe had been working on has turned up in London; upon further investigation, Winkler and Hösch had found that the doctor's girlfriend Inge herself is responsible for the leak. In fact, she's also been seducing the German agent who has been following her, as well as the double-dealing Hösch and possibly many others. Horrified and angered by the betrayal, Rothe is hardly in the mood for Winkler and Hösch's cavalier attitude about the situation, calling him a lucky man to have found out just in time and freely referring to his beloved Inge as a "slut." In fact, draining a rabbit of its blood (an act which disgusts the Abwehr colonel), Rothe soon has the small mammal's blood on his hands— literally. When he goes to the locker room and changes into his regular clothes before leaving, while looking in a mirror, he accidently wipes the blood on his face as the music swells to a loud pitch as in a horror film.

At home, Rothe never once acknowledges his fiancée, Inge (played by the gorgeous Renate Mannhardt, still attractive with her hair in a bun and in a well-worn sweater). After he leaves the room, Inge is nagged by her doting, yet pain-in-the-ass mom, Frau Hermann (Johanna Hofer), about feeding the cat. However, once Frau Hermann departs and Inge attempts to soothe whatever it is that's bothering Rothe, Lorre allows us to see his doctor's bestial rage at his intended without resorting to the usual hysterics he performed during his Warner Brothers years. Coldly refusing to respond to her entreaties, and ignoring her when she offers to light his cigarette (*he* lights it instead; can't have Lorre on-screen for even a moment without a butt). Thinking she is going to get a big smooch from Rothe, she realizes too late that he is going to strangle her with her own pearl necklace, his rising figure blocking her from our view as the music reaches its horror-crescendo.

In the present day, Hösch reminds Rothe that, after the killing, he was rescued "by the State." Soon, Colonel Winkler shows up and in record time he and the Gestapo clean up the awful mess, which includes sweeping the whole ugly matter under the rug. Soon, we have a state-sanctioned radio station announce that Frau Hermann committed "suicide by strangulation with a belt." The point is made quite plainly by director/scenarist Lorre: Rothe's brutal murder of Inge will be ignored and covered up by the State and Rothe is to go on as if nothing happened, just as the Nazis' mass murders were ignored all through the war years and hastily shunted aside by postwar Germans so that they could carry on without either shame or guilt.

In the next scene at the cemetery, Lorre avoids the clichés of the burial and the minister saying a prayer at the grave. Instead he focuses his camera on the ancient face of Frau Hermann crumpled in despair. It's not too much of a stretch to say that she is not only sad for her daughter's death, but the fact that she is mourning herself; for without Inge around, who is she to mercilessly treat like a baby anymore? Ultimately, she stays with the doctor and babies *him* as a replacement for her daughter.

At his home, Lorre meets Ursula (another beauty: Eva Ingeborg-Sholz), a new boarder whom Frau Hermann has allowed to move in to her late daughter's old room. All through

IV. Final Solutions (1946–1954)

the scene with Ursula in the dining room and later in his study, director Lorre gives the scene to his charming co-star, letting her babble away good-naturedly as he offers nothing more than short sentences which respond to Ursula without giving away too much of what Rothe is *really* thinking and feeling. It is only when Ursula asks why Rothe's fiancée killed herself that a tension enters the scene. Later, back in his overcoat and smoking his ubiquitous cigarettes, Rothe wanders into Hamburg's red light district looking to make other promiscuous women pay the penalty.

In a tavern where pickups are apparently common, Rothe meets a prostitute (again, director Lorre has a good eye for pretty faces; character actress Gisela Trowe) who will take him up to her flat. What is unusual in this scene is language many audiences, especially in America, would not have heard in 1951 ("Don't talk bullshit when I'm with a client," she says to a man who fancies himself as her protector). However, when the girl takes him into her seedy, rundown building, she sees something in Rothe's face that frightens her. Calling him a murderer, she shouts for help and runs all over the staircase knocking on doors and pulling her equally seedy neighbors out onto the landings (they know of her activities and apparently fully accept them). Indeed, with shouts of "murderer" echoing up and down the stairs, the scene is highly reminiscent of Fritz Lang's *M*; but instead of missing children, the scene ends with Rothe assuring her neighbors that the whore is just drunk and the good doctor is allowed to escape once again, as is his presumed victim. The next woman will not be so lucky.

On a train to Rothenberg, Rothe meets a busty and lonely woman whose husband is away at the front (Lotte Rausch). But when an air raid starts and the passengers are herded below into bomb shelters, the woman elects to remain on board the now empty car with her cigarette-puffing companion. After she removes her coat (to emphasize her curvy figure), her look of horror is the last thing we see before Rothe approaches and the scene fades out.

Now guilt-ridden, Rothe plans suicide, but not before getting even with Hösch. After burning his own papers and stealing Hösch's gun, he figures to find his double-crossing assistant at Colonel Winkler's mansion. Instead, he finds that Hösch is not there, but instead Winkler is playing host to *Abwehr* conspirators. It is implied that these "swells," as Hösch calls them, are planning a possible coup, and there is much talk of "heroes" with poison capsules in their pockets and being interrogated at *Prinz Albrecht-Strasse* (SS headquarters), though Lorre and his co-scenarists never once spell out that this could be another *Valkyrie* or any other anti–Hitler conspiracy.

Back in the present-day, Rothe comments about a punishing bombing raid ("Thousands were dead. Thousands who wanted to live. But I, I was still alive.") It seems that during the raid, Frau Hermann and Ursula, innocent, good-natured Ursula, along with Dr. Rothe, were also listed as killed. In a flash, Rothe became Neumeister and he became the physician at Camp Elbe-D until Hösch showed up, making Rothe belatedly realize that there was no escaping the past. When Hösch drunkenly tells him that he hasn't the guts to shoot him, Rothe proves him wrong and blows him away. He returns the gun to the corpse and steals one last cigarette off him. Then, donning his overcoat and going outside into a bleak countryside, Rothe walks the railroad tracks just as a train is coming up behind him. In despair, but ultimate resignation, he chooses not to get out of the way when it finally catches up to him.

If Lorre or his backers thought that the film would belatedly open the eyes of Germans who saw the film, they were in for a rude awakening. According to Stephen D. Youngkin in his definitive biography of the actor, *The Lost One: A Life of Peter Lorre*, the author wrote:

"Lorre discovered close hand that the spirit of fascism was still alive, if not well, and more deeply ingrained than he had ever supposed at a distance. He found a devastated and demoralized, but also cynical and self-pitying people who refused to accept responsibility for Nazi war crimes."[7]

In assessing the film's predictable failure with German audiences, Youngkin wrote: "Tired of 'accusatory' films, [German] moviegoers thirsted for escape from their problems. In pictures that portrayed the "idealized pleasures of country life," they drank their fill of *Heimatschnulzen* [homegrown schmaltz], 'heather and heartache' daydreams doused in sentimental fatalism."[8] In other words, the usual pap approved of by Joseph Goebbels.

Apparently, postwar Germans preferred Kristina Soderbaum drowning herself for going out with the wrong kind of boy than Lorre's resigned suicide in front of an oncoming locomotive.

Certainly, German audiences gave it as much a cold shoulder as it gave Marlene Dietrich, Billy Wilder or any other émigré returning to the "fatherland." Indeed, at its premiere in Frankfurt on September 18, 1951, *Der Verlorene* played for only ten days. Even the film-loving French, who ended up on the side of the victors (mainly thanks to the Americans and the British) kept far away from Lorre's indictment of postwar Germany, with only Lotte H. Eisner of *Cahiers du Cinéma* singling the film out for praise.

Lorre himself lost heart about the film, cynically predicting that American audiences would ignore it and not even attempting a stateside release. Accurately assessing the political situation in his adopted homeland, Lorre said: "[But] there are times when an actor knows not to make money. I don't think the State Department would like me to indict another country's politics."[9]

In this way of thinking, Lorre was right. The victorious Soviet Union had grabbed the eastern half of Germany (and Europe as well) as ruthlessly as the just defeated Nazis had grabbed the same lands only a few years before. The Cold War was very hot in 1951, and the U.S. government, as well as Great Britain, wanted their zones of Germany to be free and anti–Communist. To indict those same people, Nazi supporters they may have been, was considered bad politics. It was one of the main reasons mass-murdering Nazi war criminals were either allowed to escape justice, given light sentences when they were caught, or hired as scientists and spies by our own intelligence community. In his Lorre biography, Stephen D. Youngkin wrote of the actor's performance as a tormented anti–Nazi German scientist in *Hotel Berlin*, drunkenly looking around his room for a mythical "Good German." Indeed, it was the so-called "Good Germans" who, through their own refusal to accept responsibility for their support of the Nazi regime, were now turning away from his film in droves. With no film offers coming in, Lorre would now be forced to return to a Hollywood that would only cast him as a two-bit sleazeball in clichéd adventures in support of leads who did not have even *half* his own talent or charisma.

It was not until the summer of 1984, a full twenty years after the actor's death, that Americans, art house New Yorkers mostly, would finally see *Der Verlorene* (including this author, who viewed it at the Bleecker Street Cinema). Critics finally found reasons to praise both Lorre and his neglected masterpiece, billed as *The Lost One*, with Vincent Canby of the *New York Times* calling it "an interesting expression of Lorre's creative personality" on August 16, 2002.[10]

"Interesting" was the least one could say of *Der Verlorene*. While Fritz Lang would brag that his original title for *M, The Murderers Among Us*, was attacked by a growing number of pro–Nazi Germans (a claim that was *never* proven), Peter Lorre actually *did* make a film showing a murderer among Germans who refused to come to terms with their Nazi past. With a plot that put the film's central character mainly among stifling boarding rooms, cold laboratories, displaced persons' camp barracks, dark streets, back alleys, cramped railway cars and bleak country landscapes where only a ghostly train chugs in and out of the frame at odd moments, Lorre out-*noired film noir*. With its euphemistic indictment of postwar Germans, *Der Verlorene* is a fascinating work whose main character of a serial killer stood in for the Nazis' selective killings of those whom they deemed inferior, and a well-deserved attack on those who looked the other way.

"No doubts or qualms, no shadows or misgivings darkened my creativity. The artist knows but one struggle—the struggle for perfection of his own work. He knows only one freedom—the unifying of his idea with his own creative vision."[11] Despite the use of "he" and "his," the person who said this was Leni Riefenstahl. On February 11, 1954, the last film she would ever both act in and direct, would be released in West Germany. Based on the opera *Tiefland* (*Lowlands*), the film had a long, twisted history before its release in a postwar Germany where the very existence of Leni Riefenstahl was a nagging reminder of a hated regime. The film itself was innocuous, yet the making of it revealed not only the typical chicanery behind any deal concerning the National Socialists, but also the inherent callousness and cruelty of the woman who made it.

Go back to 1940, when both Leni Riefenstahl and the regime she served faithfully were both riding high. Passionately believing in her "vision," whatever it was, the acclaimed director of *Triumph des Willens* had grown to an exalted position of power and influence within the National Socialist state. A friend and devoted admirer of the Führer, a sometime enemy/sometime grudging friend of Joseph Goebbels, and a beneficiary of the patronage of Göring, Himmler and especially Martin Bormann, Riefenstahl had it all in a triumphant Nazi Germany whose conquests kept multiplying. Even the expulsion and extermination of their so-called enemies within Germany, and in Europe itself, the Jews, the Gypsies, the Slavs, the homosexuals and others similarly targeted, was working out beyond even the wildest expectations of Hitler and the rest of the Nazi hierarchy. To Riefenstahl, the world, at least the one under Nazi domination, was hers for the taking. Saturated with an endless supply of funds for her projects from Hitler's private bank accounts, as well as government coffers (generously supplied by the regime's premier check-writer, Martin Bormann), Riefenstahl could film whatever she chose; and with Goebbels' propaganda ministry essentially telling the nation's critics to praise whatever project she came up with, her status as a major filmmaker, as well as her sizable ego, were secure.

All this would come to a crashing halt with a project that would signal her last performance as an actress on movie screens. Despite her anointed status as an icon of National Socialist cinema, her choices of film material always seemed to be hopelessly old-fashioned. Still believing herself to be the same lovely woman who could dance, swim, climb mountains and still get the guy at the last reel, she cast herself in a project that had been knocking around German studios for years.

Based on a Catalan 1896 play called *Terra baixa*, the property was eventually fleshed out into a prologue and three acts by Eugene d'Albert with a libretto by Rudolf Lothar. Now called *Tiefland*, the play premiered for an unsuccessful run in Prague on November 15, 1903.

Later, it would have more successful runs in Berlin and Hamburg in 1907, and finally debut at New York's Metropolitan Opera on November 23, 1908, for a very successful run, followed by thousands of performances all over Europe.

The story deals with Gypsy heroine Marta, the evil landowner who lusts after her, and the heroic shepherd she ends up with. Like most operas, it was creakier than a rusty door latch. Cliché-ridden even at the turn of the century when it was first produced, one wonders just what possessed Riefenstahl to take a crack at it, or to cast herself, 37 years old when she reportedly began filming in 1941, as its virginal Gypsy heroine. Originally, before choosing the *Tiefland* project, she was to play the title role of an Amazon queen in a vehicle called *Penthesilia*, opposite the Greek hero Achilles. However, the scope of the project would have needed location shooting in such places as Italian-dominated Libya, the procuring of thousands of horses and chariots, and the use of precious color film stock (a rare material during the war); but Hitler had to politely inform his favorite filmmaker that, due to the logistics of filming near war-torn battlegrounds, the project was not feasible. *Tiefland*, however, was far less ambitious; besides being set in a mountain and the lowland village beneath it, the opera was one of the Führer's favorites, a little detail Riefenstahl obviously kept in mind. And so, green-lighted by Hitler himself, Boorman opened the purse strings and a contract was signed with Tobis for distribution rights, giving the studio 15 percent of the profits and Riefenstahl 85 percent, respectively.

The story is still basically the same, though with one glaring exception: Knowing she could not sing a note, Riefenstahl removed all the music. In other words, this gave the characters a chance to emote some opera-like *Sturm und Drang* without actually singing to it; kind of like a western without horses.

The story has a poor Gypsy girl named Martha (not Marta, and played by the director in either a moldy black wig or dyed hair), a wagon-peddler, living in the lowlands of her Spanish village. For extra money, she dances in the local tavern. In this one scene, Riefenstahl revives her dancing career for the first time in over a decade. However, the Spanish dancing she does in the film is clearly beyond her range. Her age also works against her. She looks plainly ridiculous in Gypsy rags (though tastefully tailored) and clicking castanets to a male audience that apparently has low standards for entertainment.

Meanwhile, up in the Bavarian Alps doubling for the Pyrenees, a shepherd named Pedro (Franz Eichberger) finds that a wolf has killed a sheep in his flock. Angry, Pedro takes the wolf on in a violent, bloody, rolling-down-a-hillside fight that almost makes one forget the cornball material this film is based on. Ultimately, the shepherd, an obvious symbol of Master Race strength and perfection, kills the wolf by strangling it. Though a lively scene, it also showed Riefenstahl's clumsiness as a filmmaker; as anyone who has ever seen a wolf could tell, the creature Pedro kills is a *dog*, and not a very well fed one at that. Though the scene is intended to make the audience admire Pedro for his strength or virility, instead it fills us with rage for his killing of this poor animal.

The village is more or less under the thumb of the Marquis, Don Sebastian (Bernhard Minetti), who has been diverting the waters in the village's dam for his own bulls—with the surrounding farmers not having any water for their crops or to feed their own stock. The screenplay was by Riefenstahl and assistant director Harald Reinl, though typically, she never once gives him credit (Reinl would later direct the Old Shatterhand westerns, based on the books of Joe May, in the 1960s). However, neither Riefenstahl nor Reinl answer the question:

If the Marquis possesses such a large herd of bulls, why does he not sell them off if he is drowning in debt instead of marrying a woman he does not love? It is not the only bull Riefenstahl tries to foist on her audience during this film.

Charmed by the gangling, aged, German-accented Gypsy girl, the Marquis never wants her to leave his *hacienda*, but *La Dona* Amelia (the tragic Maria Koppenhöfer, who died of cancer at 46 in 1948) demands that Martha be kicked out before she marries him. Don Sebastian's aide comes up with a great solution: Have Martha marry some poor *schlub* in-name-only, and then *still* be able to have an affair with her. Pedro, who loves her anyway, is coincidentally the groom chosen for the project. After the marriage, the shepherd is mystified by her refusal to be touched and angered by the villagers laughing at him. Of course, Riefenstahl portrays the people of the "lowlands" as ignorant *Untermenschen*, while she and Pedro are their superiors who are destined to live high above them in the mountains. Soon, Pedro learns of the deal. On the night of his wedding to Amelia, Don Sebastian decides during a powerful wind storm that night to "visit" Martha. For all her perfectionism, Riefenstahl again screws up big time as the Marquis walks down some steps in the village and we see him being tracked by a huge Klieg light.

At the mill, Pedro and Don Sebastian have a big knife fight; but then, wounded in the wrist (just as the wolf bit him there), Pedro eventually strangles the evil nobleman. Now in love with Pedro, Martha climbs the mountain with him back to his cabin as man and wife.

Though the film is pap, script-wise, there is no mistaking the wonderful cinematography by Albert Benitz and Riefenstahl, as well as fantastic art direction by Isabella Ploberger. Commanded by Nazi higher-ups to help Riefenstahl in any way they can, directorial advisors were at her beck and call. Forced to neglect their own projects to help an arrogant woman they all had contempt for, their advice (or hands-on work) is clearly seen in this film. Whether actively assisted by them or not, however, Riefenstahl actually excels in her shots in the mountains (she had *lots* of experience there). Covered in endless mists, silhouetted against the moonlight and shrouded in cloud cover, these mountains are like a separate character that is so much more attractive to look at than any of the film's human inhabitants. Typically, it is in her direction of human beings where Riefenstahl fails. One can easily see where there are long spaces in the screenplay where a song must have been before it was cut out in the transfer from stage to film, effectively killing our chance to know what these people are feeling; and we are again reminded that it was Riefenstahl's decision to cut out the music. Despite the fact that she claimed credit for the direction as well as the entire screenplay, Riefenstahl's co-directors were (besides Harald Reinl) Dr. Arnold Fanck, G.W. Pabst, Veit Harlan, and even her former co-director/cameraman from *The Blue Light*, Hans Schneeberger.

There is some debate as to when the film was begun; some say 1940, some say '41 and others say '42. Nevertheless, the standard accepted time Riefenstahl worked on this film is something like close to five years starting in 1941, with some tinkering and fine-tuning being done even after the war. It was without a doubt the longest duration for the production and shooting of a film in German history and, along with Goebbels' backing of the ill-fated *Kolberg* near the end of the war, one of the most expensive.

Arriving at a high mountain plateau in Mittenwald in the Bavarian Alps in June of 1940, Riefenstahl was horrified that the town the crew had built would give her little maneuverability for her cameras. Pulling an ego trip not seen again until the era of Michael Cimino and *Heaven's Gate*, Riefenstahl had the entire village razed to the ground and rebuilt. The cost of the destruction and rebuilding ballooned the budget by half a million Reichsmarks; in itself, enough to cover the budget of a full-length movie—and she had not even started shooting yet. Goebbels, already smelling trouble, but powerless to interfere with the Führer's favorite filmmaker, wrote in his diary on April 2, "I won't let myself get too drawn into this affair."

As the war got worse for Germany and the film's budget mounted, Riefenstahl used her clout with the powers-that-be to pull more strings than a puppeteer on speed. As Allied bombs rained down on a besieged Germany and millions were either dying or made homeless, Riefenstahl badgered Party power-brokers to give special treatment to her cast and crew, despite the war's getting closer and closer to home. According to Steven Bach in his excellent *Leni: The Life and Work of Leni Riefenstahl*, "She bombarded Berlin with demands for continued draft deferments for her technicians at a time when young boys and old men were being drafted into civilian militias armed with shovels. Almost all deferments were rescinded, including the one [Albert] Speer obtained for Fanck, now well over fifty."[12]

Despite all the battles, back-stabbings, credit-stealing and assorted and numerous temper tantrums brought on by the director/scenarist/star, including her imperial treatment, not only of her cast and crew, but even aging mentors like Arnold Fanck, Rienfenstahl's most controversial move was her casting of the village's extras, especially the children.

As Riefenstahl had to start shooting in her makeshift Spanish village high up in the Bavarian Alps, she realized that she could still rely on the old mountain farmers as extras that she had used back in the days of *The Blue Light*. However, pretending that the locale was Spain was going to be awfully difficult when she realized that the villagers' wives and children were going to be played by blonde-haired, blue-eyed Aryans. Looking for what she called "Spanish flavor," in late September 1940, she visited, along with assistant director/screenwriter Harald Reinl and SS guards ordered to accompany her by SS Commandant Anton Böhmer, the infamous Maxglan-Leopoldskron "transit camp" outside Salzburg. As many Holocaust historians know full well, the term "transit camp" was a nice euphemism for "deportation camp," a brief but brutal stopover before being taken away for extermination. At Maxglan, prisoners were barely fed, dressed in skimpy rags, had mud in their cells sometimes up to their knees, and had to sometimes sleep with rats or other vermin. One important group of inmates that Riefenstahl needed was the camp's Roma and Sinti Gypsies. She needed villagers, particularly children, with black hair and dark skin; ethnic peoples whom Germany's racist policies had condemned to death. Peering at them as they appeared before her behind barbed wire, Riefenstahl stared intently at their faces, especially the children, hungry and forlorn, as they gazed back at her in their misery. Surviving eyewitnesses would later tell of the filmmaker's visit; how she had showed up with her SS entourage dressed in slacks and carrying a briefcase, officious to the core even when surrounded by such human suffering. With certain prisoners, whether adults or children, she would frame their faces with her thumbs and forefingers, as if looking through a viewfinder. One surviving Gypsy would recall that she said to her guards, "I can't take people like this! They need to be re-clothed."[13]

Riefenstahl would always claim that she had never personally visited the camp and selected the Gypsy inmates. For having done so would have clashed with her much repeated mantra that she never knew of the existence of the concentration camps. Effectively throwing her loyal collaborators under the bus, she would later claim that Reinl and production manager Hugo Lehner visited Maxglan and chose the Gypsies for her film (nevertheless, this did not

IV. Final Solutions (1946–1954)

absolve Harold Reinl, who was indeed at Riefenstahl's side as she chose what Gypsies she wanted to use). Soon, a contract was signed on September 24, 1941, between Leni Riefenstahl Produktions and Commandant Böhmer, as the duly chosen representative of Maxglan. The contract authorized "pay" for the Gypsies of seven Reichsmarks a day (for adults); needless to say, said pay did not go to the Gypsies, but instead went to something called the "Gypsy General Fund," an organization quickly set up in Salzburg to defray the costs of housing the Gypsies (that is, in barns and stables under strict SS guard to prevent escape attempts; they were even followed to the latrines). The funds were also used to grease the palms of SS officers since their work on Riefenstahl's film would delay their transport to the concentration camps of the East.

Twenty-three Gypsy prisoners were taken from Maxglan, 15 of them children, the youngest three months old (the website of the U.S. Holocaust Museum has the count as *fifty-one* Gypsies, both adults and children, taken from Maxglan). With typical German efficiency, it was certified that they were "not from Jewish tribes." Predictably, once she was through with them, Riefenstahl returned the Gypsies to Maxglan, where they barely got their bearings

Master race gypsy: Leni Riefenstahl in the long-delayed film version of the operetta *Tiefland* (though she removed all the music). Filmed during the war, Riefenstahl purposely used Gypsy prisoners slated to die in the Holocaust and denied responsibility for it years later.

before they were pushed, shoved and beaten onto cattle cars and taken to their final destination at Auschwitz-Birkenau. On April 27, 1942, Riefenstahl visited the Marzahn transit camp and "requisitioned" 68 Gypsies, an unknown mix of adults and children, to use for shooting at the Babelsberg studios in Berlin. On April 6, 1943, Leni Riefenstahl Produktions paid the Marzahn authorities for the use of the prisoners. However, by the time the check went out, Riefenstahl's Gypsy "actors" had already been gassed at Auschwitz-Birkenau a month before.

According to Steven Bach, "Leni later claimed, 'We saw nearly all of [the Gypsies] after the war' and they remembered the experience as 'the loveliest time of their lives,' especially as 'nothing happened to a single one of them.'"[14]

One does wonder just who among us would find sleeping in freezing cold barns and stables while being guarded by SS men "the loveliest time," but Riefenstahl's usual self-involvement and callousness were no excuse for her behavior this time. To view certain parts of the film, especially with its cliché-ridden story and stilted acting, can be an awful enough experience. But to see these Gypsy children, beautiful little angels all, running up to Riefenstahl when she crawls into the peddler's wagon in an early scene, or to see them happily running up to Pedro before his wedding to Martha, causes the film to go from an exercise in vanity for its director/star to an outright obscenity. Whenever they appear on-camera, we see these children smiling and laughing; grateful to be free from the horrors of their incarceration, they fully cooperated with Riefenstahl and project nothing but sheer joy to the audience. Indeed, it is hard to view the film itself knowing full well that these babies would be going to their deaths as soon as Riefenstahl had all the shots of them that she cared to have.

In 1946, the film, along with the studio that made it, would fall into French hands, and it would take years before she would get it back and perform final editing on it. In fact, unlike the 1930s when the French heaped praise on her for *Triumph of the Will* and *Olympia*, this time they transported her to Innsbrook (in Germany) and put her under house arrest. Declaring her an "undesirable," they gave her exactly 24 hours to pack her things and leave their zone. Three years later, she sued the German weekly *Revue* for accusing her of knowing that her Gypsy actors in *Tiefland* were going to be sent to Auschwitz. In 1982, documentary filmmaker Nina Gladitz made *A Time of Silence and of Darkness*, which also accused her of knowing that the Gypsies were headed to their deaths; after filing suit against Gladitz, Riefenstahl successfully had the film suppressed.

By 2002, under a wave of accusations from the few Gypsies to survive their suffering at Auschwitz, a Roma group took her to court for her continued denial of the extermination of the Gypsies under her care. Reluctantly, Riefenstahl was forced to admit that "Sinti and Roma had to suffer under National Socialism. It is known today that many of them were murdered in concentration camps."[15] It was emphatically *not* an apology, nor was it even an admission of responsibility for exploiting the Gypsies as slave labor (the court ruled against Riefenstahl and agreed with the Roma on this point), and certainly not an admission that she knew that they would be sent to their deaths as soon as she had finished with them. She was not even the one who made the statement; she sent out a spokesman to do it for her.

All in all, when *Tiefland* was released in West Germany and Austria in early 1954, the film bombed, though Riefenstahl would, of course, always claim that it was a great success. However, one critic acidly wrote of her performance, "When one sees her dancing here, one suspects that the world of ballet was only too happy to lose her to the world of film; when one sees her act, one concludes that, in fact, she should have stuck to ballet."[16]

Tiefland may have been, outside of its brilliant mountain cinematography, a hackneyed work made by a vain, egomaniacal woman, it may have been a corruption of the original opera, and it may have been the most expensive and time-consuming film production in Germany's history, but all of that soon fades away and one is left utterly heartbroken at the film's one lasting, painful memory: The laughing eyes of Gypsy children going to their doom.

V
AIRBRUSH (1955–1962)

Both Hollywood and Germany rewrite history as it condemns Nazism while praising "good Germans" in war-themed films

> "Propaganda becomes ineffective the moment we are aware of it."—Dr. Joseph Goebbels

Deutschland did not only have an aging and bitter Leni Riefenstahl to deal with in the mid–1950s.

The country saw the release of a slew of films dealing with anti–Nazi resistance, otherwise known as the "Good German" films. Neatly avoiding any necessary discourse on the role ordinary Germans, as well as the Third Reich's *Wehrmacht* officers, played in supporting Hitler's conspiracy to wage war and militarily conquer other nations, these films instead gave us those few principled officers who personally hated Hitler and the SS and strove to do something about it. These films, of course, gave the same Germans in the audience who had supported Hitler and his war aims a chance to feel good and tell themselves that *they* were just like these army officers who heroically sought an end to the Nazi regime.

Perhaps this subgenre was given a kick when Hollywood's *The Desert Fox*, starring James Mason as Field Marshal Erwin Rommel, was released in West Germany in August 1952. Within *six* months in the first half of 1955, four films were released concerning German officers secretly plotting to kill Hitler, and *one* showing Hitler's last days in the bunker (with a sequence in which a *Wehrmacht* officer tries to kill him). December 30, 1954, saw the release of *Canaris* (aka *Deadly Decision*), about Wilhelm Canaris, the principled head of the *Abwehr* (German intelligence) who kept up secret contacts with the Allies. When his consorting with anti–Hitler plotters was discovered by the SS, he was tried and then executed on April 9, 1945 (he was actually led to the gallows naked). The film starred O.E. Hasse as Canaris and Martin Held in a chilling performance as Canaris' opposite in the Nazi intelligence community, Reinhard Heydrich. Unusually, especially for a Germany still healing from the Hitler debacle, the film was quite frank about the former *Abwehr* chief's homosexuality.

Perhaps because it was felt the anti–Nazi resistance should be handled by a more "macho" protagonist, *The Devil's General* was released less than two months later on February 23, 1955. Starring the handsome and dignified future Hollywood actor Curt Jurgens (*né* Curd Jürgens), the film was based on the life of former World War I ace Ernst Udet, whose confirmed kills were second only to Manfred Von Richthofen. Later joining the Nazi Party, he was made director general of equipment for the *Luftwaffe*, and contributed enormously to the development of Germany's air force. Unfortunately, Germany had stretched itself too thin on too many fronts and was desperately in need of raw materials for the manufacture of bombers (despite these limitations, Udet helped develop the *Stuka* dive bomber). At first, Udet's old flying comrade, Reichsmarschall Göring, protected Udet and lied to Hitler about just why they lost the Battle of Britain to a far more skillful and productive RAF. However, Udet's flying pal could not be loyal to anyone for more than, say, two weeks, and in due time, Göring pointed his fat finger at Udet as to the reason why the *Luftwaffe* was not doing the job. Under intense pressure from the Führer and becoming disillusioned with the New Order, the former hero ace became an alcoholic. Finally on November 17, 1941, almost five months after Germany attacked the Soviet Union and a mere three weeks before Pearl Harbor, Udet shot himself in the head.

In *The Devils' General*, Jurgens, oozing middle-aged machismo, plays former World War I ace General Harry Harras, who is in charge of developing planes for the *Luftwaffe*. Unfortunately, Harras' planes have been having equipment trouble and crashing, with the general's chief adversary being an SS officer whom he treats with contempt; a very dangerous thing to do, but remember that Harras has principles. Indeed, Jurgens does play him as an honest, decent man and not the bossy SOB most German officers were in real life. The middle-aged and alcohol-needy Harras is very attracted to (and the feeling is mutual) a gorgeous 24-year old party guest named Dorothea (24-year old Marianne Koch); he is also a father figure to a confused junior officer; and he covers up for his friend at the air field who is *really* behind sabotaging the planes (in order to sabotage Hitler's war effort). In a meeting with his staff, he is told that his country is now at war with America; finding out that *Germany* declared war first clearly horrifies him and convinces him that he is among lunatics. When he takes the blame for his friend's sabotage, and in revenge on the SS colonel pursuing him, he crashes his plane onto the airfield. No happy ending here, but it did seem appropriate for the larger-than-life Harras to end it all this way.

It Happened on July 20th (released on June 19, 1955) starred Bernhard Wicki, the future director of the antiwar classic *The Bridge*, as Colonel Klaus von Stauffenberg; it is perhaps one of the few films about the heroic Count in which Stauffenberg's eye-patch is actually over the correct eye. Well-acted by Wicki and the cast, the film (also known rather ludicrously as *Jackboot Mutiny*) is crisply shot in black and white by the great G.W. Pabst. Watching a Stauffenberg film made by Germany is a refreshing experience after seeing the mostly British-accented officers and nonexistent performance of the highly overrated Tom Cruise in the more famous *Valkyrie*. Two days after Pabst's film debuted, Wolfgang Preiss starred as Stauffenberg in *The Plot to Kill Hitler*, giving German audiences yet another film in the now-growing subgenre of Kill-Hitler flicks.

G.W. Pabst had a fascinating on-screen career depicting the Germany of *both* world wars. Sandwiched between his classic *Pandora's Box* and *The Threepenny Opera*, Pabst directed the powerful, but little-known *Westfront 1918*, an antiwar film that made it into theaters in both Germany *and* the United States less than a month after the more famous *All Quiet on the*

Western Front. The Pabst film is *far* superior to the Lewis Milestone film, an effective antiwar piece without the annoying, lecturing, finger-wagging tone of the Oscar-winning Best Picture. Just by showing the hell the young German soldiers go through (including ending up in a monastery-turned-war-hospital), Pabst lets the audience see war as useless without the irritating and condescending speeches of Milestone's film. Pabst's own career afterwards was productive, but nowhere near the heights of his Weimar period work. Leaving Germany upon Hitler's rise, Pabst (born in Austria-Hungary) returned to Austria to settle some property there and was trapped in the country just as the Nazis had their *Anschluss*. Forced to return to Germany, Pabst now had to direct films for the new Nazi film industry. Fortunately, for the most part, his work consisted of costumed biographies and pointless musicals, though he gave these films far more class than they deserved.

This makes his treatment of Hitler and Nazism doubly interesting when he started filming these themes in democratic West Germany in the postwar period. Released just two months before the Stauffenberg film, *The Last Ten Days of Adolf Hitler* (or *The Last Act of Adolf Hitler* and a half dozen other titles the film goes under) for the first time on screen, showed us Hitler's bunker as it really was; not just a few little rooms with maps, but a sprawling underground city under a city. Hitler was joined not just by his senior officers but by several hundred people, cooks, secretaries, soldiers and their girlfriends, telephone operators, general staff officers and their wives, Goebbels and his wife and children. Throughout the piece, we see Oskar Werner as a good *Wehrmacht* officer, a crazed Hitler waving his fist a lot and constantly obsessed with his framed portrait of Frederic the Great, and a general air of doom hovering over the male and female inhabitants of the bunker as they dance, laugh, drink to excess, and of course make love even as Russian missiles are raining down from above. Indeed, much of this accuracy is due to Pabst's hiring Hitler's last secretary (and his youngest), Traudl Junge, as technical advisor (she was paid 1500 Deutschmarks, according to IMDB). Junge's memoirs would also be the source material, along with Joachim Fest's *Inside Hitler's Bunker*, for the fascinating *Downfall* in 2004. Besides Junge's contributions, *The Last Ten Days* was also based on the novel by historian/jurist Michael A. Musmanno. All in all, Pabst's film makes a mockery of *Hitler: The Last Ten Days*, starring an overly made-up and overacting Alec Guinness.

Back in America, Hollywood would give us their own version of the "good German." In *The Sea Chase*, John Wayne, of all people, played a good German skipper during the war. However, he is stuck with the villainous Lyle Bettger as a fanatical Nazi, whom the Duke ends up punching out soundly. Over at Fox in 1957, Robert Mitchum was an American captain and a now Hollywoodized Curt Jurgens played a German U-boat captain in *The Enemy Below*. They are both depicted as intelligent and decent men who do not like war, but do their duty anyway. In fact, Fox cunningly used this World War II tale to push the antiwar message, stacking the cards by making Jurgens not an SS murderer but an officer in the German navy. Jurgens himself praised the fact that, for the first time in a Hollywood film, a German officer was being portrayed as a human being (we assume compared to the portrayals approved by the BMP during the war period). Indeed, like *The Sea Chase*, there seems to be just *one* fanatical Nazi sailor on Jurgens' sub, and, of course, he proves to be a wimpering coward when the chips are down.

Interestingly, the original screenplay had both decent skippers dying in an explosion when a battleship collides with the U-boat at the film's climax. However, according to a memo

Top: Never apologize for the miscasting, pilgrim: Lana Turner and big John Wayne as two unlikely Germans in Warner's *The Sea Chase*; another in a series of films made at the time depicting so-called "good Germans."

Bottom: Troubled waters: Robert Mitchum (with hand to mouth; the extras are unknown) as the American captain in a seafaring game of cat and mouse with Curt Jürgens's Nazi sub captain in *The Enemy Below*. It was yet another Hollywood depiction of former wartime enemies, this time Nazi crewmen, as being no different than us.

by Harry Brand, Fox's Director of Publicity, dated June 26, 1957, six months before the film's targeted Christmas release, a new ending was decided upon. According to Brand, at the end of his synopsis of the film, he (or someone else) crosses out the last sentence "taking the two skippers to their deaths" and adds "right after the three men are hauled to safety by the crew members of the returning lifeboat."[1] Indeed, at the end of the completed film, both officers, former enemies (with the German skipper and his crew now prisoners of war who will face merciful treatment in the U.S.) will now bond as friends, a touching finale signifying brotherhood between former enemies. However, one can certainly wonder what the reaction would've been from a *Jewish* sailor in Mitchum's crew; perhaps in the 1950s, former enemies can bond *only* if they are gentile and only if they forget all that has happened to Germany's many victims.

On New Year's Day, 1958, a week after the release of *The Enemy Below*, a far less cerebral offering on the subject of National Socialism would be released to an appalled public. Directed by B helmsman Richard Cunha, this low-budget camp classic revised the old Monogram/PRC formula of merging the dynamics of the science fiction/horror film with the scourge of Nazism.

She-Demons is today considered a camp laugh-fest for many audiences; however, it highlighted, a mere dozen years after Allied armies broke into the concentration camps, how real-life Nazi horrors and the suffering of their victims were now to be put on a clearly comic book level.

Snotty rich socialite Jerrie Turner (played by the B movies' most statuesque blonde, and star of the *Sheena* jungle girl TV series, Irish McCalla), explorer Fred Maklin (Tod Griffin) and radio man Sammy Ching (a rare role for an Asian in the genre, the talented Victor Sen Yung) on a yacht belonging to Jerrie's rich dad. Needless to say, the boat gets blown off course and the usual "three-hour tour" ends up on a lonely, uncharted island. When U.S. air force planes fly over the island, it is not to search for the lost boat, but to use the island for bombing practice.

Soon, they find the boat's pilot, Kris (Charles Opunui) murdered. Following the trail of blood, the trio finds a bevy of scantily-clad women dancing very badly. Then a group of men in Gestapo uniforms arrive led by a big man named Igor (Gene Roth, who had played both Nazis and Communists). Sammy blurts out to the hero that the uniforms are that of "the Nazi Gestapo!" Afterwards, the women are herded into a bamboo cage. Igor whips a woman tied to a tree, and when the Gestapo man leaves, Fred finds that the woman has died. Getting too close to the cage, Sammy is almost eaten alive by the women, who apparently still have the same curvy figures, but now also have horrible, disfigured faces.

Finding a secret tunnel that leads into a cave/laboratory (or a laboratory/cave), the intrepid trio hide when Igor enters, but Jerrie is discovered. Hoping to make the statuesque blonde his main squeeze, Igor is interrupted by Fred and the two men fight. Taking it outside, the hero knocks the big Nazi creep into the bamboo cage, where the hungry she-demons devour him.

Soon, the three are captured by other Gestapo men, and taken to Colonel Karl Osler (Rudolph Anders—hurray!). Fred quickly recognizes Osler as a Nazi scientist who tortured concentration camp inmates during the war and is wanted by the "International War Commission"—whatever that is. He is now experimenting with the badly dancing beauty contestant winners (of whom there are many on this uncharted island) and extracting their glands in order to restore the face of his disfigured wife, Mona (Leni Tana). Though not once apologizing for his collaboration with Hitler (shades of Leni Riefenstahl and Veit Harlan!), Osler does lamely admit that the girls he experiments on *do* tend to turn into murderous beasts when he is finished with them.

Ultimately, the air force returns again and bombs the island; added to this, Mona helps Jerrie release Fred and Sammy. Osler is sizzled by lava, the Gestapo thugs die, and Mona reveals her own hideous face to our heroes before joining her husband in a fiery death. Soon, the three find their rowboat and Fred ends up with the formerly snotty Jerrie.

Indeed, not until *Hogan's Heroes* would the Nazis be this dumb, with Irish McCalla having absolutely no trouble sneaking around Osler's Gestapo guards as if they were blind. At another point, Fred is able to accurately shoot one of them in the face with a Luger from a distance of 200 feet. However, director Richard Cuhna, who co-wrote the screenplay, is at least able to find some *intended* humor when Sammy ventures that Osler will use *them* to restore Mona, to which Fred tiredly replies, "Who'd want a wife with our face?"

The film's saving grace is Rudolph Anders, an actor who can portray Nazi scum in his sleep. Almost winking at the audience, he is amused by the name Fred gives to the disfigured girls: "*She-demons!*" he exclaims happily, laughing at the film just as much as the audience. However, later, while trying to put the moves on Jerrie, and in full SS officer uniform, he threatens her friends: "You forget, I used to run concentration camps. Human life means nothing to me." Though the anti–Nazi Anders is reminding American audiences of the camps, the vehicle in which the line is presented is still on the level of schlock; an unusual comment on the Holocaust in the same film that includes murderous beast-women.

Though a laugh riot today, back in the late 1950s, *She-Demons* was the first film in the post–Production Code era that emphasized the more grotesque and sleazy sci-fi elements in the Nazi tenets to create a superior race. In subsequent low-budget efforts in this new Nazi/sci-fi subgenre, mad Nazi scientists would endeavor to either revive Hitler, put his head back on his body, or try to bring SS killers back to life, a plot that would influence the Nazi-zombie sub-subgenre which would culminate in the over-the-top, cartoonish *Dead Snow* movies of the 21st century. Already, it seemed a long way from when Allied soldiers liberated places like Auschwitz and witnessed firsthand man's inhumanity to man.

"Without doubt, there would be no need for faith..."—Erich Maria Remarque. Practically on the heels of the release of *The Young Lions* with its controversial portrayal of a "good Nazi" by Marlon Brando, Universal, the studio that produced the film version of *All Quiet on the Western Front* and would constantly return to the novels of Erich Maria Remarque, decided to film his 1954 novel, *A Time to Love and a Time to Die*. Very few questioned the author's obvious firsthand knowledge of wartime conditions during World War I since the author had been a wounded veteran of the trenches in 1918. However, by the time he switched his attention to the next world war, a conflict where he did *not* have firsthand battlefield experience, the result was a continuation of the "good German soldier" who lacked the barbarity of an SS thug, and instead, like Brando's pathetic distortion of Irwin Shaw's Christian Diestl, "thought of peace a thousand times a day."[2]

The cards were indeed stacked when Universal-International had Douglas Sirk shoot the film version of Remarque's novel from August to December 1957; around the same time 20th Century–Fox was shooting *The Young Lions* all over Europe. Though both films, made a good dozen years after the fall of the Third Reich, have vast differences, one cannot help but see far too many similarities—like for instance the canard that young Nazi soldiers were really good, decent boys no different from our own fighting men, but were trapped in a dreadful conflict in which both sympathetic protagonists were doomed: Lieutenant Christian Diestl getting blown away by an American G.I.; Private Ernst Graeber getting blown away by a Soviet guerrilla. In a kind of twisted version of that old *Boys' Town* cliché that "There are no bad boys; only boys who haven't been given a chance," the two films seem to be saying, "There are no bad Nazis, only Nazis who haven't been given a chance to kill even *more* people...."

A Time to Love begins, as Sirk's titles proclaim, on "The Russian-German Front, 1944." Private Ernst Graeber (All-American leading man and Universal-International star John Gavin) is with his platoon in the Soviet Union, obviously in retreat since they've passed through the same territory before. Graeber's pals are a varied bunch, though one notices that every single one of them, like the leading man, has a distinct *American* accent; this casting choice on Sirk's part was probably to show that these Aryan Supermen were, in reality, no different than us. Chief among this motley group of All-American Nazis is the cynical machine-gunner Private Immerman (Universal western star and former stunt man Jock Mahoney):

When a lady offers a Nazi a Tiparillo: John Gavin as the American-accented good Nazi soldier and unknown female extra as a very naughty lady in the film version of Erich Maria Remarque's *A Time to Love and a Time to Die*. The best part of Douglas Sirk's film is shooting on-location in war-torn Germany.

For the veteran cowpoke actor, his performance as the black-humored soldier is a revelation, and points up to what a shame it was that Hollywood did not use more of his dramatic talents for A films rather than bread-and-butter action movies.

Also standing out among these good-hearted boys is the baby-faced and sensitive Private Hirschland (making his film debut, Jim Hutton), a new soldier who hates the constant killing. Though the unit is commanded by the sympathetic Captain Rahe (German actor Dieter Borsche), the platoon is also saddled with Gestapo spy Steinbrenner (Swedish actor Bengt Lindstrom). Everyone in the unit hates Steinbrenner because he's a Nazi and, in the twisted logic of this movie, they apparently don't think *they* are. Also, they unrealistically treat him like crap, especially Immerman. Another glaring omission of the film is the nonexistence of extermination squads like the Waffen SS, the Order Police and the *Einsatzgruppen*. From June 22, 1941, onward, after the Nazis struck across Communist-occupied Poland and invaded the Soviet Union, the mobile killing squads of these three groups were to roll into the country in the wake of the *Wehrmacht* advance. After the regular German army attacked Red army positions, the SS Special Police Battalions were to follow them in and wipe out all the countryside's Jews and Slavs. Yet for some reason, Steinbrenner seems to be the *only* hardline Nazi among the German occupiers; openly hated, mocked and treated with contempt, it never occurs to Immerman or any of the others that Steinbrenner could report them, which could endanger their families back home. Again, as in *The Sea Chase* and *The Enemy Below*, the placement of one lone Nazi fanatic among the regular German servicemen is meant to accentuate the basic decency of the Germans.

After three "guerrillas" are captured, they are ordered shot by a firing squad, consisting of an enthusiastic Steinbrenner, as well as the reluctant Graeber and Hirschland, who is horrified by it all. Depressed by his actions and what he'd witnessed, Hirshland ultimately shoots himself (off-screen).

Certainly, during this scene, and in fact, all through the whole two hour and 14 minute movie, one will notice that the various soldiers and officials, whether German or Russian, all seem to sound alike. This is because the voices of the various German actors sounded garbled (the entire film was shot in Germany with American leads, but also German supporting players). Again, Universal went to premiere voiceover artist Paul Frees to save the day. The actor already had a busy career doing the voices of every other cartoon character in Creation. Already signed with Universal to dub in the voices of the various outlaws in the studio's *Last of the Fast Guns* (starring this film's Private Immerman, Jock Mahoney), it seems that every soldier Graeber comes in contact with has Frees' distinctive voice (it's not that Frees, a good actor, did not try to make them all sound different, but there is something that sounds so distinctly *Paul Frees* about every one of these characters). Despite Frees' obvious vocal versatility (he *also* does the voiceover for the film's trailer), the decision to redub every other voice with his distracts us from Graeber's own problems.

Given a three-week furlough (Dutch character actor John van Dreelen plays the officer at the train depot who suddenly cancels the leaves of other furloughed soldiers), Graeber returns to his bombed-out town. If anything, one must admire Sirk's skill in using these real bombed-out ruins as a powerful reminder of the war's deadly outcome. In the summer of 1957, much of Germany had *not* been rebuilt to its former splendor and one must applaud Universal's decision to allow Sirk to shoot on location; more than any studio-bound set, these ruins are a distinct plus that are amazingly absent from the film's more popular rival, *The*

Young Lions. Despite the poor script by Orin Jannings (which might have had some input from Remarque himself), Sirk's utilization of these ruins adds to the tragedy of a defeated and broken Germany and is the film's main attraction. One can be turned off by all the unrealistic American-sounding actors, but at least Sirk reminds us of the flavor of Remarque's novel by the sight of a once-proud and now obliterated Germany.

Back in his hometown, Graeber attempts to search for his parents. During his trek, he meets another varied group of German humanity. There is the doctor's daughter Elizabeth (Swiss actress Lisolette Pulver) whose father was taken off to a concentration camp; there is the garrulous American-sounding German soldier Boettcher (Don DeFore); the happy-go-lucky Reuter (Keenan Wynn); Graeber's former classmate, now powerful Gauliter, Oscar Binding (Thayer David); his former teacher, the anti–Nazi Professor Pohlmann (the author himself in his *only* acting role: Erich Maria Remarque), who is harboring a Jew named Joseph (Charles Regnier), and various flotsam and jetsam of German humanity as they flee constant Allied bombardment and gripe (mildly) about the hardships of war. In fact, opposite a groundbreaking classic like Bernhard Wicki's *The Bridge*, which was shot in West Germany around the same time, *A Time to Love and a Time to Die* does not make war look so bad at all.

Throughout his leave, the lonely Graeber will argue with Elizabeth, but love wins the day and the two people decide to marry before the private has to return to merry old Stalingrad. During these scenes, one *does* sympathize with the two lovers, who are both likable characters (and played by good performers). However, despite their romantic idylls and the warm, fuzzy feeling one gets from their many romantic scenes, they don't hold a candle to the scene where Graeber, desperately searching for Elizabeth after her house has been bombed, runs through already bombed-out ruins as Allied bombs explode around him. Sirk's skill in these scenes is on full display as John Gavin's stunt double runs from one ruin to another, which the Universal special effects department rigged with live explosives and promptly blew up the moment Gavin's stunt man starts running. Obviously, Universal-International had the hollowed-out structures blown up with the full permission of West German authorities and, unlike the studio's usual tacky explosive effects used for their other films, Sirk got every penny of the production's special effects budget for these scenes.

Finally, after all the *Time to Love* portion of the film is out of the way, the *Time to Die* part comes along and Graeber returns to the Russian front. Amazingly the old gang is still there and in one piece. However, when the fun-loving Immerman spots a keg of beer in a pool of water, he goes for it and a bomb is dropped on him; here we see Mahoney's stunt man training kick into full gear, since the explosive goes off and he's throwing *himself* away from the charge, not a stunt double. When three men are arrested as guerrillas, they are taken by Graeber and Steinbrenner to a makeshift guardhouse. The Gestapo man plans to murder the prisoners, but Graeber stops him; when Steinbrenner aims at him, the private fires his rifle first, killing him. With a sly look on his face (the first time we actually see the character being capable of deceit), he decides to let the prisoners go. After releasing them, he wanders off and reads the letter from his wife saying that she'll have a baby. Before you can say "Only the good die young," one of the partisans grabs the late Steinbrenner's rifle and fires it at Graeber, killing him. We see, in death, the young soldier, reach out for the letter, now floating away in a pond under a bridge. If this death scene looks nauseatingly familiar, remember that it was written by the same man who gave us *All Quiet on the Western Front*. However, instead of reaching out for a butterfly and getting shot dead for his trouble, *this* young German soldier reaches out for yet *another* life-affirming symbol, his wife's letter of good news for the future, after getting gunned down by a callous enemy. Certainly, both of these scenes, written to drive home the tragedy of war by sacrificing our likable young German hero, instead only shows us that the soldier should *never* have dropped his guard! If anything, the needless deaths of these likable characters makes you hate their murderers, a reaction very much at odds with Remarque's antiwar message.

The acting is not bad, with Gavin a likable actor who gives a sincere performance (as does Pulver), but the future ambassador to Mexico is obviously *not* German, a distinct disadvantage in an antiwar piece set in the Fatherland. Ditto Don DeFore and Keenan Wynn, who could have, with a little change in dialogue, been two recruits in an American barracks; albeit over-aged ones. Out of the various Yankees in the film, only the underrated Mahoney shines as the cynical Immerman; though not German, he uses his voice very well, putting into it a grating undertone of contempt that adds to his character. One German performer (actually Polish) stands out, despite the fact that he's dubbed: Klaus Kinski as a Gestapo officer. When Graeber comes to Gestapo headquarters to find out what they want from Elizabeth, Kinski responds that it's to return something of her father's—in fact, it's her *father*—now burned down into ashes (he was thrown into a concentration camp) and coldly presented to Graeber in a small box. Sirk uses stark shadows around Kinski, accentuating his ugly face in the semi-darkness, as the Gestapo man proclaims their business finished. It is without a doubt the scariest moment in a film set during wartime Germany that had far too few of such chilling scenes; but it was a harbinger for Kinski's future career as a cinematic madman (he was reportedly a madman *off* screen as well).

If anything, the film demonstrated how two nations with completely opposite ideologies still had similar views concerning the Nazi juggernaut and the people who supported it. Both Israel and the Soviet Union (a nation of Jews and a nation that persecuted Jews, respectively) banned the film for its unusually sympathetic portrayal of Germans in World War II.

In their New Year's Eve, 1957, review of the film's rough cut, the unknown writer of *Variety* declared:

> *A Time to Love and a Time to Die* is less a panorama of the battle horrors of the Second World War, though these are implicit, than a poignant telling of the anguish of being in love while civilian bombings rage, and decency is held hostage to vicious character traits. In unfolding the Erich Maria Remarque novel, producer and director have been long on "heart" and "sentiment" and the result is a bitter-sweet love story.

In his *New York Times* review of the completed film on July 10, 1958, the usually acerbic Bosley Crowther was not about to let the film's many flaws escape his attention, especially the cast's woefully inadequate accents:

> At least, we are told these are Germans, though the general impression conveyed is that the soldiers are nice Americans who just happen to be dressed in Wehrmacht uniforms.
> The hero is played by John Gavin, a good-looking, awkward young man whose speech, attitude and dull delivery betray the tyro from Hollywood. And the hero's good friends in the army are played by Keenan Wynn and Don DeFore, who might as well be acting as automobile salesmen in Sioux City, Iowa.
> This again is a fault of the picture—it simply does not ring true. It has an air of studied contrivance and artificiality. Lilo (Lisette) Pulver, for instance, is winsome as the German girl, but she acts, under Douglas Sirk's direction, with the airs and manners of a well-fed ingénue. Except for a trace of a German accent, you'd never dream she's been near a bombed German city in World War II.

Crowther wasn't about to let the author's acting debut off the hook either: "Stumbling about in a small role of an aging school teacher is Mr. Remarque, who might better have saved himself embarrassment by staying as far away from this pastiche as he could." The reviewer of *Motion Picture Daily*, by contrast, would call the author's performance "mighty good" on April 1, 1958.

In the meantime, in late 1950s West Germany, former Hollywood B maven Frank Wisbar was going to have his own take on the debacle at Stalingrad: "One can't help feeling it's an invitation to commit suicide"—so said General Friedrich Paulus upon hearing that the Führer promoted him to the rank of field marshal just before his surrender at Stalingrad.

The whole awful story of the defeat and capture of the German Sixth Army at Stalingrad, as well as the blundering lack of foresight and lunatic decisions made by the Führer and his loyal bootlickers in the Nazi high command, would echo down through history. The German army, militarily one of the best in *any* century, was now going to be led into a quagmire from which they would never recover; a disaster which was a harbinger for even more disasters that would face this once proud army, who obviously did not see themselves as rapacious conquerors and murderers of innocents, but a class of warriors descended from men like Frederick the Great, Bismarck and Hindenburg. The fact that they would more likely be put in a class with men like Himmler, Heydrich and Eichmann, men who did not play by the rules of proud military traditions, apparently did not dampen their spirits or enthusiasm for waging war against people who did them no harm. To this day, the *Wehrmacht* is seen as a "kinder, gentler" brand of Nazi terror; to many historians, they were the military elite, not the madmen of the SS; to them, it was soldierly professionalism, not the killing of Jews that was uppermost on their minds. And yet, people forget that, were it not for the *Wehrmacht* storming into Russia and other lands to the east, there would not be mobile killing squads like the Waffen SS, Order Police, and the *Einsatzgruppen* following in their wake and killing every "racial inferior" in sight.

Failing to get into the German Navy, Friedrich Wilhelm Ernst Paulus joined the 111th Infantry Regiment of the Imperial German Army as an officer cadet in February 1910. When World War I broke out, Paulus saw action in France, soon became a staff officer, and was eventually promoted to captain by war's end. After the war, he became a company commander of the 13th Infantry Regiment stationed at Stuttgart. New responsibilities soon came with new rank as Paulus soon rose in the army hierarchy. General Guderian would praise him as "brilliantly clever, conscientious, hard-working, original and talented,"[3] but also despaired that he was not decisive enough to lead, and wondered whether he could handle a *really* responsible command post.

After being promoted to major general in May 1939, Paulus was named Chief of Staff of the German Tenth Army, which, for some reason, would be renamed the *Sixth* Army. The new general was front and center when he and his men stormed into western Poland (while the Soviets took over the eastern half), and the following year he and the Sixth were part of the spring offensives in Belgium and Holland. Promoted to chief of the German General Staff, Paulus helped draft the plans for the coming Operation Barbarossa, the invasion of the Soviet Union. Leading the Sixth Army, Paulus heeded the Führer's order to change his path from Moscow to Stalingrad, what many military historians would see years later as a tactical blunder that helped cost Hitler a decisive victory. From the fall and winter of 1941 and all through the following year, Paulus and the Sixth Army fought the Red Army to a veritable standstill; but as time wore on and Paulus' supplies of food and ammunition dwindled, the general was starting to see the writing on the wall. Devoid of warm winter clothing to survive a brutally long Russian winter (remember that Paulus himself was part of the planning group for the invasion), as well as more weaponry and ammo to counter the Red Army's seemingly limitless supply (and, unlike the Germans, *they* had warm winter gear), the Sixth Army's situation was indeed desperate. By November 1942, the Red Army launched Operation Uranus, which had nothing to do with the eighth planet in the solar system, but a great deal to do with surrounding the Sixth Army in a tightening noose they could never escape from.

Radioing Berlin for new orders to break out of the trap (or "break ranks"), Paulus was somewhat dismayed when Hitler ordered him to hold his position "to the last man" and not retreat. It was never fully explained just why Hitler and his minions decided to stay in Stalingrad with disaster staring them in the face, except perhaps the Aryan supremist ego and vanity that wouldn't allow them to surrender to people they saw as Slavic *Untermenschen*. When Field Marshal Erich von Manstein launched Operation Winter Storm in December to relieve the Sixth Army, which needed at least some kind of attempt by the beleaguered men to break out of their trap, for some strange reason, Paulus refused. Obeying his Führer, Paulus decided to hold his men in fixed defensive positions and not retreat to safer ground, frustrating Manstein's attempt at a rescue. Keeping his men where they were, Paulus watched them die by the thousands, even as Hitler finally ordered a breakout, but also ordered that the Sixth would have to hold onto Stalingrad as well, something way beyond the means of Paulus' starving and ill-equipped men.

On January 8, 1943, the Red Army commander, General Konstantin Rokossovsky, called a ceasefire and offered the Sixth Army food, warm clothing, medical treatment and the promise that they could emigrate to any country they wanted to after the war was over.

As we would later see, it was the typical Bolshevik BS. Of the close to 100,000 German soldiers captured at Stalingrad, nearly half of them died on the long march to prison camps in Siberia, with thousands more dying of starvation, disease and firing squad while being held by their supposedly merciful captors. Only 6,000 of these men would survive to return to their conquered nation after the war.

However, seeing the situation as hopeless, Paulus *still* felt the need to wire the Führer for permission to surrender. Again, Hitler refused, ordering him to hold "fortress Stalingrad" to the death. After January 25, with the Soviet takeover of the airstrip the Germans used to land supplies, again Paulus radioed Hitler for permission to surrender. Five days later, Hitler again turned him down; however he *did* give him a consolation prize for all his suffering and promoted him to the rank of Field Marshal. Paulus knew what that little gesture meant. It was said that in the history of the German military, no officer with the rank of Field Marshal ever surrendered to the enemy; the implication was for Paulus to blow his own brains out before the Red Army overwhelmed them. Now regretting his original decision to obey Hitler and stay where they were, indeed, disillusioned with everything his Führer ever stood for, Paulus remarked acidly to General Max Pfieffer, "I have no intention of shooting myself for this Bohemian corporal." A loyal Catholic, Paulus not only refrained from committing suicide but he ordered his men not to stand openly on trenches or hilltops so they could be shot dead by the surrounding Red Army.

Typically, under Stalin's orders, the bulk of the men who surrendered would be murdered by the Soviets either through violence, starvation, disease or neglect. However, Field Marshal Paulus was a different story altogether. Seeing a high-ranking Nazi officer as a good propaganda tool, Stalin ordered that he be spared the fate of the men under him (so much for sympathy for the proletariat). Paulus was to openly call for Germany's surrender and the Soviets appointed him to something called the National Committee for a Free Germany, which, of course, meant a Germany controlled by the Soviet Union. A witness for the prosecution at the Nuremburg War Crimes Tribunal where his testimony helped indict former comrades, Paulus eventually settled in East Germany and continued his new career as a Soviet mouthpiece. When asked by journalists in the mid–1950s about how the captured German soldiers from the battle of Stalingrad were holding up, the ex–field marshal told them to tell the wives and mothers awaiting their loved ones in Germany that their husbands and sons were alive and being treated well. In reality, however, most of the soldiers had already died on the march from Stalingrad, with these "wives and mothers" never once having been informed by the Soviets that their loved ones had died over a decade before.

Now appointed chief of East Germany's "Military History Research Institute," a Communist organization that was emphatically *not* going to have accurate material dealing with World War II (for instance, the Nazi-Soviet Pact is never mentioned), Paulus himself finally died of amyotrophic lateral sclerosis ("Lou Gehrig's Disease") on February 1, 1957. His wife and children had not seen him since he left for the Eastern Front in the summer of 1942…

Based on the novel by Austrian writer Fritz Wöss, the wonderfully titled *Stalingrad: Dogs, Do You Want to Live Forever?* was released in West Germany on April 7, 1959. A semi-fictional retelling of the battle for Stalingrad told from the German side, the film veered sharply from the typical Hollywood pap of war-themed films like *A Time to Love and a Time to Die*. In fact, in defiance of the typical Soviet depiction of the *Wehmarcht* as brutal monsters who murdered the populace and had no redeeming characteristics, the German film accomplished an almost impossible task: It portrayed the soldiers, even their Russian enemies, as all-too human; but it also slammed Hitler and the Nazi hierarchy for ordering the Sixth Army to hold their positions to the death. The production had seasoned German actors to perform their historic roles (unlike the usually non–German international co-productions where all the Nazis have British accents). The production's most interesting feature, however, was the man who helmed the film, an underrated and talented filmmaker who was more than familiar with both Nazi rule and Hollywood schlock.

Born Franz Wysbar, the director would later Americanize his name into Frank Wisbar. A helmsman who had a knack for using light and shadow and with a sharp eye for good art and set direction, Wisbar was a German filmmaker who excelled in directing fantasies during the Weimar years. Many of these films are lost, but one classic survives: the lyrical *Fährmann Maria*. The plot of this film, released in Germany in 1936, was odd even by esoteric European standards, and certainly an unusual production to be green-lighted during the Nazi era. After a ferryman dies, the ferry is taken over by a woman (played by the tragic Sybille Schitz). When she takes a wounded fugitive on her ferry, she must fight to keep him alive when the figure of Death seeks to take him. Ultimately, she sacrifices her own life for the man she loves. How such a fascinating romantic fantasy could come from a man who would later direct *Secrets of a Sorority Girl* and *Devil Bat's Daughter* is itself a fascinating tale. Wisbar's dark fantasy films met with some disapproval by Nazi censors, with the strident Goebbels himself frowning on the making of horror and science fiction projects, to say nothing of fantasies where Death seems to win out. Under pressure to conform, Wisbar, like so many other artists, left Germany and eventually made it to Hollywood. Unfortunately, after 1938, Wisbar would not make another film until 1945; by then, he was signed with the moribund PRC studios and forced to contribute to their usual output of low-budget tripe. However, all was not so horrible as it seemed; he was able to remake his own *Fährmann Maria* as the more horror-sounding *Strangler of the Swamp*, one of the few examples of a talented director circumventing PRC's chintzy budgets to come up with an underrated gem (though German refugee Edgar Ulmer certainly succeeded in this also).

Returning to Germany (the western half) after the war, Wisbar revived his career, with a new Denazified German film industry more than willing to welcome back former émigrés. Wisbar helped introduce actor Horst Buchholz to international audiences with *Wet Asphalt* in 1957, a parable on the scourge of yellow journalism and a rare acknowledgment in the German cinema of the time of Nazi war criminals still residing in the country. With *Stalingrad: Dogs, Do You Want to Live Forever?*, Wisbar (who co-wrote the screenplay) etches a portrait of German fighting men in a no-win situation and superior officers who cynically could not care less.

Wehrmacht Lieutenant Wisse (Joachim Hansen) is ordered to report to the Russian front at Stalingrad to act as liaison for Romanian army regulars. The unit is under the command of one Major Linkmann (veteran German character actor Wolfgang Preiss), a selfish and glory-hungry martinet who is jealous of Wisse's easy camaraderie with the men. Though General Paulus (Wilhelm Borchert) will also feature in this film, the rage of the screenwriters is directed at the fictional Linkmann, an officer who not only obeys the Führer blindly, but keeps himself out of the line of fire as his men are killed for lack of ammunition and starve to death for lack of food.

Throughout the film, Wisbar uses newsreel footage of the Russian front to enhance the proceedings; however, he *also* shoots unusually powerful tableaus of soldiers slogging through deep snow, with dead men lying in mounting snow drifts and tanks slowly rolling through the scene like mammoth ghosts. In fact, the shots themselves suggest a dream world where the soldiers crossing before the frame will soon be as dead as the soldiers frozen in the ground. These are shots that belong more in a horror film, and prove that Wisbar had lost none of his talent for creating chilling imagery.

Throughout the film, as Wisse bonds with his starving men and Paulus gets sarcastic when Hitler again turns down his request to break out of the siege (we never hear about Paulus' original decision to obey Hitler's directive to hold their positions), we see the Führer usually with his back to the audience or in semiprofile as he continues to firmly reiterate that the Sixth Army has to defend their positions to the death. When Linkmann orders a captured stockade of food and supplies burned to the ground so the Red Army won't get it, Wisse defies orders by having his men grab all the supplies they can and *then* orders it burned.

Another plus for the film is Wisbar's shooting on-location in the bombed out ruins of Göttingen in Lower Saxony. Like Douglas Sirk in *A Time to Love and a Time to Die*, Wisbar fully exploits these ruins to depict, not a burnt-out Germany, but a burnt-out Stalingrad, with both armies hitting each other with mortar and tank fire amidst the rubble of a war torn nation. Unlike Sirk's Hollywood production, Wisbar is allowed to show blood and gore, with torn bodies without arms and legs and torn faces on tattered uniforms. This is also emphasized during Wisse's visit to a German field hospital with the company chaplain. The scene is bleak, with wounded soldiers crowded all over the floor, many of them without limbs. At one point, when a friend of Wisse's dies, he covers the corpse with a blanket, but then after he leaves, another wounded soldier grabs the blanket off the corpse and covers himself for warmth.

After all the cliché-ridden war films where the hero covers up the corpses of dead buddies with blankets, it was almost a pleasure to see this cliché busted so realistically. When the voice of Göring comes over the radio and announces that the men are doing a great job beating the Russians, Wisbar cuts to several of the men, now not only in physical pain, but thoroughly disgusted. A hardline Nazi corporal wants to keep the radio on despite the anger of the wounded (there was a penalty for German soldiers who turned off radios when either Hitler, Göring or Goebbels was making a speech), but the chaplain angrily smashes the radio to bits. Again, Wisbar's tableau is twofold; combining a sympathy for the wounded men who fought at Stalingrad while expressing contempt for the wrongheaded Nazi leaders who foolishly sent them there. Another difference between Wisbar's film and the Universal production is the fact that the Stalingrad the Sixth Army is slogging through is deep in snow while Universal's Stalingrad has John Gavin and his buddies in a beautiful park on a sunny day (only when the film is set in Germany proper amidst actual bombed-out ruins does the film excel).

Among Wisse and his men, frustrated by the powers-that-be for turning down all requests for food, warm clothing and weapons, there is not only camaraderie, but a constant supply of realistic foul language that never once appears in Universal's depiction of the Russian front. Indeed, it was not until the 1970s and Hollywood's depictions of the Vietnam War that soldiers on American screens were routinely allowed to curse out in the open; European filmmakers never had this problem.

Ultimately, the selfish Linkmann, realizing that all is lost, grabs a captured Russian coat and hat, puts them on, and makes a run for the Red Army garrison pinning the Germans down. Seeing this, an angry Wisse shoots him down as he flees. At this point, the fanatical Linkman seems to be taking a page out of Edward Albert's portrayal of a cowardly major in *Attack*, which was made in 1956 (in real life, Albert was a naval hero during World War II, having been awarded the Bronze Star for personally using his craft to rescue dozens of wounded Marines during the battle of Tarawa). Ultimately forced to disarm and surrender, the men are marched by the Red Army to their captivity. In fact, we already see soldiers drop to the ground, a good implication what will happen to the survivors on this death march.

Stalingrad: Dogs, Do You Want to Live Forever? was everything *A Time to Love and a Time to Die* should have been and clearly wasn't. Wisbar's film also has only one woman in it, the Russian Katja (Sonja Ziemann), who was helped by Wisse back in Germany and is now able to return the favor by helping him escape the Red Army when he grabs a dead Russian's coat and hat and pretends to be one of them.

Never released theatrically in the United States, *Stalingrad: Dogs, Do You Want to Live Forever?* continued Frank Wisbar's lucrative return to the screen in his native land, with a prolific career producing, writing and directing both films and TV shows almost up to his death on March 17, 1967, at the age of 67.

The times were certainly changing in Germany (the *western* half, that is), with young, up-and-coming German artists rejecting the now stereotypical "good German" films in favor of actor-turned-director Bernhard Wicki's powerful antiwar film *Die Brücke* (*The Bridge*), released in West Germany six or seven months after Wisbar's indictment of Nazi blunders in Stalingrad. Based on the novel by Gregor Dorfmeister, himself a teen veteran of the *Wehrmacht* in the final days of the war, the film details the lives of six youths who are forced to join the German army even as they face imminent defeat. With unusual support and understanding, their Nazi superiors order them to guard a bridge near their homes, an easy task with no

V. Airbrush (1955–1962)

danger involved. However, gung-ho for the Fatherland and trying to prove themselves "men," the boys end up fighting an approaching American tank and infantry snipers. The boys are killed off (except for one, who, it is implied, will go mad) and some Americans are killed as well, all needlessly. Powerful, evocative, and beautifully shot in black and white, the film was an eye-opener for young Germans sick of both Nazi lies and their parents' convenient forgetfulness concerning wartime atrocities committed in the name of patriotism. Though they were both on record as being pacifists, neither Wicki nor Dorfmeister ever explained just how a persistent call for peace was going to defeat brutal totalitarianism of either the Nazi variety or any other kind.

As the new decade arrived, Allied Artists, closely watching the huge international success of Erwin Leiser's two-hour German documentary *Mein Kampf*, knew that interest in the Third Reich could be big box office if they were able to come up with a famous Nazi name that would have instant recognition for the paying public.

When Mossad agents finally captured a famous Nazi war criminal who was also one of the architects of the Final Solution, the studio knew that that would be their next project. Just as the assassination of Heydrich would inspire the dual filmings of *Hangmen Also Die* and *Hitler's Madman*, the capture and subsequent trial of this war criminal stunned the world and galvanized the public's attention on the little nation of Jews that sought justice for the dead.

Their catch was a man who reportedly abhorred violence, but as an important official in charge of transporting Jews to concentration camps, he still distinguished himself, even among an already contemptuous group of Nazi monsters, as unremittingly evil.

"I will leap into my grave laughing because the feeling that I have five million human beings on my conscience is for me a source of extraordinary satisfaction." So said SS *Obersturmbannführer* (Lieutenant Colonel) Otto Adolf Eichmann at war's end in 1945. One of the most homicidal men in a thoroughly homicidal Nazi elite, like many of the Third Reich's major players his origins were average, even ordinary, indicating nothing that would point to a life and a career marked by anti–Semitic hatred and murderous bloodlust.

Born on March 19, 1906, in Solingen, Germany, to a Calvinist Protestant family, at eight years old he moved to Linz, Austria, with his family when his father took a position as a commercial manager for the Linz Tramway & Electrical Company. Like Reinhard Heydrich, the young Eichmann was proficient at playing the violin; and, like Heydrich, as a youngster he fell in with various right-wing groups whose aims were pro-militarist and rabidly anti–Semitic; in Austria, these were certainly not hard to find. A poor student, he eventually joined a mining company started by his father; but after a few months, he left and wandered about at a series of clerical jobs. After a two-year stint as a sales clerk for a radio company, in 1927, he worked for five years in Salzburg as a district agent for the Vacuum Oil Company AG (in far too many "biographies" of Eichmann, it was erroneously reported that he was a "vacuum cleaner salesman"). During this period, being a faceless bureaucrat of little imagination and even less staying power, Eichmann took the advice of a family friend who advised the dour and bourgeoisie bland to join a new political movement which promised the overthrow of the democratic Weimar Republic, the creation of a powerful military and a severe curtailing of "Jewish influence"; the family friend was a high official of the SS named Ernst Kaltenbrunner. After joining the Austrian Nazi Party on April 1, 1932, Eichmann enlisted in the SS seven months later, where his duties were to guard Party headquarters in Linz and protect speakers at pro–Nazi rallies.

After Austrian Chancellor Engelbert Dollfuss banned the Nazi Party in early January 1933 and Hitler took power on the 30th, Eichmann returned to Germany. His star rose gradually in the SS, and in 1934, he requested a transfer to the *Sicherheitsdienst*, the intelligence section of the SS, where he became an "expert" in matters related to both Freemasons and Jews. In fact, to set himself apart from his rivals in the SS and SD, he learned Jewish culture, and even picked up some words in Hebrew, all while he prepared classified reports to the Nazi leadership on the growing Zionist movement coming back into being in pre-independence Israel. In the meantime, Eichmann's rank in the SS kept rising until he was made SS *Untersturmführer* (Second Lieutenant) in 1937. After the *Anschluss* of Austria, Eichmann was promoted to SS *Obersturmführer* (First Lieutenant) and also appointed to head the Central Agency for Jewish Emigration in Vienna.

During those years, the Third Reich rigidly enforced their anti–Semitic "Aryanization" laws, which empowered the government to confiscate all Jewish homes and property, usually at the point of a Gestapo gun, and force the victims to sign over everything they had. Thus, now penniless, these new Jewish refugees were forced to leave the country; this enabled Aryans in both Germany and Austria to buy up confiscated Jewish businesses and property literally at a "steal." Adolf Eichmann, as head of the so-called "Jewish Agency," was a major player in this policy, forcing Jews to hand over everything they worked for all their lives and frequently threatening Gestapo harassment, or worse, until they gave all they had to the State and then cleared out. During this persecution, Eichmann and his many cronies in his agency reaped great profits personally by grabbing much of their Jewish victims' savings and enriching themselves as well as the State. During his reign, an estimated 100,000 Jews fled Austria, many never to return.

After Germany attacked Poland on September 1, 1939, and war was declared, Nazi policy towards the Jews turned from forced emigration to forced *deportation*. Three weeks later, Heydrich ordered the mass deportation of all Jews, not only in Germany, but all areas controlled by the Reich. During this period of rapid policy changes, on December 19 Heydrich appointed Eichmann to head Sub-Department IV-B4 of the Reich Security Main Office, which was detailed with transporting Jews from all areas occupied by the Reich into ghettos in Poland. In this function, Eichmann had to procure trains to transport thousands of Jews into cramped ghettos where disease, overcrowding and starvation were rampant. During the entire task, Eichmann's main concern was not alleviating the Jews' suffering as they were being forcibly deported, but getting the job done as quickly and cheaply as possible.

After hosting the infamous Wannsee Conference on January 20, 1942, Heydrich appointed Eichmann as his personal liaison to all the various departments involved in this new Nazi policy: Instead of being kicked out, the Jews were now to be taken away to be murdered. Eichmann quickly became an enthusiastic point man for this new plan, a logistical nightmare for most Nazi officials, but a unique challenge to the former paper-pusher from Linz. With his new powers, Eichmann energetically oversaw mass deportations of thousands of Jews, Slavs. Gypsies and other "undesirables" to Auschwitz, Sobibor, Treblinka and other extermination camps, coddling some officials, threatening others, as he obtained dozens of trains needed to transport his victims on their final journey. He studiously collected information on Jews, confiscated their property and scheduled the trains.

After Germany invaded Hungary on March 19, 1944, Eichmann arrived later that spring to take full control of the deportation of Hungarian Jews to Auschwitz II–Birkenau. Startled by the Allies' rapid advance towards Germany, the Hungarian government, fearing Allied reprisals, halted all deportations on July 6; coincidentally, seeking to dispose of any evidence of genocide, Himmler also ordered a halt to the deportations. However, Eichmann, whose hatred of Jews had grown into a mania, defied these orders and was able to procure more trains to continue the deportations. His efforts had already sent more than three-quarters of Hungary's Jewish population to their deaths, with some 437,000 people promptly gassed as soon as they arrived at Auschwitz.

Then, during October and November, with all train transport halted by the Allies, Eichmann personally oversaw a forced march of thousands of Jewish victims from Budapest to Vienna; starving and suffering from various illnesses and endless abuse, many of them died on the way. With the Red Army closing in, Eichmann fled to Berlin where he and his staff at Department IV-B4 promptly began destroying incriminating records.

Though captured by the Americans, Eichmann was able to escape a work detail at the Cham detention camp. It is said that during this time he was ably assisted by Odessa, the powerful organization consisting of still-fanatical former SS officers. Indeed, Eichmann's (and for that matter, Mengele's and thousands of other Nazis') easy flight from justice could not have been made without the help of sympathetic friends belonging to some shadowy organization whose power reached much further than those of most official government agencies (some fascist-leaning figures in the Vatican *also* assisted Nazi war criminals to escape to South America). Meanwhile, during the Nuremburg trials of 1946, the former commandant of Auschwitz, Rudolf Höss, revealed much of his former friend and collaborator's crimes during his time as head of Department IV-B4. Even so, three years and two months after Höss was dangling from a noose for his own heinous crimes, Eichmann was able to obtain papers to travel to Argentina, ultimately sailing from the Italian port of Genoa on June 17, 1950. Once in Buenos Aires, he settled comfortably into the city's powerful German émigré community, which, needless to say, consisted of former SS officers. No longer Adolf Eichmann to the outside world, his new name was "Ricardo Klement." It was well-known that the fascist government of Juan and Eva Perón knew that escaped Nazis, especially those guilty of Crimes Against Humanity, were respected citizens of their country and they had absolutely no intention of turning them over to the Allies.

Though he would move periodically from one job to the next, Eichmann was relatively safe and content in his adopted homeland for the next ten years. And in all that time, he never once suspected that one day the children of the very people he had so enthusiastically murdered were going to pay him a little visit.

Originally called *Six Million Murders*, the proposed project had its title changed to *Operation Eichmann* by the time of the film's release on March 15, 1961 (it was still referred to under its former title in Allied Artists correspondence as late as October 1960). Produced on Allied Artists' traditionally low budget, the film was directed by western helmsman R.G. Springsteen, an unusual choice for this kind of material, but hired obviously for his ability to bring a film in on time and under budget. However, it was the screenwriter who was the company's most interesting choice. Calling himself "Lewis Copley," the scenarist was none other than Communist Party member Lester Cole, blacklisted for the past dozen years since being kicked out of MGM in 1948. Kirk Douglas had already broken the blacklist by crediting Dalton Trumbo for *Spartacus* in 1960, but for some reason Cole still refused to use his own name for the Eichmann project. This choice of Cole as the screenwriter might seem unusual for some, but here, the Communist scenarist merely continued the anti–Nazi tone of his 1944 screenplay for Columbia, *None Shall Escape*. Only this time, by 1960, he was able to show more atrocities in the concentration camp scenes than under the usually reluctant Joseph Breen.

Before the title credits of *Operation Eichmann* come up, we see Eichmann himself (an outstanding performance by Werner Klemperer) defiantly indict an unseen jury as he speaks from a courtroom. However, we soon flash back to the crimes that put the former SS lieutenant colonel and head of Department IV-B4 in this situation. Eichmann chairs a "secret meeting at SS headquarters in 1941, during the early days of the war." Two of the participants in said meeting are Auschwitz commandant Rudolf Höss (John Banner) and Major Kessner (Lester Fletcher). It is here that we see that *Eichmann alone* creates the means of extermination that figured prominently in the Holocaust. This, of course, was only partially true; he handled much of the transporting of Jews into the camps and the confiscation of their property, especially in Hungary. Still, it is obvious that this "secret meeting at SS headquarters in 1941, during the early days of the war," is meant to be the Wannsee Conference, which was actually hosted by Heydrich, not Eichmann, and that it took place on January 20, 1942. Also established is Eichmann's righteous airs, as he witheringly condemns Kessner for possessing a ring once owned by a murdered Jew, contraband that he believes to be "contaminated." Starting with this scene, Klemperer infuses Eichmann with an arrogance bordering on mania for get-

Murderers' row: German-Jewish actor Werner Klemperer (center) as Adolf Eichmann, with unknown Nazi extras in Allied Artists' *Operation Eichmann*, which was released shortly after Israel's Mossad captured him in Argentina.

ting the task of exterminating six million Jews completed within two years. Indeed, as written by Communist Party member Cole, Eichmann is depicted as a kind of pseudo-capitalist whose control over the mechanics of mass murder make him less a tin pot clone of the Führer than a profit-seeking captain of industry. In a later scene, he even demands that the gas chambers work 24 hours a day, not 16.

We see him at dinner with Höss' wife and children; in fact, Springsteen opens the scene with a shot of a full dinner table as compared with the starving victims of the camps. However, during the dialogue at the table we see both Klemperer and Banner, two friends who would find fame just four years later on TV's *Hogan's Heroes*, in two roles radically different than the comedic Nazis they would play on the show.

With no wife and family in the film, the Colonel (apparently Cole had him promoted from lieutenant colonel) has been getting a little on the side with a pretty blonde named Anna (pretty blonde Ruta Lee, who would later guest-star on *Hogan's Heroes*). In reality, because of his duties, Eichmann kept far away from his wife and family, which apparently did not bother him much. In the film, he is seen as an incorruptible martinet; stubbornly he presides over the firing squad of a guard who took bribe money to allow prisoners to escape.

At Auschwitz, Eichmann personally orders the gassing of dozens of Jews, including the mother of young David (Jim Baird). Despite the brutality of this scene, however, the filmmakers *still* had to contend with the man who inherited Breen's job, Geoffrey Shurlock. Less pompous and strident than his predecessor, Shurlock nevertheless had his own nitpicking rules about scenes depicting the Holocaust. In a letter to Allied Artists producer David Diamond on October 28, 1960, Shurlock wrote:

> While we realize the validity of showing some of the stock material and captured Nazi films of the horrors perpetrated at the various concentration camps, we must urge to the utmost that very careful discretion be exercised in the shots to be incorporated in your picture. We here have seen a large amount of footage of this type of material and know the grizzly [sic] contents thereof. While these horrifying scenes might be suitable for a select audience, we know that much of it is not suitable for inclusion in an entertainment film. It is upon this basis that we urge your very careful consideration and discretion.[4]

Despite the censor's apparent squeamishness to scenes depicting genocide in an "entertainment film," Springsteen ordered a paring-down of concentration camp footage and apparently this restraint flows into the scenes of machine-gunning in the camps, which look like just what they are: Crimes Against Humanity being committed on a sparse movie soundstage. Only in the shower scene, where Jewish families, including their children, are gassed to death does the reenactment attain a level of horror and revulsion, as screaming human beings (including the hero's mother) are suffocated by bursts of Zyklon B. However, even this touch of realism is undercut by showing the victims fully clothed.

When Allied armies come closer, Eichmann commandeers trucks to transport their victims to the camps in Germany, like Dachau. However, this detail of a convoy of trucks removes the forced death march ordered by Eichmann in late 1944 since desperately needed trucks were not to be had. With the Allies ahead of them, Eichmann vindictively orders all prisoners in the trucks, including Jewish children, to be machine-gunned by the soldiers. This scene has elements of Cole's screenplay for *None Shall Escape*, in which Jewish prisoners are machine-gunned while still in their railway cars as some of them attempt to fight back. However, after Eichmann's men open fire, many of the adults protect the children with their own bodies, a sacrifice David will never forget.

Unfortunately, Geoffrey Shurlock again insisted that if the filmmakers decided to show a massacre, it had to be family-friendly:

> The slaughter of the victims in the trucks, on this page, should be conveyed not more than by suggestion. As described in the script, these scenes seem so horrifyingly brutal as not to be approvable in your finished picture. Reverting to the second paragraph of this letter, we here again must urge upon you the greatest possible restraint, to avoid offending audiences everywhere. We feel that the point involved can be thoroughly conveyed without going into nauseating detail.[5]

After the Nazis' defeat, Springsteen shows us happy crowds celebrating, but then he cuts to a somber scene of a synagogue where the Jewish congregants mourn their dead. Here we have the irony of a Jewish Communist screenwriter depicting Jews in a house of worship (Cole had denied his own religion for decades). Then we see the scenes of American commanders touring the camps; "Some great Americans came," says the narrator as we see Eisenhower and Patton entering Auschwitz, the irony being that, despite Patton's initial revulsion, he went right back to spouting his own hateful anti–Semitism and professed admiration for the Nazis. Here, Springsteen defiantly gives us all the Nazi atrocity scenes that Geoffrey Shurlock had warned the filmmakers not to show.

On the dodge, Eichmann shows up at Anna's apartment with stolen jewels, apparently forgetting his previous nitpicking Aryan purity. However, in Israel, David has started his search for Eichmann. He tells us that he is the head of a group of "volunteers," and never once during the film do we hear the word "Mossad." In fact, Cole and the filmmakers never once mention Simon Wiesenthal, a former concentration camp survivor who had been looking for Eichmann, Mengele and other Nazi war criminals since the late 1940s. Ultimately, when Eichmann wound up in Argentina in 1950, Wiesenthal knew that he needed some muscle backing him up; lacking the funds, the official standing, and political clout to have his men arrest Eichmann when he was well protected by the Peróns, the Nazi hunter ultimately turned his files over to the Israelis. However, though there is an implication that David and his friends have government backing for their hunt, this part of the plot is never clearly stated. Similarly, after Eichmann's escape from an American P.O.W. camp, the film shows him being helped by wealthy former SS men, including a now-powerful Kessner, but never once are they referred to as Odessa.

Meanwhile, David and his wife Sarah, who was almost killed in the truck shooting with him, argue over having Eichmann killed. ("Are we to try him six million times for six million deaths?") In the ensuing scenes, Cole gives us more moral quandaries, but fortunately the decision is made to capture Eichmann and put him on trial, with a well-made noose in the former SS officer's future. However, the Mossad, if indeed that is what they are supposed to be, better move fast since Eichmann's own former SS cohorts want him in the ground as well. Arrogant as always and still foolishly believing that he is in charge, Eichmann's defiance of "little Kessner" soon makes him a target. When the heat gets too hot for Eichmann in Argentina (which did not happen), Kessner orders a bruiser named Hans to trail him.

Fleeing on foot from Hans on a Buenos Aires highway (which looks suspiciously like an L.A. freeway) Eichmann is also chased by David and his men in their car. After knocking aside Hans, they shove the war criminal into their car and David shows the now-frightened Eichmann his concentration camp tattoo on his arm, informing him that he will now be put on trial. "They'll learn," says David, "and they'll remember!" The film ends with Eichmann's look of defeat, quite unlike the defiant words he spouted during the pre-title sequence.

Nazi hunters II: Donald Buka and Steve Gravers (with gun) in a publicity shot from *Operation Eichmann*. Though essentially portraying Israeli agents, the name "Mossad" is never once mentioned in the formerly blacklisted Lester Cole's screenplay.

Certainly, the critics took note of the quick filming to take advantage of the current trial. In his *New York Times* review of May 4, 1961, Howard Thompson wrote:

> As might be expected, a film company has galloped towards the box office with a feature on Adolf Eichmann—"Operation Eichmann." Obviously a rush job, this standard melodrama, with factual trimmings, opened yesterday at neighborhood theaters. Carefully underlined with dire warnings and indignant narration, this curiously ambivalent picture laces history with familiar cloak-and-dagger flourishes.

Critics would justifiably praise Klemperer ("a powerful performance" said *Film Daily*). Decades later, long after playing Colonel Klink opposite John Banner and former concentration camp survivor Robert Clary on *Hogan's Heroes*, the actor would play the Jewish character,

Herr Schultz, in a successful Broadway revival of *Cabaret* on October 22, 1987 (it ran till June 2, 1988).[6]

In reality, captured on May 11, 1960, Eichmann's pursuit and trial would be better handled in future decades by better filmmakers who had much larger budgets at their disposal. This film, however, avoided the complicated machinations and intricate planning that went into the kidnapping of the former SS murderer. Isser Harrel, a man of great integrity, was the chief of Mossad at the time. Now armed with Wiesenthal's voluminous and highly informative files on the head of Department IV-B4, Israel's Prime Minister David Ben-Gurion at first ordered Harrel to bring in Eichmann dead or alive (at the time, Mengele was also on Mossad's radar). This order was later altered to capture Eichmann alive and bring him in for trial—the better for the world, especially the *goyim*, to see the horrors they allowed to happen for so many years.

Grabbed close to his home off Garibaldi Street (Mossad had set up agents around the house for months), Eichmann tried to resist, but the agents were bigger, tougher and, let's face it, *much angrier*, and had no problem throwing the former Nazi big shot into a waiting car. They filled him with dope and kept him on ice for nine days as they checked and re-checked his identity. After even more drugs were pumped into him by a Mossad doctor on midnight May 20, the long, dangerous journey began. With Eichmann in this semi-woozy state, he was dressed in an El-Al uniform and the agents, in similar uniforms, ushered him past Juan Perón's Finest all the way onto a waiting plane and out of the country (they had pretended they were just the usual standard drunken airline pilots). They all arrived safely in Israel on the 22nd. The following afternoon, Prime Minister David Ben-Gurion announced Eichmann's capture to the Knesset, Israel's parliament. The entire chamber, including the gallery, stood up and applauded.

Israel would weather the usual outcries and complaints from an ignorant United Nations General Assembly.

"Banality of evil" or not, former SS *Obersturmbannführer* Adolf Eichmann was hanged by the neck until dead a few minutes after midnight on May 31, 1962, one year and two and a half months after the film's release.

Though Eichmann may have gone to his death with a kind of bitter resignation, one thing was certain. He wasn't laughing as he dropped through the trap. "The victor will not be asked whether he told the truth."—Adolf Hitler. On the night of August 31, 1939, a group of SS men and *Abwehr* agents, dressed as Polish soldiers, attacked the German radio station in Gleiwitz, Upper Silesia, near the Polish border. Under the command of SS *Sturmbannführer* Alfred Helmut Naujocks, the Germans brought along a Jewish inmate from the Dachau concentration camp, pumped him full of drugs, and also dressed him as a Polish soldier. Known as *Sender Gleiwitz,* the station was seized and an *Abwehr* man broadcast an anti–German message in Polish on the station's transmitters. Fransciszek Honiak, a 43-year old, unmarried German Silesian farmer known to be sympathetic to the Poles, had been arrested by the Gestapo the previous day; the SS dressed him up as a Polish soldier, gave him a lethal injection and brought his body along on the raid, dumping it at the station where it could be found. They also pumped several bullets into him. Similarly, the Jewish Dachau prisoner that had been drugged before he was brought to *Sender Gleiwitz,* was beaten and bloodied by the SS to make him unrecognizable and shot dead. Code-named *Operation Canned Goods*, the raid was the idea of SD chief Reinhard Heydrich and head of the Gestapo, Heinrich Müller; though it was a sure thing Propaganda Minister Dr. Joseph Goebbels *also* had sizable input into the plan since he would have full control over how the "Polish outrage" would be broadcast on German airwaves the following day.

German provocations had occurred all along the Polish border, yet *Gleiwitz* was the one Hitler would use as the "last straw," the final provocation which violated German sovereignty (in another incident, SS men disguised themselves as drunken Poles and wrecked the customs house at the border town of Hochlinden). The Soviets, the Nazis' new partners in world domination, had signed their infamous pact a mere week before the attack. *Canned Goods* was conceived to lay the groundwork for a German invasion of Poland, a plan the Soviet Union was well aware of, since plans had already been laid by Red Army staff officers to invade Poland from the *east* two weeks after the German incursion. This was part of the "secret protocols" of the Nazi-Soviet Pact (military invasions are *rarely* spontaneous; they take *months*, or at the least, several weeks, to plan).

At 10:00 a.m. on September 1, Hitler spoke to the Reichstag: "I am wrongly judged if my love of peace and my patience are mistaken for weakness, or even cowardice...." Though many are familiar with Adolf Hitler's "love of peace," in December 1945, former SD *Obersturmbannführer* Naujocks testified at his trial for war crimes and spilled the beans on the plan.

On April 22, 1961, East German audiences saw the release of *The Gleiwitz Case*, a part-documentary/part reenactment of the events leading up to the so-called "Polish provocation" that launched World War II.

Directed by Gerhard Klein and released by DEFA, Communist East Germany's revival of the old UFA studio, *The Gleiwitz Case* was shot in crisp black and white, not only giving the film the feel of a documentary, but a nightmarish one at that.

Hannjo Hasse plays Naujocks, and after we see the plan being formed by Müller and his superiors, we see the Polish-speaking SS men chosen for the mission. As he travels towards the Polish border by rail, Naujock expresses confidence that Germany will defeat the "Polish pigs." Later, speaking to the men whom he is to lead, he reminiscences about the kind of violent raids his SS platoon usually made on Germany's enemies: "Reds, Jews, émigrés, masons, sundry riff-raff. They didn't write that into the Versailles Treaty of Shame. Man, that was exhilarating."

His constant crazy little smiles and sheer enjoyment in oppressing others clearly reveal a lunatic, though the real Naujocks was anything but. Still, the filmmakers give us a quick flashback into Naujock's life; a hop-skip-and-jump bio that the Communist filmmakers use to indict other influences in his life besides Nazism. In fact, as soon as he declares, "We'll show no mercy! The world can count on it!" the scene shifts to him being baptized, a blatant indictment of religion in this future madman's psyche. Later on, his father and his teachers will instill in the young man anti–Semitism and nationalism. Before you know it, he is taking an oath to the SS and his career as a mass murderer is on its way. Still, Klein's subtle staging of the scenes is fascinating. For instance, we never *once* see the young Naujocks; instead, we see his life from his viewpoint as he visualizes those he knew and influenced his thinking.

Interestingly, when the SS grabs a prisoner to take with them and murder at *Sender Gleiwitz*, he is not a Jew from Dachau, but a prisoner of no special religious denomination from *Sachsenhausen*, the concentration camp known mainly for housing *Communist* prisoners. All through the film, Klein presents the events leading up to the raid as a Kafkaesque nightmare, with severe close-ups of Müller, Naujocks and other SS officers' faces to make them look far more frightening than they would appear normally. Especially nightmarish is Naujocks' personal shooting of the poor camp prisoner and his screams of agony at the end of the film. Needless to say, the government-backed filmmakers do *not* mention the Nazi-Soviet Pact, or that the Soviets were fully aware that Germany would use this provocation to invade western Poland by early September.

Still, despite the usual Bolshevik omissions, *The Gleiwitz Case* is a fine piece of filmmaking; running a mere hour and five minutes, the film gives us an interesting twist on German duplicity, as well as Nazi figures almost as frightening as those in William Cameron Menzies' *Address Unknown*.

Almost a year later, Allied Artists would return to the world of Nazi film bios that they had explored with *Operation Eichmann*. Only this time, it would be the number one Nazi himself.

"The private life of Hitler revealed for the first time!"[7] So claimed the over-the-top tagline for Allied Artists' latest foray into Nazi mania. Indeed, just as the hit TV series *The Untouchables* inaugurated a whole new series of B films based on real-life gangsters from the 1920s and '30s, so too did Erwin Leiser's phenomenally successful feature-length documentary on the Third Reich, *Mein Kampf*, set in motion a new subgenre of pseudo-biographies of Nazi leaders (even an episode of *The Untouchables* featured the Nazis). By April 1961, shortly after the successful release of *Operation Eichmann*, Allied Artists already had a script for a new film about Hitler. However, if the audience might have seen some of these scenes before, it is probably because the film, again detailing the rise of Hitler and the Nazi Party, is practically an uncredited remake of Paramount's *The Hitler Gang* from nearly twenty years before. To top off this harking back, one of the screenwriters is Sam Neuman who wrote the semi-comic *Hitler: Dead or Alive*! For co-screenwriter E. Charles Straus, this was his *only* screenplay ever. Fortunately, the film is directed by old hand Stuart Heisler (his last film; after this he would direct the cult TV western *The Dakotas*), and scored by Universal horror composer Hans J. Salter.

Unlike *The Hitler Gang*, this film starts at the time of the Munich *Putsch* in 1923. However, as in the Paramount film, Hitler (an overacting Richard Basehart) is at Landsberg Prison dictating *Mein Kampf* to a slavish secretary (who, for some reason, is not Hess); they call a skeptical Gentile cellmate "a stinking Jew," spit at him and Hitler plans world conquest. Except for a few anti–Semitic epithets from Hitler (when a psychiatrist tells him about his "problem," the Führer rants, "Jew science!"), the film takes pains, as far too many other American filmmakers have, to downplay the Holocaust. Indeed, the film seemed to be far more interested in showing Hitler as a mental case without once emphasizing the greatest example of mental derangement in all the monstrous acts he ever committed.

In time, Hitler leads the Nazi Party, which features Martin Kosleck in his *fourth* turn as Dr. Joseph Goebbels (Kosleck is so good at this role, that he should have had a picture all to himself rather than just supporting Hitler). Also, the film features *Operation Eichmann* alumni and future Sergeant Schultz, John Banner as the cynical Gregor Strasser; there's also veteran screen villain Berry Kroeger as Ernst Röhm (with a toupee); and another *Eichmann* player, Lester Fletcher as Röhm's "pal," Lieutenant Heines; John Mitchum (Robert's son) as Göring, William Sargent as Claus von Stauffenberg and Russian actor Gregory Gaye as Erwin Rommel.

At his half-sister's villa, Hitler meets his niece Geli (German actress Cordula Trantow).

V. Airbrush (1955–1962)

Here, the film departs sharply from John Farrow's pseudo-documentary approach and becomes bad psychodrama, with emphasis on the psycho part. Neuman and Straus give Hitler a mother complex which causes him impotence; alternately, he is both aroused and repelled by the attentions of women; implied by the filmmakers, this is why he is murdering so many people. Unfortunately, by focusing on Hitler's sexual problems, the filmmakers address his rampage through Europe and his murders of millions in, more or less, a perfunctory, quickie manner. Instead of his war of conquest, we see him reach longingly for Geli (and later, Eva Braun) and then pull his hand away at the last minute in frustration and rage. This film was not about Hitler; it was about Norman Bates with a swastika armband.

Later, in Munich for Party business, Hitler is jealous of Geli's dancing with a Hitler Youth member. In their hotel room, Geli purposely opens the door to her adjoining room; she *wants* him to do something with her. Of course, thinking of his mom, the seduction does not work. Later, he orders his men to have her shot. Certainly, this scene is far different from the one in the Farrow film; in that one, Geli is *not* the aggressor. However, though there has always been a heavy implication that Geli did not commit suicide and was murdered on Hitler's orders, there has never been any absolute proof; in both films, his men murder her. Later, as

Springtime for Hitler: Nazi refugee filmmaker Erwin Leiser's documentary *Mein Kampf* was an international hit that triggered a glut of films and TV dramas depicting the Third Reich. This marquee is of the Rivoli theater on Broadway and West 50th Street in Manhattan.

the Reichstag is burning (again, as in *The Hitler Gang*, this film plainly accuses the Nazis of starting the fire themselves and framing the Communists), Hitler again meets Eva Braun (skilled German actress Maria Emo). In a quick bit that echoes Jimmy Stewart's obsessive control of Kim Novak in *Vertigo*, the Führer tells Eva how to wear her hair. In a later scene, despite his impotence, there is an implication that the blonde Hitler groupie has been able to seduce him. This goes against the statements of several ex-girlfriends who maintained that Hitler did *not* have a mother complex or was impotent. However, his being a clinical psychopath was never disproved.

Almost as an afterthought, the film returns to its claims to history and shows Hitler taking over Europe, with help from *lots* of stock footage of the type that was put to much better use in Leiser's *Mein Kampf*. After Hitler studies war maps in the Wolf's Lair, which, with Allied Artists' meager budget, looks like a tiny office, Colonel Stauffenberg leaves that briefcase and then boom! Just to point out, with the flimsy old card table the briefcase was pushed behind, there was no reason Hitler should not have been blown to bits! Soon, the Führer calls for reprisals and Stauffenberg and his staff are hanged, the filmmakers neglecting to show that the heroic officer was actually killed by an SS firing squad.

Soon, Hitler is in that bunker with Eva, Goebbels and company. Though limping around and possessing a stiff arm, these were not necessarily injuries. According to German author Joachim Fest, much of Hitler's infirmities might have come from a severely damaged psyche that wanted to make him look more sympathetic. Still, he rants and raves of being betrayed and let down by his men, such as his wanting General Steiner's army group to mount a counterattack, but the general did not have enough men or arms to take on the Russians (this was historically true). Unlike the real bunker which housed hundreds of people like a small self-sufficient underground city, thanks to Allied Artists' low budget, we just see a handful of advisors in a couple of small rooms. In this film, Eva is the only woman here; this not only removes literally dozens of women who were secretaries, servers, cooks and telephone operators, but it also does not show Magda Goebbels and her kids (whom she would poison before she and Goebbels also killed themselves). Ultimately, Hitler rebukes Eva's claim to the title of "Frau Hitler" and the two kill themselves off screen: End of film, as the narrator tells us of Hitler's evil, as if we needed reminding.

Richard Basehart's performance wildly alternates between rare quiet moments and out-and-out ham. As it turns out, this was hardly Basehart's fault; a good actor, he was reportedly told to change his original subtle performance. According to the TCM website, "When they saw the rushes, studio bosses objected to Basehart's restrained performance, and insisted on reshoots with the star in full hysteria mode."[8] In fact, Basehart's Hitler is a raving lunatic all through the film; and though Hitler *was* a lunatic, the filmmakers basically took the ranting Hitler of the public speeches and had him this way even when he and Eva are in the bedroom during an intimate scene (or as intimate as Basehart's Hitler could get). Again, thanks to the emphasis on showing Hitler as foaming at the mouth 24/7, we wonder just *how* this man was able to control his temper long enough to have all these military victories or win the loyalty of millions of Germans for twelve long years. Ranting and raving from the first reel on, the performance literally had nowhere else to go.

And though Kosleck and Banner are good. the film's best acting is from its women, with Cordula Trantow (nominated for a Golden Globe for the film) and especially Maria Emo outstanding in their thankless roles as victims of Hitler's abuse.

V. Airbrush (1955–1962)

In a letter to Allied Artists executive Lorene Buntrock, dated April 7, 1961, the PCA's Geoffrey Shurlock was not only against showing Hitler's impotency and "sexual attachment to his mother," but he argued against a scene in the psychiatrist's office in which the doctor "seems to argue for the therapeutic need of an affair with Eva." Outraged, Shurlock wrote, "This kind of justification of extramarital sex relationships would be a violation of the Code."[9] All in all, it was certainly novel for a censor to argue that a man who murdered millions was *really* going over the line when he had sex outside of marriage.

However, Shurlock lowered the boom on another controversial topic of those days: "In addition, there is an element of homosexuality. It is rather broadly hinted that Roehm [sic] exercises a homosexual hold on Hitler, and Roehm's own proclivity this way is clearly and distastefully drawn. The same is to be said with his introduction of homosexuality among large numbers of the top officer staff of the S.S."[10]

Here, Shurlock's details were wrong; Röhm was the head of the SA, not the SS. Still, the controversy over the film's depiction of homosexuality would remain a major sticking point on whether Shurlock and the PCA were willing to allow the film to be shown in violation of the Code. However, the PCA also brought to the studio's attention the need to water down Geli's promiscuity, right down to the little detail of having her *not* lie back on a couch. At another point, Shurlock insisted that "Geli [does] not lie on the grass after kissing her 'Uncle.'"[11] On another issue, it was ruled that whenever the word "bastards" was used, it was to be replaced with either the words "vermin" or "dogs"[12]; when they wanted to be really fancy, a character could say "pigs."

Again, as in Farrow's film, another Nazi could not drape his arm over Hitler's shoulder; in this case, Röhm. Also cut was the SA leader's playfully smacking Heines' rump with a shoe.[13] As it is, there are literally pages and pages of correspondence that exist in which officials of the PCA and the filmmakers negotiate dozens of cuts to the film to eliminate all implications of homosexuality among Hitler and the Nazi elite; yet *still*, there are little signs here and there, especially in the Night of the Long Knives scene, where Röhm doesn't hide his obvious affection for Lieutenant Heines and his dialogue with Hitler where the SA leader certainly implied that *something* had happened between them in the old days; such as Röhm mentioning a little incident between them "that goes back to our barracks in 1919!" Or Röhm's line indicting Hitler: "You can't permit me to live because I am the proof of your own corruption!"[14] At another point, in a letter dated from May 29, Shurlock insisted that the character of Putzi not "act like a fairy."[15]

Demented, delirious, filled with sexual frustrations and sleazy implications of then-forbidden

Voyage to the bottom of the Reich: The future Admiral Nelson of the *Seaview*, Richard Basehart, as the Führer himself in Allied Artists' *Hitler*. A good actor, Basehart was forced by the studio to overact. The film also triggered the wrath of the Production Code office in its attempts to depict Hitler's impotence and mother complex, as well as Ernst Rohm's homosexuality.

desires, as well as a wildly ranting performance from its leading man, Allied Artists' version of *Hitler* is a camp classic from an era in American film struggling with what was and was not permissible before a rapidly changing public. Certainly, it was not Allied Artists' last foray into the Third Reich; the next time the studio would attempt to show the rise of Nazism, it would be set to music and directed by Bob Fosse a decade later.

By the mid–1960s, as Stanley Kramer's excellent *Ship of Fools* showed how the coming Nazi terror affected a group of ship's passengers and crew in pre-war Germany, other filmmakers would endeavor to parrot the camp approach of Richard Cuhna's *She Demons*—but on a *much* lower budget.

VI

MESHUGANNAH (1963–1980)

Mad doctors, Nazi zombies, attempts to revive Hitler, death camp perverts and Ships of Fools

> "So you're the *superior* ones! The slappers of women, the torturers of old men!"—*They Saved Hitler's Brain*

"Soon Hitler will return! We will rewrite history! And the Third Reich will endure, not for a thousand years, or a hundred thousand years, but forever!" So proclaimed the character of Professor Ernest Von Hauser in the sparsely released (mostly in theaters and drive-ins in the South) B-grade opus to merge cheap science fiction with Third Reich atrocities. Shot in Texas and released in 1963, *The Yesterday Machine* continued the formula, first started in the postwar era by *She-Demons*, of having one of Hitler's top scientists conducting the same dangerous experiments he had during the war to further the Führer's agenda of conquering the world.

College football champ Howie Ellison (Jay Ramsey) is trying to fix his stalled car on a lonely road as his cheerleader girlfriend Margie De Mar (Linda Jenkins) twirls her baton and practices her moves while the radio plays. It has nothing to do with the plot, but who cares? When the two come too close to a lonely farmhouse, they run into two Confederate soldiers; during their escape, Howie is shot and wounded and Margie disappears. The case gains the attention of Police Lieutenant Partane (the sadly declining Tim Holt) and reporter Jim Crandall (James Britton), both of whom happen to be World War II veterans. They find that Howie was shot with an actual iron ball from the days of the Civil War. Also investigating the disappearance is Margie's big sister, Sandy (Ann Pellegrino), who sings at the local nightclub.

When Jim and Sandy return to the location where Margie disappeared, they find themselves in a time warp back to 1789. Soon they return to the 1960s and are inevitably captured by two Nazi thugs, though their hats seem to belong more to the Weimar constabulary than the SS. The two also meet ex–Nazi scientist, Professor Ernest Von Hauser (the hammy Jack Herman), who has invented a "time machine" which looks more like several Art Deco lamps.

Despite Von Hauser's passionate speeches about the Führer and rage against the victorious Americans (at one point, he calls Jim "my Yankee friend," an interesting epithet in a film made down South), the mad doctor also stops the film for a full ten to fifteen minutes to explain his theories to the convincingly skeptical journalist. One can hardly describe Herman's performance except perhaps that he had been channeling John Carradine, though without that old ham's talent. Eventually, an English-speaking Egyptian slave girl (Olga Powell) whom the doctor transported to the 1960s for some reason, stabs one of the Nazi thugs to death and Jim and Sandy are able to escape. During a shootout, Jim kills the other Nazi guard (apparently Von Hauser's huge, terrifying army of Nazi marauders consists of just *two men*) and the arriving Lt. Partane shoots Von Hauser as the time machine sends his body back in time. Partane then destroys the machine and the others are freed.

Now a camp laughfest on DVD, *The Yesterday Machine* continued the 1960s trend of putting Nazism on a clearly comic-book level. Back in Burbank, Warner Brothers had been working on their own version of a comedy featuring Nazism. *Mr. Limpet* was a comic novel written during the war (1942) by the prolific Theodore Pratt. Having bought the rights to the book, Warner Brothers had finally gotten around to working on a script in 1961, but filming did not begin until 1964, when the studio renamed the project *The Incredible Mr. Limpet*. In a scenario just as wacky as any of Professor Van Hauser's speeches, Don Knotts is the milquetoast from Brooklyn who wishes himself turned into a fish. The newly transported fish (complete with spectacles) can now aid the war effort against the Third Reich's navy. Here, we have basically an animated Walt Disney–like cartoon rudely interrupted by the appearance of National Socialists. If anything, praise should go to Oscar Beregi, who had played many a Nazi over the years, for a hilarious performance as a German admiral, with his "*Das Limpet!*" becoming one of the film's funniest lines. For an actor who had only a few years back played the unrepentant concentration camp officer in the powerful *Twilight Zone* episode *Death's Head Revisited*, the performance was just another example of Beregi's rarely noted versatility.

The Incredible Mr. Limpet failed at the box office, despite the good performances of Don Knotts, Jack Weston and Oscar Beregi. But Warners was not through with mixing the elements of science fiction with National Socialism.

"In the end, the head cries, 'Bury me, bury me.' Hopefully, this will be the box office response to this project of producer-writer-director Herbert J. Leder." This critique, excerpted from the September 14, 1967, anonymous review in *Variety*, neatly sums up the general reaction to a production Warner Brothers' British unit had released in England in 1966, but eventually crossed the ocean to an eagerly awaiting American audience in the fall of the following year. *Variety* and several other reviewers were able to finally view this masterpiece a mere week and a half before its American premiere in Boston on September 27. It is perhaps an understatement that audiences the world over were not disappointed—it was every bit as bad as *Variety* had said.

The above-mentioned Herbert J. Leder was a triple threat schlock producer-writer-director; a New Yorker who settled in England and provided some American-style, off-the-wall madness to the usually staid and talky sci-fi products to come out of England in the late 1950s and 1960s. Though he made a handful of films, all of them Bs, he actually excelled with his first screenplay for the British sci-fi *Fiend Without a Face*. His work on the script was certainly helped along immensely by the original short story on which the film was based, Amelia Reynolds Long's *The Thought Monster*, as well as first-rate special effects. By the time Warners decided to film Leder's screenplay in 1966, his penchant for the unbelievable had

VI. Meschugghanah (1963–1971)

been brought to the fore; it only proved that without good source material (like Long's story) and the fact that Leder was both producer and director as well as writer, audiences were going to be in for a rough time. Perhaps channeling the scripts of past B Nazi/sci-fi schlock like *She-Demons*, *The Yesterday Machine*, and especially the non–Nazi themed *The Brain That Wouldn't Die*, Leder continued the 1960s trend of turning the many atrocities committed in the name of National Socialism into something on the level of *Frankenstein's Daughter* and *The Amazing Transparent Man*. Unfortunately, with the man in charge of the purse strings writing the screenplay and directing as well, audiences were going to be in for long, talky scenes in cheaply furnished drawing rooms, badly lit lab sets and populated by a cast of no more than a eight or nine actors, most them in bit parts.

Our story begins in merry old England. According to a synopsis from the files of Warner Brothers' home studio in Burbank, "Dr. Norberg (Dana Andrews), a brilliant ex–Nazi scientist, operates a laboratory in an English castle where, with his sadistic assistant, Karl Essen (Alan Tilvern), he experiments with living organs." Right away, we're expecting the usual schlocky ingredients. Norberg is visited by former Nazi officers General Lubeck (Karel Stepanek) and Captain Tirpitz (Basil Henson), who are backing the scientist's plan to reanimate 1500 Nazi soldiers frozen at war's end, so that they can take over and rule the world! (It had to be Nazi *soldiers*; would scientists of the Third Reich use suspended animation to freeze Nazi *stenographers*?) One particular experiment gone wrong are a wall full of detached arms formerly belonging to SS men, which can do things like move around once in a while, but that's about it; we also see a few Nazis in *Wehrmacht* uniforms frozen behind a glass encasement. However, we are told (*told*, not shown) that 1,500 soldiers who are supposedly hidden in caves all over the planet are ready to march at a moment's notice. Also on the premises are former Nazis who have become empty headed, murderous zombies; in other words, they had not changed much since they first followed Hitler.

Unfortunately for the Aryan cryogenicists, Norberg is visited by his pretty niece Jean (British actress Anna Palk) and her friend Elsa (Kathleen Breck). Essen's sudden bursting in with the announcement of their visit causes Norberg to screw up an important brain operation. Though welcoming the two women, Norberg tells his rather lame assistant that he needs another brain from ... *somewhere*! Since Essen falls into the usual category of mad doctor's lab assistant who screws up his boss' work and thinks he can correct the situation by simply murdering a living human being for the organ the doctor needs—well, that's *exactly* what he does! Sneaking into Elsa's room at night, he drugs her, murders her, and then puts her in the proximity of a zombie so it looks like *he* murdered her. The psychotic assistant convinces Norberg to use Elsa's brain for his experiment; soon, he disposes of her body and keeps her head alive and locked in a cabinet.

Also invited to Norberg's castle of fun is an American scientist named Ted Roberts (Philip Gilbert), invited because of his own experiments, like keeping alive the head of a dead dog, though the film never quite explains why he would do such a thing. Norberg and Essen show Jean a phony typewritten note they claim was left by Elsa saying that she left for London. Though Roberts has seen a woman wearing Elsa's clothes getting on the departing train, he has not seen her face; this is good because the face, mutilated beyond repair, belongs to Essen's evil mom, a former Nazi who had been worked on by victimized villagers. Jean, however, smells a rat, and investigates her friend's mysterious disappearance. Adding to her skepticism is the fact that Elsa, even as a decapitated head, is telepathically communicating with Jean and letting her know that she is still more or less alive. Down in Norberg's lab, Roberts is shown Elsa's head and is sworn to secrecy; impressed by seeing a moving head on a table, Roberts agrees to help Norberg with his work.

When Essen attempts to kill Jean because she knows too much (the attempt fails), Norberg angrily has the murderous lab assistant put into the freezing chamber with the dead Nazi soldiers and lowers the temperature until he freezes to death. Meanwhile, Lubeck and Turpitz decide to give a try to killing Jean by having her water poisoned. However, as she is about to drink it, Elsa telepathically causes Jean to drop the glass. Horrified by all this, Roberts, who has fallen for Jean, decides to reveal all to her about her uncle's evil experiments, including the fact that Elsa is more than just your usual head case. He also reveals that one of the zombies, the most murderous of them all in fact, is her own Nazi father! As Bette Davis said in *All About Eve*, "It gets *better*!"

Deciding to find her father, Jean sends Roberts to go fetch Inspector Witt (Tom Chatto). When Norberg finds her in his lab (you would think that such important and secretive experiments would be kept in a place that was *locked*), he tells her about her father. But a pistol-packing Lubeck enters and soon he and Norberg struggle over the gun; unfortunately they get a little too close to that wall of detached arms. Now with the telepathic powers of the girl with the decapitated head from *The Brain That Wouldn't Die*, Elsa uses her mind to have the dead arms come to life and strangle the two men. Unfortunately, the evil Tirpitz seems to have gotten away; despite the fact that Warner's synopsis has the former Nazi captain "arrested while trying to leave the castle," no such scene exists in the finished film.

When Jean's father attempts to strangle her, he is gunned down by Witt, who arrives with Roberts. All go to Elsa and listen to her as she sadly begs the trio to "Bury me … bury me…"

In the *Hollywood Reporter*, September 14, 1967, John Mahoney wrote: "A murky and dank return to the caverns of the Mad Scientist, the film supplies sufficient gore to make a fast cleanup among the less discriminating multitudes." They also said that Dana "Andrews is adequate, despite infrequent recollections of an unconvincing accent." Palk's performance is described as "okay," but her appearance in this film would open the door many years later for her casting in the far more violent *The Horrors of Snape Island*.

In its review of September 14, Mandel Herbstman of *Film Daily* wrote that *The Frozen Dead* "churns up some lively and chilling adventures. The excitement at times is high, but so is the credibility gap. It proceeds along formula lines that should create response among the patrons. It also has inventive touches."

Unfortunately, Herbstman never explained just what the "response" was among the patrons, nor the film's "excitement," nor its supposedly "inventive touches."

If Dana Andrews, who at the time was suffering from alcoholism, did not drink during this production, it would be a surprise. The actor had declined horribly since his heyday of the 1940s and 50s, and his German accent is, to put it kindly, a bit *inaccurate*. Palk is cute and sincere and the others in the tiny cast are, for the most part, the usual British actors trying to do German accents. Warners was reportedly impressed enough with Leder's work on the film to have him write and direct *It!*, a ripoff of the Golem theme starring Roddy McDowall as the mad scientist and Jill Haworth (Anna Palk's future co-star on *The Horror of Snape Island*) as the usual "girl in distress."

All in all, *The Frozen Dead* continues the growing Nazi/sci-fi subgenre, artfully reducing Nazi atrocities, as well as their ambitions for world conquest, into comic-book schlock; with

VI. Meschugghanah (1963–1971)

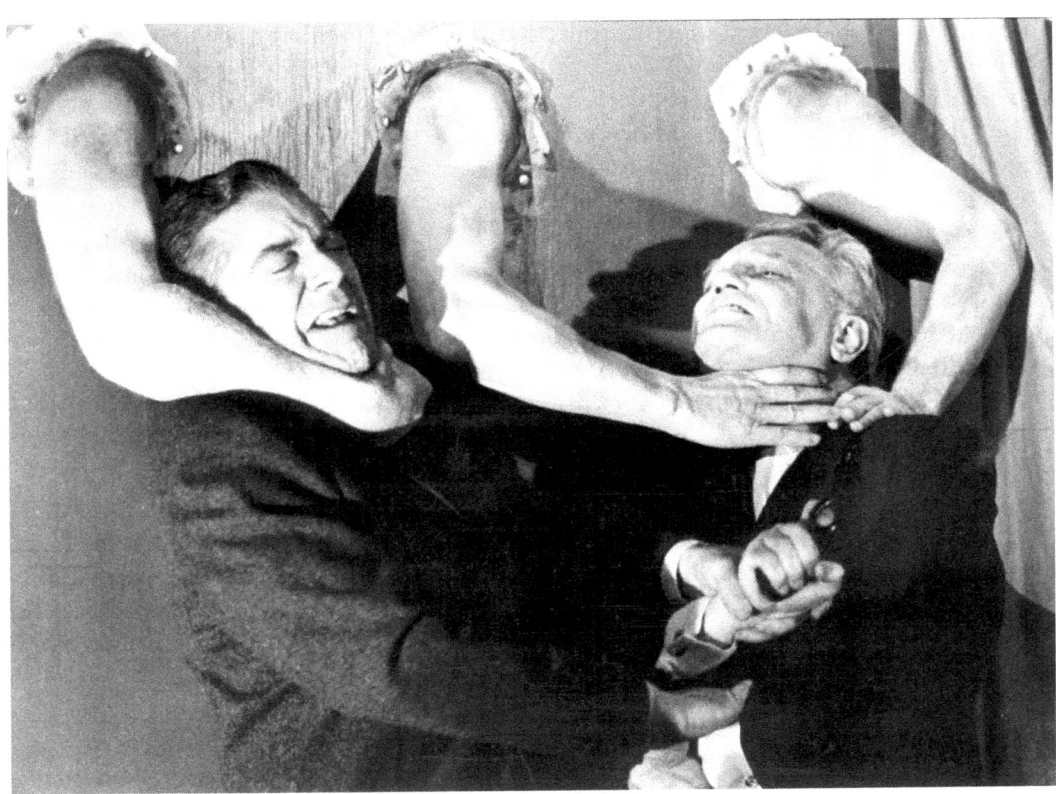

Right to bear arms: Dana Andrews and Karel Stepanek as Nazi war criminals experimenting in reviving SS soldiers in *The Frozen Dead*. Low budget and badly written, the film helped pave the way for films merging National Socialism with sci-fi schlock.

decapitated heads with special telepathic powers and detached arms which kill, though not necessarily for the Führer or the Reich, but just for the hell of it.

Though reduced to the level of camp, even in the shadow of Best Picture nominees like Stanley Kramer's *Ship of Fools* (released in America just a year before *The Frozen Dead* was released in England), the subject of Nazi brutality would get a significant boost from a film financed by veteran producer Sam Spiegel and released by Columbia in 1967. Headed by Spiegel's usual international cast and based on a bestselling novel by the prolific German author Hans Helmut Kirst, this film skillfully compared the work of a serial killer to the barbarism of the Nazi State. In fact, it even made them one and the same.

"A general is no less expendable than anyone else. In fact, it might be good for morale if the troops saw a dead general now and then."—Major General Matthew B. Ridgeway[1]

Hans Hellmut Kirst was born in Osterode in East Prussia on December 5, 1914. At 19, he joined the *Wehrmacht*, as well as the Nazi Party, and would survive the war to finish his service with the rank of First Lieutenant. Commenting on his membership in the now-reviled organization years after the war, he lamely explained that as a young man, he had "confused National Socialism with Germany."[2] But then, after Germany's defeat, *everybody* basically said the same thing; though he did honestly admit that he did not at first believe the horror stories about Nazi atrocities. "One did not really know one was in a club of murderers,"[3] he explained.

Perhaps to expiate his own feelings of guilt and self-loathing for having been a "member" of this so-called "club," Kirst would explore the German military's role in World War II, accentuating both the back-stabbing politics and ruthless cold-bloodedness of the Nazi leaders he himself had served so faithfully for twelve long years. In some 60 novels, most of which were translated into several languages, Kirst used his experiences serving the Nazi State and its suffocating bureaucracy to show individual heroes who fought the system, giving the reader a moral figure to identify with; such a hero was the soldier Gunner Asche, who kept his integrity and fought the Good Fight against Nazi chicanery in many of Kirst's novels. In many ways, Kirst gave us the kind of hero he had wished he could have been, but clearly wasn't; just like his officer who sabotages a Nazi garrison in his first book, published in 1950, *The Lieutenant Must Be Mad* (remember that Kirst ended the war as a First Lieutenant).

In 1962, he published *Die Nacht der Generale*, translated as *The Night of the Generals*. Three years later, the novel was nominated for an Edgar Award by the Mystery Writers of America. In Warsaw in 1942, a prostitute is slashed to death up in her room; however, when a witness sees the killer leave, through a door crack, he quickly notices the red stripe down the leg of a military uniform—indicating that the killer was a general. Since the murdered woman was an informer for the Germans, a captain in the military police gets involved, ignoring his superiors and tenaciously tracking three suspects who could not vouch for their presence on the night of the killing. Another bestial killing of a prostitute occurs two years later in occupied Paris, and it is not until twenty years later that justice is finally done.

In 1966, already involved with the productions of *The Chase* and *The Happening*, megaproducer Sam Spiegel also took on the reins of the international British and French coproduction (eventually released by Columbia) of *The Night of the Generals*. Gore Vidal, one of the many writers who contributed to the script, would claim that he told Spiegel to get a new hot, young director to do the film, but the producer was adamant in hiring veteran (some thought has-been), former Hollywood helmsman Anatole Litvak. One of the reasons for Spiegel's insistence on hiring Litvak was because the Russian-Jewish director owned the rights to Kirst's novel (though the script is *also* allegedly based on a chapter of *The Wary Transgressor* by mystery writer James Hadley Chase).[4] Continuing the infuriating stubbornness for which he was famous, Spiegel also hired Peter O'Toole as the murderer General Tanz, and Omar Shariff as *Abwehr* officer Major Grau (changed from the novel's military police captain) by insisting that he pay them the same paltry wages they were both making in their pre-star days before they hit it big in *Lawrence of Arabia*.

In the film, a Polish prostitute is stabbed more than a hundred times in a sleazy room in Warsaw. Though the Quisling police inspector and German officers reject the witness' claims that the killer is a German general, Major Grau of the *Abwehr* (Omar Shariff) explains that the victim was one of their agents. He constantly tries to see the three *Wehrmacht* generals who are suspects, but they put him off. The three are the clearly neurotic General Tanz (Peter O'Toole), the fence-sitting General von Seiditz-Gabler (Charles Gray), and the sardonic General Kahlenberge (Donald Pleasance). As one can tell in this production, a film begging for historical accuracy and appropriate casting, three of the German roles are played by British actors and one is played by an Egyptian. In fact, except for Sharif and Joanna Pettit, *every* German role is played by British actors. At several points, the actors playing military adjutants almost lapse into Cockney (Patrick Allen is a good actor, but one cannot see him as a Nazi officer under *any* circumstances).

VI. Meschugghanah (1963–1971)

Mainly to get him off their backs, Grau is promoted to Lieutenant Colonel and transferred to Paris. However, two years later, the three generals themselves are also transferred there. It seems that Kahlenberge is part of the plot by a group of *Wehrmacht* officers to kill Hitler, with the Führer making that July 20 visit to the Wolf's Lair (Stauffenberg is played by an old actor, unusual since the martyred officer was a relatively young man). To get rid of the pro–Nazi Tanz for a while, Kahlenberge orders Corporal Hartman (the British Tom Courteney) to chauffeur the general around Paris museums and nightclubs. Frustrated (in more ways than one) that he cannot spend the time with his girlfriend Ulrike (American Joanna Pettit), who happens to be Seiditz-Gabler's daughter, Hartman witnesses Tanz's rather bizarre martinet behavior.

When the July 20 plot fails, Tanz shoots Grau dead as the *Abwehr* officer tries to arrest him. After Tanz murders a French girl he had Hartman pick up for him, he frames the corporal and, at gunpoint, forces him to flee Paris and go on the run. The war ends, and twenty years later the Hamburg police are trying to solve the horrible murder of a prostitute. French Interpol inspector Morand (Philippe Noiret, the *only* actor in the film whose accent matches the nationality of his role), who had been friendly with the anti–Nazi Grau during the war, realizes that Tanz, recently released from prison for war crimes, is the killer. He eventually finds Ulrike, who is now married to the fugitive Hartman, the one living witness to Tanz' crimes. Trapping the murderous general at a wartime reunion of his men, Noiret allows Tanz to go into an empty banquet hall and shoot himself.

It is quite possible that General Tanz was based on a real-life SS commander who, like Kirst's murderer, was a tank commander (in the film, we see Tanz wipe out a whole neighborhood in Warsaw with flame-throwing Panzer tanks just to get a handful of Resistance fighters). *Obersturmbannführer* Joachim Peiper was the commander of the 1st SS Panzer Division *Leibstandarte SS Adolf Hitler*, one of the most infamous Waffen-SS tank corps. As historian John S.D. Eisenhower wrote of him in *The Bitter Woods*:

> Peiper was an ideal man to lead the advance elements of the SS formations. Tough, arrogant, and hard-core Nazi, he was another who possessed what Hitler admired as "fanaticism."
> He was famous for his ruthlessness. Formerly an adjutant to Heinrich Himmler, he had performed notable feats of daring with his tanks in Russia—where he allegedly burned two villages and killed all the inhabitants. Some of the SS troops he was to lead in the Ardennes campaign had served for a long time on the eastern front, where brutality of all sorts was commonplace. Others were boys, but fanatic believers in the Führer. Softheartedness would have no place in this offensive, a most difficult assignment for which Joachim Peiper was a natural selection.[5]

Reinforcing this observation, Peiper would later say to a member of his staff, "You have no idea how fine it is to fight in a tiger tank, and how easy it is to kill Russians."[6]

His men had murdered 84 captured American soldiers in Malmédy a few days before Christmas 1944. And though Peiper was not present at the massacre, and would indeed later claim that he never ordered his men to murder prisoners, others were familiar with the SS commander's murderous sprees in practically every location he and his men were sent to.

In *The Night of the Generals*, Peiper's cold-bloodedness, so common to all SS commanders and troops, is transferred into one cleanliness-obsessive *Wehrmacht* general. Added to this ruthlessness is a man who sublimates his sexual frustrations, not only in the mass killing of Resistance fighters, but in the mutilation and disemboweling of prostitutes. The brutality of the Third Reich mixed with sexual deviations, a larger comment on those who massacred for the Nazi State and those other serial killers who murdered for their own sick drives. Or

Serial-killer, Nazi style: Tom Courtney (left) as an innocent *Wehrmacht* corporal and Peter O'Toole as the psychopathic general in the film version of former Nazi soldier Hans Helmut Kirst's novel *The Night of the Generals*. Produced by Sam Spiegel, the producer badly underpaid O'Toole and filled the cast with British actors playing Nazi officers.

as Grau says to Morand: "Then let us say what is admirable on the large scale is monstrous on the small. Since we must give medals to mass murderers, why not give justice to the small ... entrepreneur."

Unfortunately, the lead, a fantastic actor in his own right, was blasted by the critics, with Bosley Crowther referring to the "too wanton and waxy performance of Mr. O'Toole" in a February 3, 1967, *New York Times* article. *Time* magazine wrote, "As the villain, Peter O'Toole exhibits the now celebrated twitching upper lip and glazed stare that some viewers have seen once or twice too often."[7] Indeed, angered by the bellicose Spiegel's underpaying him despite his superstar status (supporting player Donald Pleasance was earning much more than O'Toole *and* Sharif), the actor played Tanz as a nut job from his entrance up to his last shot.

As contributing scenarist Gore Vidal said years later: "He [O'Toole] comes on insane, there's no development, and you know he's the murderer from the first moment that you see him.... He is so mad in his first scene that he has no place to go except stay insane all the way through the picture, and this was all resentment at Sam."[8]

The cost of the actual shooting and production of the film before the cost of advertising and promotion (negative cost) was $5,522,135.69,[9] *The Night of the Generals* lost money; and it would take the Nazi Germany–set perversions of Luchino Visconti's *The Damned* that

VI. Meschugghanah (1963–1971)

J'accuse!: Ex-Nazi serial killer Peter O'Toole (left) is finally trapped by French Interpol detective Philippe Noiret (center) at a Nazi reunion banquet in *The Night of the Generals*. O'Toole's psychotic Nazi tank commander might have been based on the life of SS General Joachim Peiper, whose men committed the Malmédy Massacre.

would capture the attention of international audiences. Ironically, the film's star, Dirk Bogarde, had been in the running for the role of Major Grau, but the suggestion was shot down by Spiegel due to his discomfort with the actor's homosexuality.

The summer of 1968 saw the sparse release of *They Saved Hitler's Brain*. Continuing the Nazi–science fiction subgenre, the film had few, if any, good things about it, though it *is* hard to keep a straight face when one sees the decapitated head of an extremely skinny Hitler being carried around under a dome like a macabre hatbox. Originally shot in 1964 and, starved for financing, the film would not be completed until 1968. The film actually begins with an espionage-agent prologue with actors with long hair driving late 1960s cars who obviously share no scenes with the more conservatively dressed cast from 1964. Perhaps Professor Von Hauser was lending the producers his time machine.

Nazism also was a major background for Euro-trash flicks made by Jess Franco and other sleaze-meisters, as monstrosities like *S.S. Girls* and *Ilsa, She-Wolf of the S.S.* (actually shot in Hollywood) accentuated Nazi sexual depravities for the soft-core porn/violent snuff film market. *The Night Porter*, though shot later in 1974, was a pretentious European take on the Nazi/S&M formula which reunited Bogarde with his *The Damned* co-star Charlotte Rampling as, respectively, a former concentration camp SS officer and his ex-prisoner, whose physical relationship (which apparently consists of the Nazi's beating her between acts of oral sex and fornication) is renewed when she meets him again many years later when he is the manager of a hotel. Instead of her turning him in to Mossad, the two are rolling around the floor of her room before you can say "I was only obeying orders." Bogarde and Rampling, two wonderful actors, are unfortunately saddled with this sleazy film, with the Holocaust once again reduced to the background of a particularly sick porn movie.

At the end of the tumultuous 1960s, with the Vietnam War taking more attention from the American public than did the global war fought by a previous generation, one comedian, in his cinematic decline, decided to parody the Third Reich.

"There's a better film on the cutting room floor...." At the time, not too many people would have disagreed with comedian Jan Murray, who had just finished co-starring in a World War II comedy produced and directed by a man who was seen by most moviegoers as a comic icon.

Jerry Lewis was a star in films for 21 years before he finally made his first comedy about the Nazis in late 1969. One might recall the only other time in all those years that his screen character would make a comment referencing Nazi horrors—back in 1950 in the film *At War with the Army*, costarring his then-partner Dean Martin. In a blistering comment on army bureaucracy, Lewis' harassed private would whine at one point: "The first thing I'm gonna do overseas is surrender. A concentration camp's gotta be better than this!" As Lewis biographer Shawn Levy wrote in his *King of Comedy: The Life and Art of Jerry Lewis*: "A Holocaust joke coming from a Jewish comedian in 1950: It's not just embarrassing to laugh at this stuff—it's downright degrading."[10]

Nevertheless, Jerry Lewis still stands as one of the great comic geniuses of American film, a writer, director and producer of funny movies; the first triple threat in film comedy since Chaplin. Unlike his predecessor, however, Lewis stayed far away from the political; his films were there to make you laugh, period. So one does wonder why, in 1969, with the country heavily involved in an unpopular war in Vietnam, he decided to make a film, a comedy yet, where a private army of American soldiers attempts to neutralize a high-ranking Nazi general. Despite the fact that the Nazis were still seen as universally evil, it was a time when movie audiences were seemingly tired of patriotic films, even if they were slapstick comedies. Though films set during World War II were still popular, these too would soon disappear as, thanks to the debacle of Vietnam, *all* wars would be seen as pointless. And thanks to Mel Brooks' *The Producers*, which made black comedy out of a bad musical featuring Nazis, World War II itself would be seen as a joke in a way that would have shocked audiences just a few years before.

By the late 1960s, Lewis' career had declined considerably from the superstar years of just a few years before. The assassination of President John F. Kennedy and the Vietnam War killed off much "innocent" film entertainment, with Jerry's "idiot" persona being one of the first to suffer. His films were losing money; kicked out of Paramount in 1966, he made a few films for Columbia, one for Fox, and finally ended up at Warner Brothers. For the studio of Jack Warner, *Which Way to the Front?* would be the first time they would show comic Nazis since Don Knotts sank the German navy in *The Incredible Mr. Limpet*.

At rise, multimillionaire Brendan Byers (Jerry Lewis) is bored; in a hilarious entrance, he turns to the camera revealing a pacifier in his mouth. When Byers is called before his draft board, instead of using his influence to back out of it, the millionaire seizes the chance to join

VI. Meschugghanah (1963–1971)

up and do something for his country. In fact, a screen character had not possessed patriotic zeal like this since *The Incredible Mr. Limpet*, though Byers has a far more interesting way of fighting the war than turning into a cartoon fish. Rejected by the military (the draft board is headed by western veteran Myron Healey), he reacts in the usual spastic way a Jerry Lewis character would react—and it's still very funny. There he meets a nightclub comic pursued by gangsters (standup comic Jan Murray), a henpecked husband (underrated comic actor Steve Franken, who would return to work for Lewis again in his comeback film *Hardly Working* in 1979), a young man (Dack Rambo), Byers' butler (John Wood) and chauffer (Willie Davis). Using his wealth, Byers has himself and his friends suited up in bright, colorful uniforms that would attract even the worst German sniper. Easily sailing his yacht from America and into European waters without once being stopped by the American navy, the group is almost torpedoed by a Nazi U-boat. However, the sub's captain (that old portrayer of Joseph Goebbels and many other Nazi characters, Martin Kosleck) figures that the yacht is an American trap sent to lure them into the open!

Once they get to occupied Italy, they go through many comic situations before they capture Field Marshal Kesselring (also played by Jerry) who is a double for Byers. After getting the field marshal out of the way, Byers, as Kesselring, is to order a retreat, allowing American and British troops to capture all previous Nazi-held positions. In fact, once they capture Kesselring, after tying and gagging him, it is never explained what happens to him; Lewis leaves this issue unresolved. Another interesting touch Lewis the director makes is the fact that all the men in his makeshift "army" are disguised in the uniforms of *Wehrmacht* officers, but he has Steve Franken, who plays the group's meekest character, as the only one wearing an SS uniform.

However, in a scene in which the phony Kesselring is to give medals to heroic German soldiers, Lewis injects an unusual note of patriotism as well as Jewish revenge fantasy. Introduced to three soldiers by his adjutant (ventriloquist/actor Paul Winchell), Kesselring is told of their "heroism," with each soldier actually guilty of murdering Americans. In turn, Kesselring brutalizes the soldiers, punching, kicking and stabbing them, all the while singing their praises and pinning medals on their chests (one of the soldiers is played by Jerry's blonde-haired son, Ronald, as "Lieutenant Levitch," Jerry's real last name).

Meeting a cabal of German officers (led by comic/voiceover artist Benny Rubin), Byers learns that Kesselring had actually plotted with the others to assassinate Hitler. He is even given a briefcase with a bomb to blow up the Führer; an interesting subplot with Lewis suddenly becoming a slapstick version of Colonel Klaus von Staffenberg.

Meeting Hitler (former child actor Sidney Miller), after a series of bad jokes and even a bad comic ballet played to the theme from *Love Story*, Byers leaves the bomb and Lewis cuts to a shot of the Führer's lair blowing up. We do not know if Hitler had been blown to bits or whether he escaped death as he did on July 20, 1944, but since Lewis never has him return, we can safely assume that he bit the dust. Indeed, not until Hitler was shot to pieces in Quentin Tarantino's semi-comic remake of *Inglorious Bastards* (titled of course *Inglourious Basterds*) would we see the Jewish revenge fantasy of Hitler meeting violent death at the hands of Jewish protagonists (Byers is not Jewish, but the man playing him most definitely is). By the end, Byers buys himself and his crew out of an American P.O.W. camp and before you know it, they end up disguised as Japanese sailors (complete with stereotypical makeup, even Willie Davis!) where they can now sabotage the Japanese war effort.

The film, inspired partly by *The Producers*, partly by Chaplin's *The Great Dictator* (with Lewis in a dual role as both Nazi and anti–Nazi, respectively), was poorly distributed by Warner Brothers, where it usually ended up on double bills in neighborhood theaters and received short play-dates. Lewis would remain bitter at Warners for years because of their botching the release of *Which Way to the Front?* in his own country, even as the film's box office went through the roof in Europe, especially France (which *always* loved Jerry) and Germany, whose citizens greatly enjoyed a comedy zinging their nation's dark past.

In his *New York Times* review of September 5, 1970, Howard Thompson wrote: "Disguised as goateed Nazi officer and spewing a guttural falsetto, Lewis is quite funny for a while. But it wears thin. Fortunately, it takes two to tango, even in Jerry Lewis' Third Reich."

"Jerry Lewis' Third Reich." Little did Thompson know that the iconic comedian was not yet through with the subject of Nazi chicanery.

It is said that in the spring of 1971, as *Which Way to the Front?* was still making money in Europe, and long after it bombed in America, Belgian producer Nathan (Nat) Wachsberger offered Jerry Lewis the chance to direct and star in a film version of a 1960s script by former publicity agent Joan O'Brien and TV critic Charles Denton (based on an idea by O'Brien) called *The Day the Clown Cried*. The story dealt with a clown, a former international circus star, imprisoned in a Nazi concentration camp who is ultimately ordered to lead Jewish children to their deaths.

Lewis would later claim in his autobiography that he told Wachsberger: "My bag is comedy, Mr. Wachsberger, and you're asking me if I'm prepared to deliver helpless kids into a gas chamber? Ho-ho. Some laugh—how do I pull it off?"[11]

Nutsy: Comedy icon Jerry Lewis as the American millionaire doubling as a Nazi general in Warner's *Which Way to the Front?* Lewis remained bitter that Jack Warner booked the film into double-bill theaters. It bombed in America, but was a hit in Europe.

However, Jerry, who would always consider himself a reincarnation of Charlie Chaplin, thought it over, however, ultimately feeling that the film would have something important to say about the Holocaust, a subject he had been avoiding in his many years as a filmmaker—and the film would be a good Chaplinesque showcase for his talents. The project had attained the status of a cult-like legend in the past 44 years, most of it fanned by Lewis himself, despite his supposed annoyance at interviewers who asked questions about it.

Principal photography began in Sweden in April 1972. However, after a few weeks of shooting, Jerry started to get disturbing reports that costume houses, film labs and other facilities that serviced the production were not being paid; also, actors and technical personnel had been issued rubber checks. In fact, despite Wachsberger's waving around a guaranteed release by prestigious Europa Films and other elaborate perks, it turned out that Jerry was sold a bill of goods. Apparently, the derelict producer forgot his responsibilities

VI. Meschugghanah (1963–1971)

Jerry's kids: Jerry masquerades as a *Wehrmacht* officer in *Which Way to the Front?* From left to right: Paul Winchell, Dack Rambo, Jerry Lewis, John Wood, Steve Franken and Jan Murray. A year after this farce, Jerry would go to the opposite extreme and attempt to make the controversial (and barely seen) *The Day the Clown Cried*.

and ran out of money way before filming reached the halfway mark. This forced Lewis to pay everyone's wages and production costs out of his own pocket, which was already sapped by lawsuits from bilked investors from the old Jerry Lewis Cinemas. Never once having visited the troubled set or even taken Jerry's frantic phone calls, Wachsberger had more to hide than his shady ledger books. In fact, it turned out he never even had the rights to Denton and O'Brien's script, with the former publicity flack getting just $5,000, but not the balance of the $50,000 she was to receive prior to the start of filming. Though Jerry would justifiably point an accusing finger at Wachsberger, O'Brien would always maintain that the comedian himself knew that he was making a film without her and Denton's permission. "Jerry knew the option had expired," said O'Brien, "but he decided to go ahead."[12]

Lewis publicly proclaimed that Wachsberger failed in his financial commitment to the project, prompting the angry producer to sue the comedian for breach of contract, and claiming that he (Wachsberger) possessed the negative film and had more than enough footage to finish it in post-production *without* Lewis. However, one-upping him, Jerry would always claim to possess a complete rough cut of the film and hoped to finish it by January 1973. In reality, *neither of them* had the rights to release the work since O'Brien kept a tight rein on those rights. In a belated attempt to get O'Brien and Denton on his side, Jerry invited the former publicity maven and her TV critic collaborator to a screening of his rough cut of the film. Unfortunately, once they saw the film, the plan backfired and a hardened O'Brien and Denton promised *never* to grant permission for the film's release. "It was a disaster," was O'Brien's description of Jerry's work on the film. "Just talking about it makes me very emotional."[13] No less disgusted than his writing partner, Denton added, "Jerry is lying in his bunk wearing a pair of brand-new shoes after theoretically having been in a concentration camp for four or five years."[14]

In the original script, the clown, Karl Schmidt, is an egotistical, exploitative, contemptuous SOB who hates everyone but himself. Described as "mediocre" in the original script, in Lewis' version the clown becomes a talented, under-appreciated comedy genius who had fallen on hard times (kinda like the man playing him). Renamed Helmut Doork (get it?), the clown becomes a pathos-driven, Emmett Kelly–like performer who is ordered to keep Jewish children amused as he leads them, in Pied Piper fashion, into the gas chambers. Unfortunately, the idea for merging comedy with the Final Solution would be picked up by European filmmakers decades after *The Day the Clown Cried*, with works like *Life Is Beautiful* and *Jacob the Liar* getting international critical acclaim, which perhaps demonstrated how insensitive those critics were.

Years later, as Jerry barked retorts at fans who inquired about the film (inexplicably heaping contempt on his adoring fans, Lewis always seemed to be *slightly* more respectful to critics), he admitted that the film was horrible (especially after actor Harry Shearer publicly said so after being shown Jerry's cut of the film[15]). In December 2015, Lewis contributed his copy of the film to the Library of Congress with the proviso that it would not be seen for ten years, by which time the comedian would turn 99. Charles Denton died on September 10, 2002, and Joan O'Brien died on November 12 two years later. Despite the deaths of the two writers, however, as of this writing, their estates *still* refuse Jerry the right to release *The Day the Clown Cried*, something he was well aware of while cunningly sparking interest in the film even as he kept saying how bad it was.

Jerry Lewis is still one of the greatest comedians of all time. However, as the makers of the awful *Life Is Beautiful* and other "concentration camp comedies" should have learned long ago, there's nothing funny about the genocide of a people.

VII
GHOSTS (1981–2015)

Concentration camp children appear as next-door neighbors, we find out what it's like to be Hitler's secretary, and Nazi zombies return (with a vengeance!)

> "I suppose that's what I'm doing, isn't it? Pretending to be a person from the other side of the fence."
> "A Jew, you mean," said Shmuel.
> —*The Boy in the Striped Pajamas*

In 1972, the Nazis would return in the landmark film version of a long-running stage musical. Indeed, for the next 44 years at least, it looked like the future, in popular culture anyway, *did* belong to them.

Cabaret was a successful Broadway musical, based on John Van Druten's 1950s play *I Am a Camera*, which in turn was based on the Weimar-era writings of journalist Christopher Isherwood. Outside of the various romantic and sexual pairings, not to mention fantastic Oscar-winning performances by Liza Minnelli and Joel Grey, aside from Bob Fosse's groundbreaking direction and always quirky, but flawless choreography, the film version, departing sharply from the stage musical, allows its Nazi characters to hover menacingly in the background, with their scenes literally increasing in power just as the National Socialists themselves increased their power the closer the film's time period gets to 1933. We see a lone Hitler Youth member soliciting contributions in the Kit-Kat Club only to be tossed out by its manager; later, as the nameless MC (played by Joel Grey) does a number where he slaps a chorus line of girls, in the alley, the young Nazi's friends are beating and kicking the daylights out of the club manager.

Midway through the film, Fosse stages an absolutely brilliant sequence when a good-looking young man starts to sing *Tomorrow Belongs to Me* in a crowded beer garden. Focusing his camera on the boy's youthful face as he sings beautifully, we are suddenly jarred out of our comfort zone when Fosse pans down to the boy's blood-red swastika armband. Gradually, everyone in the beer garden is on their feet during the rousing song and raising their arms in a Hitler salute, with the stanza "until the world is *mine*" already conveying a sinister meaning.

Fosse also focuses his camera on a sad old man, who is possibly Jewish, seated alone at the table; obviously, in this new perfect Aryan society, the future will *not* belong to him. To assuage German sensibilities, Allied Artists originally cut out the supposedly controversial scene, an insightful tableau which would have indicted, even indirectly, ordinary Germans in the rise of Nazism. Thankfully, months later it was restored, and remains one of Fosse's best; a scene clearly revealing the almost seductive attraction of the Nazi evil to a lost people—and how these people had to ultimately wake up to reality in the cold light of day...

Very few people, except maybe those in the intelligence communities of certain nations, and of course Nazi war criminals, knew of the existence of the Odessa, the vast organization of former members of the SS. Eternally proud of their crimes, still rabidly anti–Semitic and all-powerful, it was planned and put in operation as soon as it was deduced that Germany would lose the war. Shadowy, sinister and highly dangerous, they could have been created by Fritz Lang (who, unusually, never made a film about them). That former international-journalist-turned-bestselling-author Frederick Forsyth would finally bring them out into the open was not a surprise; the surprise was that our government, nor anyone else, bothered to tell us about them.

The Odessa File was a phenomenal bestseller and, as phenomenal bestsellers go, Hollywood came calling and Columbia snatched up the rights before you could say *"Arbeit Macht Frei!"* Set around the time of JFK's assassination, Forsyth juggles several plot strands. There is the young German freelance journalist Peter Miller who, after the suicide of a Jewish concentration camp survivor, reads the old man's diary, and decides to hunt down real-life SS captain Eduard Roschmann, who was then living comfortably in South America (as were so many of them). Then there's the Odessa, then hiring top German scientists to work on missile guidance systems for atomic warheads that Odessa planned to sell to the Egypt of dictator Gamel Abdel Nasser, who would use them wipe out Israel. There are scenes depicting the real-life officers of Israel's Mossad, Shin-Bet and Military Intelligence. There are even scenes with Miller getting information from Simon Wiesenthal. The plan for Nasser to use German scientists in the early 1960s to develop his missiles was absolutely true. Unfortunately, Miller's pursuit of Roschmann, and then an Odessa killer's pursuit of Miller, is one long bore, with little action, but *lots* of contrivances. Indeed, our hero does not get struck on the head until the last fifteen or twenty pages.

Heil never smile again: Oliver Collignon as the singing Hitler Youth leader (with Mark Lambert's voice dubbed in) in the memorable beer garden scene in Bob Fosse's film version of the Broadway hit *Cabaret*. Fosse depicted the Nazis as a sinister force literally waiting in the wings, with scenes of violence used as a brutal counterpoint to the over-the-top numbers in the Kit-Kat Club.

Instead, Forsyth succeeds in the early, and very painful, concentration camp flashbacks, and in capsule-sized character studies of the various players Miller has to deal with. The Columbia film sped up the action considerably, with Miller (played with a fluctuating accent by Jon Voight) pushed in front of a train (unsuccessfully) in the first half hour. Unfortunately, not long after this bit of action, one of Odessa's minions tries to warn Miller to give up his pursuit

Making the trains run on time: Jon Voight as the German reporter hunting real-life Nazi war criminal Eduard Roschmann (played by Maximilian Schell) in the film version of Frederick Forsyth's *The Odessa File*. The popularity of the novel and film helped revive the hunt for Roschmann and the Odessa group.

of Roschmann at an airport lounge (a scene from the book). So, Odessa tries to kill Miller, *then* threatens him?

There is a good fight scene between Miller and the Odessa killer, with the former SS man falling through a skylight onto a jutting spike. In the final confrontation with Roschmann, which was in the novel (Roschmann is played by anti–Nazi Austrian Maximilian Schell), after the Nazi villain's usual bellicose defense of his deeds sprinkled with vicious anti–Semitic epithets, when the Nazi grabs a gun, Miller is forced to shoot him dead. In the novel, Roschmann is allowed to escape to South America; however, Miller has won, since he has indirectly forced the SS captain and the others in the organization to disband (in the novel's climax, the SS killer pursuing Miller is shot in the head by a Mossad agent pretending to be an Odessa man). Forsyth *had* to have Roschmann escape since he was still at large at the time. However, in 1974, after the book was published and the Columbia film was released, the sadistic SS captain was back in the unwanted glare of the world's spotlight, making his bosses at Odessa *very* uncomfortable. It is said that Roschmann died in La Asunción, Paraguay, on August 8, 1977, less than four years after the release of the film. It was never proven beyond a doubt if the dead man was indeed Roschmann or, if he was, whether Odessa murdered him to stop all the unwanted attention on their group.

Still, skeptical that the corpse was Roschmann, Simon Weisenthal said, "I wonder who died for him?"[1]

When *The Hindenburg* was released by Universal on Christmas Day, 1975, it is highly doubtful that the many survivors of the incident could possibly have envisioned a film version of their suffering that was less insightful than it was tacky. Having recently triumphed at the box office with *Jaws*, Universal Pictures was still in their pseudo-biography phase with bad recreations of iconic Hollywood, like *W.C. Fields and Me* and *Gable & Lombard*. With the disaster movie vogue in full swing, the studio took the explosion of the Nazi dirigible over Lakehurst, New Jersey, and concocted, with very little substance, a make-believe scenario dealing with an anti–Nazi saboteur blowing up the legendary blimp (Hitler himself dismissed the explosion as an "act of God"). In other words, a Nazi version of *Airport*. The story has George C. Scott, our erstwhile Patton, as the disillusioned *Luftwaffe* officer Colonel Ritter, whose son, a fanatical Nazi, is fighting for the Führer. Now the colonel is appointed to head security aboard the Hindenburg. Unfortunately, he has to deal with SS man Vogel (Roy Thinnes), for whom he has contempt. And so, once again, we have the now-traditional "good German" pitted against a fanatical SS thug. Also along for the flight is World War II veteran Charles Durning, with an atrocious German accent, as the blimp's captain, and Anne Bancroft, of all people, as a badly-accented German countess. Standing out in the all-star cast, however, is concentration camp survivor (and ex–*Hogan's Heroes* player) Robert Clary as the ship's entertainer. Fully exploiting Clary's innate talent for mime, the film features the French-Jewish performer doing a comic bit zinging the Nazis, much to the anger of the captain and other pro–Nazis aboard. Despite Robert Wise's direction, and Clary's performance, however, the film failed, possibly as much for its pompous self-importance and unintentional humor as for its implausible what-if fantasy scenario. The present author's wife, Colleen, has seen *The Hindenburg* at a local movie-house on Northern Boulevard in Queens, and can attest to audience reaction at one particular point. For instance, at the end, the film's newsreel-like narrator announces who lived and who died in the tragedy; when it is mentioned that a passenger's *dog* lived, the entire audience burst into laughter.

VII. Ghosts (1972–2016) 183

Aryans in trouble II: The miscast Anne Bancroft and former Patton George C. Scott in *The Hindenburg*, Universal's laughable version of what may have triggered the fire on the doomed Nazi dirigible.

The following year, Paramount released the film version of William Goldman's *The Marathon Man*, with the author mixing the black ops of rogue CIA agents with Nazi war criminals. Needless to say, Sir Laurence Olivier's Nazi dentist ("Is it safe??") far outclasses Dustin Hoffman's whiny, little "hero" who is the laughingstock of the local street gangs. Within two years, Oliver would "switch sides" and play the Wiesenthal-like Nazi hunter in the film version of Ira Levin's wildly implausible novel *The Boys from Brazil* (a film angrily dismissed by the *real* Wiesenthal). Unfortunately, as directed by Franklin Schaffner (who won an Oscar for *Patton*), *The Boys* is an unintended laugh riot destined for camp status. Unlike his Nazi dentist in *The Marathon Man*, Olivier's performance was awful. Nevertheless, the esteemed actor seems brilliant opposite the usually dull and pompous Gregory Peck, who obviously did *not* have the range or the talent to convincingly play the raving, Hitler-like Dr. Mengele (paging Rudolph Anders!). His climactic fight with Olivier's Nazi-hunter, complete with ear-biting and face-scratching, is downright embarrassing for two elderly Oscar-winners (in the novel, there is no fight). In the film, Mengele is killed by guard dogs; though the more realistic ending would come on February 7, 1979, when the former SS *Hauptsturmführer* would suffer a heart attack while swimming off the coast of Bertioga, Brazil, and drown. Dare one venture that he saw *The Boys from Brazil* before taking his swim?

The old men from Brazil: Veteran actors Sir Laurence Olivier and Gregory Peck in the film version of Ira Levin's bestseller, *The Boys from Brazil*. The two stars, cast as a Simon Weisenthal–like Nazi hunter and Dr. Josef Mengele, respectively, thoroughly embarrass themselves in this camp laughfest.

Over in England, *Shock Waves* was released in 1977, one of the first films to recast Nazi soldiers as killer zombies. Both Peter Cushing as a Nazi war criminal scientist and John Carradine as a skipper try to make sense of this violent film, with revived Nazis rising from the island's swamps to knock off the usual group of hapless young people shipwrecked on the usually uncharted isle. In Spain, sleazy filmmaker Jess Franco, as well as horror icons Lucio Fulci and Jean Rollin, would give us their own version of Nazi zombies, with even more young people (particularly scantily-clad young women) getting maimed, mutilated and, more or less, murdered *en masse*, by former Nazi soldiers, both SS and regular *Wehrmacht*. Little did Fulci, Rollin and Franco know that Nazi zombies would make a stupendous comeback in the 21st century.

The Formula was released just in time for Christmas of 1980 (December 18). Produced by the man who wrote the novel on which it is based, Steve Shagan (he also produced *Voyage of the Damned*, also based on his novel, which itself was based on an actual incident), the film features the usual good performance by George C. Scott as the police detective hero and an unfortunately, but predictably, *awful* performance by the increasingly pompous and clownish Marlon Brando. Steeped in the left-wing paranoia of the preceding counterculture decade, the film begins with a wartime flashback. Richard Lynch is a Nazi general caught trying to smuggle "the formula for synthetic fuel" into snow-capped Switzerland. Captured by an unusually sympathetic American major (Robin Clarke), the audience is treated to the classic

A crude awakening: George C. Scott (left) as the investigating detective and an overly made-up (and highly overpaid) Marlon Brando as an oil company executive in the film version of Steve Shagan's *The Formula*. With a prologue set in wartime Germany, this paranoid opus clumsily mixes Nazi chicanery with the then-current oil crisis.

line: "From now on, the world's going to be one big, happy corporation. No more secrets, no more enemies. Just customers."

It's *highly* doubtful that any American officer or government official, even the pro–Nazi, pro-capitalist Dulles brothers, would have openly proclaimed a postwar world led by American corporate interests to a Nazi general while the two were still on the battlefield! By the way, since Lynch is driving his truck towards the Swiss border just before the end of the war, there would have been no snow *anywhere* in early May.

Raiders of the Lost Ark was a refreshing throwback to the old Republic serials. Unlike the alliance between ex–Nazis and Big Oil in Steve Shagan's paranoid epic, the Nazis returned to their former costumed-villain glory. A full decade and a half before showing the Final Solution in *Schindler's List*, director Steven Spielberg fully enjoyed his work on *Raiders*, with the Jewish helmsman relishing the task of sending literally dozens of screen Nazis to their horrible and well-deserved deaths. At the film's climax, when all seems lost, it is the Hebrew Ghosts of the Ark who save the day for Indiana Jones and Marian by literally melting, in graphically horrible detail, every screaming Nazi in that cave, a kind of fantasy revenge on their enemies denied the Chosen People far too many times in reality.

Swing Kids was not that well-known, yet it is a fascinating take on a little-explored aspect of Nazi repression—their censoring of American jazz, with a small band of young jazz-loving

Facing the music: Christian Bale and Robert Sean Leonard (standing) as the jazz-loving, rebellious German youth fighting Nazi squares in *Swing Kids*. Though casting young actors with pronounced American accents, the film *does* explore a rare subject in the Nazi film subgenre.

resisters called "Swing Kids" smuggling in jazz records and dressing like hepcats. Though most of the German characters have American accents, the British Kenneth Branaugh is a standout as a Gestapo officer (*and* he refused screen credit).

The screen version of a Stephen King novella, *Apt Pupil*, features Brad Renfro as the youth fascinated by the ex–Nazi officer he meets (Ian McKellan), picking up some of the old man's worst traits. By the end of the film, with the aged McKellan committing suicide, the youngster becomes cruel and cold-blooded, but he does not become the serial sniper who has a deadly shootout with police at the end of King's story.

Downfall was released in Germany on September 8, 2004. Starring Bruno Ganz as Hitler and based on both Joachim Fest's *Inside Hitler's Bunker* as well as the memoirs of Traudl Junge, the last (and youngest) of Hitler's secretaries, *Downfall* was perhaps the most accurate version of Hitler's last days in that doomed bunker, with G.W. Pabst's *The Last Ten Days* running a close second (and even then it had Oscar Werner as the usual Good German officer who actually tries to kill Hitler, something that never happened—in the bunker anyway). The film closely follows its literary sources, though at times it does seem to be an uneven mix between Fest's painfully researched history and Traudl Junge's personal point-of-view memoirs. Ganz' performance fairly blows away many previous Hitler performances, especially Alec Guinness' highly overrated one. We see Hitler's psychopathia on full display: wild mood swings between angry tirades and maudlin self pity, pathetic fantasies of a surprise victory and pure terror that the war is lost and his own death is imminent, with a side-trip of pure contempt for the German people whom he felt "failed" him and richly deserve their suffering. We also see the *Wehrmacht* general staff, whom we *almost* feel sorry for as they trod gently around their progressively unbalanced leader while trying to defend Berlin with practically zero manpower, arms or realistic plan of attack.

Traudl herself had already appeared in *Blind Spot: Hitler's Secretary*, a feature-length documentary with the filmmakers interviewing the old woman as she reminisced about her time in the bunker. Though claiming innocence of Hitler's character due to her age, Junge (birth name Gertraud Humps) was married for eleven months during the war to an SS lieutenant, so she couldn't have been *that* naïve. Still, it is the real Junge who briefly appears at the beginning of *Downfall* as a kind of authoritative ghostly presence from the past. A technical advisor for Pabst's *The Last Act* in 1955, Junge had died in Munich on February 10, 2002, two years before the making of *Downfall* and, ironically, the same day *Blind Spot: Hitler's Secretary* was released for the first time at the Berlin International Film Festival.

The Boy with the Striped Pajamas revealed its British origins by being released in England before anywhere else on September 12, 2008. And if the credits showing a co-production between Miramax and BBC Films were not added evidence, the now-familiar British-accented German characters will dismiss any doubt. This is a shame because the film is a well made version of John Boyne's moving 2006 novel. Seen from the point-of-view of a German boy who happens to be the son of a newly-appointed concentration camp commandant, the story is a powerful evocation of brotherhood even in a totalitarian country as the German boy (Bruno) befriends a Jewish boy (Shmuel) who happens to be behind barbed wire in the concentration camp next door. In the novel, Bruno lives a privileged life with his family in cosmopolitan Berlin as the son of a respected SS officer. However, though the father is ordered to take command of Auschwitz in the novel (which Bruno refers to as "Out-With," just as the Führer is referred to as "the Fury"), in the film it is never clearly spelled out what the name of the camp is, though it is implied that it's Auschwitz.

Uprooted and taken away from his many friends in Berlin, the lonely German boy fatefully meets the last person those of his world would want him to befriend. As time goes on, the boys' growing friendship blossoms even in the specter of a racist Germany, with the Jewish boy schooling the innocent German in what it's like to be on the other side of the barbed wire fence. Ironically, their friendship, started in the innocence of childhood, will also be a harbinger for both the novel's and the film's tragic conclusion. If anything, the film is marred by the all too British accents of the major characters (with David Thewlis as the commandant father). British child actor Asa Butterfield is good as Bruno, but Jack Scanlon's English accented Shmuel is somewhat of a distraction for a character who is supposed to be from a Jewish Ghetto, not the East End. In the novel, Shmuel is not introduced by Boyne until *exactly* the middle of the book, with Bruno first seeing the boy in the striped pajamas as a ghostly figure in the distance who progressively gets larger as he finally gets close enough to see him sitting forlornly on the ground with an unusual grey pallor to the boy's skin that Bruno had never seen before. As soon as they meet, we just feel that *this* particular friendship can only end in tragedy, with the Holocaust pervasively destroying the children of the perpetrators as well as its many victims.

Dead Snow was released in Norway on January 9, 2008, a unified Germany on March 7, and the United States, New York City specifically, on a hot summer day, June 9. The film is a clear throwback to the Euro-trash zombie movies of the '70s, though now with 21st century CGI and much better makeup. The film is also a rare but not unusual marriage of the still-successful zombie subgenre and Nazi terror, only this time the horror of Nazism was not the danger of being shipped to the East as an inferior, but being *eaten alive* by dead soldiers who had formerly been Hitler's minions. There is the usual hapless group of pretty and privileged young people, in this case medical students (which kind of makes you want to see them punished even *more*), who drive up in the Norwegian backwoods for a little R & R and instead finding R.I.P. (though even *this* is denied them since zombies rarely rest in peace).

The film gets off to a great start as we see a lone woman skiing down the mountain slopes around the usual "cursed village." As Edvard Grieg's classical piece *In the Hall of the Mountain King*, is playing on the soundtrack, the poor girl is being pursued by a group of hulking marauders in shadow whose faces and clothes are never fully seen. At one point as she pauses to turn back to see if her pursuers are still following her, the music stops and we see nothing but the cold mountain scenery and hear the whisper of an icy wind—that is, until a horribly scarred face appears for a spilt-second on camera and the pursuit, as well as the music, continue. Despite her grisly death (which takes place practically off-screen as we hear her horrible screams), it is easily the scariest sequence in the entire film, with the Grieg piece used for maximum effect.

The group shows up afterwards and soon they meet an old man, the usual horror-film device warning the future victims of the unspeakable terror to come. We are told of a treasure of gold, and a platoon of Nazi soldiers led by a Major Herzog who "killed a lot of people" (as if Nazis restrained themselves from violence). Later on, the med students are systematically eaten, have themselves turn into zombies, and are in turn killed again; there are mutilations aplenty as not only the students, but the Nazi zombies themselves, are gutted, hacked, mutilated, gored and smashed in the brains, the Norwegian filmmakers piling on the buckets of blood with an enthusiasm that would embarrass Herschel Gordon Lewis. During one painful sequence, when one Nazi zombie has his guts pulled out, the hero, Martin, finds himself hanging over the edge of a cliff with the intestines of the Nazi-zombie being the only thing he's hanging on to. It's cartoonish in the extreme, and unfortunately rejects the more restrained approach we saw at the beginning. Towards the end, when Martin is bitten in the arm, he's forced to cut off the infected limb with a chainsaw, an almost unconscious homage to Bruce

Campbell losing *his* arm in Sam Raimi's *Evil Dead III* (or was it IV?).

Six years later came the predictable sequel, *Dead Snow II: Red vs. Dead*. Far more cartoonish than the original, if that was possible, the film dispenses with the detail that Martin was half Jewish, and also ignores the fact that Herzog and the Nazi zombies were after the treasure (the twist ending of the original had Martin finding one gold coin left in his car just as Herzog appears outside his window). Continuing where the original left off, Martin wins out over Herzog by having the zombie lose *his* arm. Needless to say, their arms are switched, causing all sorts of lunacy. Soon it is decided that, in order to defeat the Nazi zombies, Martin and his zombie hunting friends have to revive a platoon of *Soviet* zombies to defeat them. The absurd premise has it that Herzog and his men murdered these Red army soldiers after they were brought to Norway; indeed, why would the German general staff order a transfer of Red army soldiers from the Soviet Union all the way to *Norway* to be murdered?

Death's head battalion: Orjan Gamst as Nazi zombie Major Herzog in *Dead Snow*. This over-the-top film and its sequel took the Nazi-zombie subgenre to its logical extreme, with black humor, gore, mixed-up severed limbs and an overall cartoonish plot.

More lunacy occurs when Herzog and his zombies steal a World War II Panzer tank from a museum; of course, we're supposed to accept the fact that all World War II museums always have *real* tanks on display that are not only fully operational, but also full of Diesel fuel and armed with live shells. Of course, we assume that if you accept the Nazi zombie premise to begin with, *anything* goes. Still, during the final confrontation with Major Herzog, Martin is able to give the zombie a withering slam at a certain National Socialist foible, telling him that the Nazis, having conquered much of Europe, were winning the war, but they eventually lost it because they got greedy. "And you know what?" says Martin before Herzog's own tank is about to fire a shell decapitating the zombie, "You going to lose *again!*" Not since *Indiana Jones and the Last Crusade* has a climactic fight scene both inside and outside a Panzer tank been this good.

A Film Unfinished got a limited theatrical release on August 18, 2010. The film, shot in Nazi-occupied Poland, was a long delayed powerful answer to the 1940 Nazi film *The Eternal Jew*, though even this is a simplification since its power goes so much further. Using pieces of film shot by Nazi cameramen backed by armed SS troops in the Warsaw Ghetto in May 1942, Israeli filmmaker Yael Hersonski gives the world a shattering portrait of anti–Semitic propaganda touted as "authentic" by Nazi murderers. Originally titled *Das Ghetto* by Goebbels' propaganda ministry and shot within a period of thirty days, the unfinished film without a soundtrack was discovered by archivists in Communist East Germany.

In a co-production between a unified Germany and Israel, with linking narration and interviews with Jewish survivors of the ghetto, this work both saddens and enrages as we witness the lies about the Jewish people the Nazis tried so hard to foist upon the world. We see Jews sitting in restaurants and having access to an abundant amount of food as starving children beg outside; we see Jewish families who normally were living twenty to a room now having their own apartments and living far too well; we see supposedly unconcerned Jews literally stepping over dead bodies, now having turned into skin and bones; we see Nazi cameraman Willy Wist, of course now suddenly regretting his participation in *Das Ghetto* as he uncomfortably addresses an Israeli's camera; we see naked Jewish women get into a so-called "ritual bath," with the audience just imagining leering Nazi thugs off-camera enjoying the women's embarrassment. We are also read the diary entries of Jewish Council head Adam Cherniakov, who was forced to do the Nazis' bidding, which included using his own apartment to film several scenes depicting Jews living the good life. After the Germans started deporting Jews to Treblinka in late July, the guilt-ridden Cherniakov committed suicide by taking a cyanide pill.

It is the testimony of the survivors, these shattered souls watching the painful images on a movie screen in a projection room who show the greatest courage, again living through the hell they would never forget. One woman shies away from looking at the screen, horrified at the starving, skeletal figures before her: "What if I see someone I know?" she sadly asks. The scenes show the faces of these doomed Jews, the eyes that were once soulful and alive were now hollow and empty, as if these people knew that their days were numbered. Later still, we see other Jews forced to literally shovel people who were once human beings, but were now nothing but skeletons, down ramps where they are dumped into pits. The scene is heartbreaking and still shocking when we consider that these corpses got this way without having even gone to Auschwitz.

This was but one example of what the so-called civilized world was ignoring even as they proclaimed their own basic decency.

When he won the Oscar for Best Director and Best Picture in 1994 for producing and directing *Schindler's List*, Steven Spielberg beseeched the millions of viewers around the world to listen to "the ghosts." His words were not only meant to commemorate the victims of the Nazi Holocaust, but to warn against the all too possible chance of more genocides occurring in the future. For as of this day, in the more "enlightened" 21st century, the disease of global anti–Semitism returned with a vengeance; and as the democracies welcomed more inclusion of diverse peoples than ever before in their long, mutual histories, other places around the world slid back into Nazi-like intolerance and barbarism. It was as if in all that time since the end of World War II we had not learned a thing.

In the movies, we had seen the many faces of the Third Reich on screen. We had seen

Nazis as conquerors, spies, bigots and terrorists, but we had also seen them as vampires, zombies, super-capitalists, mad doctors, noble heroes (in films made by the Nazis themselves, of course), "Good Germans," war criminals, woman-hating serial killers, perverts, bumbling clowns and all–American fascists. They were the perfect screen villains, and the most effective ones, because they were frighteningly real. And yet, most of the time filmmakers did not show us *how* real they were. In hundreds of westerns made by Hollywood and other filmmakers, none of them dared show actual Indian atrocities visited upon any white character who had the misfortune to be captured by them, certainly not according to historical accuracy anyway. In the fictional films depicting the Third Reich, the very real crimes against humanity of the Nazi regime would almost never be shown to the audience, with postwar newsreels being the only true representation of Nazi atrocities on screen. And since the majority of these documentary films were made by the victors, they did not explore the topic of vacillation or delay among the Allies for ending the scourge of Nazism and rescuing its many victims much sooner.

And even with what we know about the Third Reich and the madmen who ruled it, film biographies were not always accurate, nor were actors cast in roles that brought the most accurate impersonations. To Hollywood and the various nations who depicted Nazism, they were not only an evil to be shunned, but a *foreign* evil, even when postwar Germany itself finally depicted them on screen. *No one* wanted to take responsibility for the Nazis' rise, but everyone wanted to condemn everyone else but themselves for the same thing. No nation owned up to the cancer allowed to grow in Germany; and when they all got together to commemorate the 70th anniversary of the fall of Nazism, any mentions of responsibility for not having done enough to stop them were absent from the speeches of the many world leaders who attended ceremonies.

There had been many Hollywood scripts even in the early 1930s that criticized Hitler's reign; the Breen office was certainly not pro–Jewish and the German embassy could certainly raise a stink, but why didn't the Jewish film studio moguls say anything? Was it because they felt America would not accept what was happening to the Jews, that they would be accused of spreading "Jewish influence"? Perhaps they had denied their own heritage so long so they could fit in America that they could not find the voices to protest the ill treatment of their own brethren in Europe. Either way, the results were the same by 1940: Condemn Nazis, but not their genocidal policies.

It's been said countless times that those who don't learn from history are doomed to repeat it. But it's never been said enough that there are places where citizens aren't allowed access to that history so they can learn from it…

Chapter Notes

I—Infection

1. Stephen Bach, *Leni: The Life and Work of Leni Riefenstahl*, p. 50.
2. Richard Taylor, *Film Propaganda: Soviet Russia and Nazi Germany*, p. 137.
3. Peter Gay, *Weimar Culture*, pp. 133–134.
4. Stephen Bach, *Marlene Dietrich: Life and Legend*, p. 118.
5. Thomas Doherty, *Hollywood and Hitler, 1933–1939*, p. 4.
6. Ben Urwand, *The Collaboration: Hollywood's Pact with Hitler*, p. 25.
7. Doherty, *Hollywood and Hitler: 1933–1939*, p. 3.
8. *Ibid.*, p. 4.
9. Patrick McGilligan, *Fritz Lang: The Nature of the Beast*, p. 175.
10. *Ibid.*, p. 176.
11. *Ibid.*
12. *Ibid.*
13. *Ibid.*, p. 180.
14. *Ibid.*
15. McGilligan, *Fritz Lang, The Nature of the Beast*, p. 180.
16. *Ibid.*, p. 176.
17. *Ibid.*, p. 180.
18. *The Testament of Dr. Mabuse*, Wikipedia; David Kalat, *The Strange Case of Dr. Mabuse: A Study of the Twelve Films and Five Novels*.
19. Everson, *Classics of the Horror Film*, p. 33.
20. David Welch, *Propaganda and German Cinema: 1933–1945*, p. 62.
21. Ralf Georg Reuth, *Goebbels*, p. 82.
22. Welch, *Propaganda and the German Cinema, 1933–1945*, p. 63.
23. Goebbels' interview with the magazine *Licht-Bild-Buhne*, October 13, 1933, qtd. in Welch p. 63.
24. David Stewart Hull, *Film in the Third Reich*, p. 44.
25. Welch, p. 63.
26. *Ibid.*, p. 68.
27. *Ibid.*, p. 69.
28. Susan Sontag, "Fascinating Fascism," *The New York Review of Books*, February 6, 1975.
29. Steven Bach, *Leni: The Life and Work of Leni Riefenstahl*, p. 71.
30. *Ibid.*, p. 75.
31. *Ibid.*, p. 76.
32. *Ibid.*
33. *Ibid.*, p. 77.
34. *Ibid.*
35. *Ibid.*, p. 79.
36. *Ibid.*, p. 81.
37. Bach, p. 98.
38. *Ibid.*, p. 108.
39. Leni Riefenstahl, Wikipedia.
40. *Ibid.*
41. *Triumph of the Will*, Wikipedia.
42. *Ibid.*
43. David Thomson, *The New Biographical Dictionary of Film*, p. 822.
44. Susan Sontag, *Fascinating Fascism*, The New York Review of Books, February 6, 1975.
45. Bach, *Leni: The Life and Work of Leni Riefenstahl*, p. 257.
46. *Ibid.*, p. 258.

II—Rage

1. Friedrich Wolf, Wikipedia.
2. *Professor Mamlock*, Internet Broadway DataBase.
3. Doherty, *Hollywood and Hitler*, p. 192–193.
4. *Ibid.*, p. 194.
5. Friedrich Wolf, *Professor Mamlock: A Play*, 1935.
6. Olga Gershenson, *The Phantom Holocaust: Soviet Cinema and Jewish Catastrophe*, p. 18.
7. *Soviet Film Replaced, Motion Picture Herald*, September 2, 1939, in Doherty, *Hollywood and Hitler, 1933–1939*, p. 351.
8. Urwand, *The Collaboration: Hollywood's Pact with Hitler*, p. 214–215.
9. *Ibid.*, p. 216.
10. *Ibid.*, p. 217.
11. IMDB, *The Mortal Storm*, tagline.
12. Donald Dewey, *James Stewart: A Biography*, p. 213.

13. Michael Munn, *Jimmy Stewart: The Truth Behind the Legend*, p. 104.
14. Margaret Herrick Library, *The Man Who Killed Hitler* file.
15. Erwin Leiser, *Nazi Cinema*, p. 152.
16. *Ibid.*, p. 153.
17. *Ibid.*
18. *Ibid.*, p. 154.
19. *Ibid.*, p. 152.
20. Lichtblau, *The Nazis Next Door*, 16.
20. Quote from Jewish barber in *The Great Dictator* (1940).
21. Joyce Milton, *Tramp: The Life of Charlie Chaplin*, p. 377.
22. Richard Overy, *The Battle of Britain: The Myth and the Reality*, p. 17.
23. *Ibid.*, p. 17.
24. M. Muggeridge, editor, *Ciano's Diary, 1939–1943*, p. 275, in Overy, p. 21.
25. Welch, *Propaganda and the German Cinema, 1939–1945*, p. 231.
26. Leiser, *Nazi Cinema*, p. 160.
27. *Ibid.*
28. *Ibid.*
29. *Ibid.*
30. *Ohm Kruger*, DVD, Special features.
31. *Ibid.*
32. *Ibid.*
33. *Ibid.*
34. Max Wallace, *The American Axis: Henry Ford, Charles Lindberth, and the Rise of the Third Reich*.
35. *Ibid.*, p. 293.
36. *Ibid.*, p. 95.
37. *Ibid.*, p. 96.
38. Charles Lindbergh, *Of Flight and Life*, p. 42, in Wallace, *The American Axis*, p. 99.
39. "Jew-Baiting," *Time* magazine, September 22, 1941.
40. "Lindgergh Diary," Wikipedia.
41. *The Wartime Journals of Charles Lindbergh*.

III—Inferno

1. Margaret Herrick Library file on *Hitler's Children*.
2. *Ibid.*
3. Tom Weaver and Gregory William Mank, *John Carradine: The Films*, p. 149.
4. *Ibid.*
5. Margaret Herrick Library, *Hitler's Madman* file.
6. *Ibid.*
7. *Ibid.*
8. *Ibid.*
9. *Ibid.*
10. Margaret Herrick Library.
11. *The Hitler Gang*, http://www.tcm.com/tcmdb/title/78145/The-Hitler-Gang/.
12. Margaret Herrick Library.
13. *Ibid.*
14. *Ibid.*
15. *Ibid.*, October 15, 1943.
16. *Ibid.*
17. *Ibid.*
18. *Ibid.*
19. *Ibid.*
20. Lichtblau, *The Nazis Next Door*, p. 16.
21. Letter from Joseph Breen to Jack L. Warner, November 6, 1944, Margaret Herrick Library, *Hotel Berlin* file.
22. Margaret Herrick Library, *Hotel Berlin* file, April 12, 1944.
23. *Ibid.*
24. *Ibid.*
25. *Ibid.*
26. *Ibid.*
27. *Ibid.*
28. Margaret Herrick Library, *Hotel Berlin* file.
29. Vicki Baum, *Hotel Berlin '43*, p. 250.

IV—Final Solutions

1. *Peter Lorre Worries: Is He Bad Enough?* pressbook for *Quicksand*, 1949, in Stephen D. Youngkin, *The Lostone: The Life of Peter Lorre*, p. 317.
2. *Ibid.*, p. 317.
3. *Ibid.*, p. 318.
4. *Ibid.*, p. 319.
5. *Ibid.*, p. 320.
6. *Ibid.*
7. *Ibid.*, p. 341.
8. *Ibid.*, p. 352–353.
9. *Ibid.*, p. 354.
10. *Ibid.*, p. 355.
11. Steven Bach, *Leni: The Life and Work of Leni Riefenstahl*, p. 205.
12. *Ibid.*, p. 219.
13. *Ibid.*, p. 202–203.
14. *Ibid.*, p. 205.
15. *Frankfurter News Pressse Kulture*, August 16, 2002, in Bach, *Lini*, p. 295.
16. Ulrich Seelmann-Engebert, *Mannheimer Morgen*, undated in Bach, *Leni*, p. 244.

V—Airbrush

1. Margaret Herrick Library, *The Enemy Below* file.
2. Bob Herzberg, *The Left Side of the Screen*, p. 263–267.
3. "Friedrich Paulus," Wikipedia.
4. Margaret Herrick Library, *Operation Eichmann* file.
5. *Ibid.*
6. Internet Broadway DataBase (IBDB).
7. IMDB, *Hitler*, tagline.
8. David Kalat, "*Hitler*," Turner Classic Movies website.
9. Margaret Herrick Library, *Hitler* file.
10. *Ibid.*
11. *Ibid.*, May 2, 1961.
12. Letter from scenarist E. Charles Straus to Motion Picture Association of America (MPAA) president Jack Vizzard, April 26, 1961, Margaret Herrick Library.

13. *Ibid.*
14. *Ibid.*
15. Margaret Herrick Library, *Hitler* file, May 2, 1961.

VI—MESHUGANNAH

1. General Matthew B. Ridgeway, *Soldier: The Memoirs of Matthew B. Ridgeway* (as told to Harold H. Martin), 1956, in John S.D. Eisenhower, *The Bitter Woods: The Battle of the Bulge,* p. 300.
2. Susan Heller Anderson, "Obituary, Hans Helmut Kirst," *New York Times,* February 24, 1989.
3. *Ibid.*
4. Natasha Fraser-Cavassoni, *Sam Spiegel,* p. 278–279.
5. Eisenhower, *The Bitter Woods,* p. 217–218.
6. *Ibid.*, p. 276.
7. Jeff Stafford, "The Night of the Generals," Turner Classic Movies website.
8. Fraser-Cavassoni, *Sam Spiegel,* p. 282.
9. *Ibid.*, p. 283.
10. Shawn Levy, *King of Comedy: The Life and Art of Jerry Lewis,* p. 135.
11. Jerry Lewis, *Jerry Lewis in Person,* p. 281.
12. Shawn Levy, *King of Comedy,* p. 378.
13. *Ibid.*, p. 380.
14. *Ibid.*, p. 381.
15. *Spy* magazine, 1992.

VII—GHOSTS

1. Wiesenthal made the comment in Vienna on August 11, 1977, and it was printed by the Associated Press; the story was reprinted by the *Free Lance Star* on August 12, 1977.

Bibliography

Ailsby, Christopher. *SS: Roll of Infamy*. Osceola, Wisconsin: Motorbooks International Publishers, 1997.

Allen, Thomas B. *Declassified: Top Secret 50 Documents That Changed History*. Washington, D.C.: The House on F Street, LLC, 2008.

Astore, William J. and Showalter, Dennis E. *Hindenburg: Icon of German Militarism*. Dulles, Virginia: Potomac Book, 2005.

Bach, Steven. *Leni: The Life and Work of Leni Riefenstahl*. New York: Alfred A. Knopf, 2007.

_____. *Marlene Dietrich: Life and Legend*. New York: Da Capo Press, 2000.

Baum, Vicki. *Hotel Berlin '43*. Garden City, New York: Doubleday, Dorin, 1944.

Behlmer, Rudy, editor. *Inside Warner Brothers: 1935–1951*. New York: Simon & Schuster, 1985.

_____. *Memos from Darryl F. Zanuck: The Golden Years at Twentieth Century Fox*. New York: Grove Press, 1993.

Black, Edwin. *Nazi Nexus: America's Corporate Connections to Hitler's Holocaust*. Washington, D.C.: Dialog Press, 2009.

Blandford, Edmund L. *SS Intelligence: The Nazi Secret Service*. Edison, New Jersey: Castle Books, 2001.

Borkin, Joseph. *The Crime and Punishment of I.G. Farben: The Unholy Alliance Between Hitler and the Great Chemical Combine*. New York: Free Press, 1978.

Boyne, John. *The Boy in the Striped Pajamas*. London: David Fickling Books, 2006.

Braund, Simon. *The Greatest Movies You'll Never See: Unseen Masterpieces by the World's Greatest Directors*. London: Octopus Publishing Group, Ltd., 2013.

Breitman, Richard. *Official Secrets: What the Nazis Planned, What the British and American Knew*. New York: Hill & Wang, division of Farrar, Straus & Giroux, 1998.

Curtis, James. *Spencer Tracy: A Biography*. London: Arrow Books, 2011.

De Jonge, Alex. *The Weimar Chronicle: Prelude to Hitler*. New York: New American Library, 1978.

Dewey, Donald. *James Stewart: A Biography*. Atlanta, Georgia: Turner Publishing, 1996.

De Wilde, John C., Popper, David H., Clark, Eugene. *Handbook of the War*. Cambridge, Massachusetts: Houghton Mifflin, 1939.

Dick, Bernard F. *Radical Innocence: A Critical Study of the Hollywood Ten*. Lexington: University Press of Kentucky, 1989.

Dietrich, Marlene. *Marlene*. New York: Avon Books, 1987.

Doherty, Thomas. *Hollywood and Hitler: 1933–1939*. New York: Columbia University Press, 2013.

_____. *Hollywood's Censor: Joseph I. Breen and the Production Code Administration*. New York: Columbia University Press, 2007.

Donovan, John. *Eichmann, Man of Slaughter*. New York: Avon Books, 1960.

Eisenhower, John S.D. *The Bitter Woods: The Battle of the Bulge*. New York: G.P. Putnam & Sons, 1969.

Everson, William K. *Classics of the Horror Film: From the Days of the Silent Film to the Exorcist*. New York: Citadel Press, 1974.

Fest, Joachim. *Inside Hitler's Bunker: The Last Days of the Third Reich*. Berlin: Alexander Fest Verlag, 2002; New York: Picador, div. of Farrar, Straus & Giroux, 2004.

Forsyth, Frederick. *The Odessa File*. New York: Viking Press, 1972.

Friedlander, Henry. *The Origins of Nazi Genocide: From Euthanasia to the Final Solution*. Chapel Hill: University of North Carolina Press, 1995.

Friedrich, Otto. *Before the Deluge: A Portrait of Berlin in the 1920s*. New York: Fromm International Publishing, 1986.

_____. *City of Nets: A Portrait of Hollywood in the 1940s*. New York: Harper & Row Publishers, 1986.

Gerhenson, Olga. *The Phantom Holocaust: Soviet Cinema and Jewish Catastrophe*. New Brunswick, New Jersey: Rutgers University Press, 2013.

Gilbert, Martin. *Churchill and the Jews: A Lifelong Friendship*. New York: Henry Holt, 2007.

Grose, Peter L. *Israel in the Mind of America*. New York: Alfred A. Knopf, 1983.

Grubb, Kevin Boyd. *Razzle Dazzle: The Life and Work of Bob Fosse*. New York: St. Martin's Press, 1989.

Grunberger, Richard. *Hitler's SS*. New York: Dorset Press, 1970.

Hake, Sabine. *Screen Nazis: Cinema, History and Democracy*. Madison: University of Wisconsin Press, 2012.

Herzberg, Bob. *The FBI and the Movies: A History of the Bureau on Screen and Behind the Scenes in Hollywood*. Jefferson, North Carolina: McFarland, 2007.

_____. *The Left Side of the Screen: Communist and Left-Wing Ideology in Hollywood, 1929–2009*. Jefferson, North Carolina: McFarland, 2011.

Hull, David Stewart. *Film in the Third Reich*. New York: Simon & Schuster, 1973.

Kirst, Hans Helmut. *The Night of the Generals*. Munich: Verlag Kurt Desch GmbH, 1962; New York: Harper & Row, 1963.

Koppes, Clayton R., and Black, Gregory D. *Hollywood Goes to War*. New York: Free Press, a division of Macmillan, 1987.

Kracauer, Siegfried. *From Caligari to Hitler: A Psychological History of the German Film*. Princeton, New Jersey: Princeton University Press, 1947.

Leiser, Erwin. *Nazi Cinema*. New York: Macmillan, 1974.

Levy, Shawn. *King of Comedy: The Life and Art of Jerry Lewis*. New York: St. Martin's Press, 1996.

Lichtblau, Eric. *The Nazis Next Door: How America Became a Safe Haven for Hitler's Men*. New York: Houghton Mifflin, Harcourt, 2014.

MacDonnell, Francis. *Insidious Foes: The Axis Fifth Column and the American Home Front*. New York: Oxford University Press, 1995; Guildford, Connecticut: Lyons Press, 2004

McGilligan, Patrick. *Fritz Lang: The Nature of the Beast, a Biography*. New York: St. Martin's Press, 1997.

Milton, Joyce. *Tramp: The Life of Charlie Chaplin*. New York: HarperCollins, 1996.

Munn, Michael. *Jimmy Stewart: The Truth Behind the Legend*. Fort Lee, New Jersey: Barricade Books, 2006.

Overy, Richard. *The Battle of Britain: The Myth and the Reality*. London: Penguin Books, 2000: New York: W.W. Norton, 2001.

Packard, Jerrold M. *Neither Friend Nor Foe: The European Neutrals in World War II*. New York: Macmillan, 1992.

Pool, James. *Hitler and his Secret Partners: Contributions, Loot and Rewards*. New York: Pocket Books, div. of Simon & Schuster, 1997.

Pringle, Heather. *The Master Plan: Himmler's Scholars and the Holocaust*. New York: Hyperion Books, 2006.

Radosh, Ronald, and Radosh, Allis. *Red Star over Hollywood: The Film Colony's Long Romance with the Left*. San Francisco: Encounter Books, 2006.

Remak, Jaochim, editor. *The Nazi Years: A Documentary History*. New York: Simon & Schuster, 1969.

Reuth, Ralf Georg, *Goebbels*. New York: Mariner Books, 1994.

Ryskind, Allan H. *Hollywood Traitors: Blacklisted Screenwriters, Agents of Stalin, Agents of Hitler*. Washington, D.C.: Regnery Publishing, 2015.

Simpson, Christopher. *Blowback: America's Recruitment of Nazis and Its Destructive Impact on Our Domestic and Foreign Policy*. New York: Collier Books, division of Macmillan, 1989.

_____. *The Splendid Blonde Beast: Money, Law and genocide in the Twentieth Century*. New York: Grove Press, 1993.

Skal, David J. *The Monster Show: A Cultural History of Horror*. New York: Penguin Books, 1993.

_____ and Rains, Jessica. *Claude Rains: An Actor's Voice*. Lexington: University Press of Kentucky, 2008.

Snyder, Louis L. *Hitler's Elite: Shocking Profiles of the Reich's Most Notorious Henchmen*. New York: Berkeley Books, 1989.

Sutton, Antony C. *Wall Street and the Rise of Hitler*. Seal Beach, California: '76 Press, 1976.

Taylor, Kathrine Kressmann. *Address Unknown*. New York: Simon & Schuster, 1938.

Taylor, Richard. *Film Propaganda: Soviet Russia and Nazi Germany*. London: I.B. Taurus, 1979, 1998.

Urwand, Ben. *The Collaboration: Hollywood's Pact with Hitler*. Cambridge, Massachusetts: Belknap Press of the Harvard University Press, 2013.

Wallace, Max. *The American Axis: Henry Ford, Charles Lindbergh, and the Rise of the Third Reich*. New York: St. Martin's Press, 2006.

Waller, Douglas. *Wild Bill Donovan: The Spymaster Who Created the OSS and Modern American Espionage*. New York: Simon & Schuster, 2011.

Weaver, Tom, and Mank, Gregory William. *John Carradine: The Films*. Jefferson, North Carolina: McFarland, 1999.

Welch, David. *Propaganda and the German Cinema: 1933–1945*. London: Oxford University Press, 1983; London: I.B. Taurus, 2007.

Williamson, David G. *Poland Betrayed: The Nazi-Soviet Invasion of 1939*. Mechanicsburg, Pennsylvania: Stackpole Books, 2009.

Youngkin, Stephen D. *The Lost One: A Life of Peter Lorre*. Lexington: University Press of Kentucky, 2005.

INTERNET SOURCES

IMDB website
Turner Classic Movies website
www.fbigov.com
    Charles Lindbergh files
www.wikipedia.com
    Joachim Peiper
    Alfred Hugenberg
    Karl Daluege
    Ernst Udet
    Adolf Eichmann
    Friedrich Wolf
    Reinhard Heydrich
    Charles A. Lindbergh
    Friedrich Paulus
New York Post
    Jerry's Holocaust Comedy, December 27, 2015

New York Times
  All film reviews by Bosley Crowther
  "An Israeli Finds New Meanings in a Nazi Film." *A Film Unfinished*, Jeannette Catsoulis, August 17, 2010
  "Islamic Nations Move to Keep Out 'Schindler's List.'" Bernard Weintraub, April 7, 1994
www.variety.com
wwwhollywoodreporter.com
  "The Day the Clown Cried." Saul Abromovitch, August 12, 2013
swwtvtropes.com
  The Day the Clown Cried. Unknown writer, Undated
somewereneighbors.ushmm.org (United States Holocaust Museum)
  Leni Riefenstahl
www.miltary-history.org
  The Battle of Britain
www.senseofcinema.com
  Der Verlorene
  Robert Keser, November 2007
www.moma.org
  "Weimar Cinema 1919–1933: Daydreams & Nightmares." Unknown author and date
www.dw.com (Deutsche Welle [German broadcasters])
  "Berlin marks 70th anniversary of the end of World War II." May 23, 2015
  "Marking the 75th anniversary of the outbreak of World War II." May 30, 2015
  "Nazis 'merciless' towards Soviets, says Gauck." May 23, 2015
  "'Remembrance has no expiration date' at Sachsenhausen, Ravensbrueck." May 23, 2015
www.thefileroom.org
  "Schindler's List in Jordan." No author or date
www.en-maktoob.news.yahoo.com
  "German FM marks WWII anniversary at site of Stalingrad." May 7, 2015
www.ynetnews.com
  "Israel marks anniversary of Nazi defeat." May 7, 2015
www.huffingtonpost.com
  "Europe Marks 70th Anniversary of Nazi Defeat in World War II." May 8, 2015

INDEX

Address Unknown 78
Adler, Luther 120–121, 122
Albers, Hans 100
All Quiet on the Western Front (film) 14, 19
All Quiet on the Western Front (novel) 14, 19
All Through the Night 60, 122
Allen, Patrick 170
Alraune 26
Anders, Rudolph 46, 97, 140, 141, 183
Andrews, Dana 167, 168
Apt Pupil 186–187
At War with the Army 174
Atwill, Lionel 77

Banner, John 154, 160
Barbie, Klaus 115, 116
Basehart, Richard 160, 161, 162, 163
Basserman, Albert 77
Baum, Vicky 105, 106, 111, 112, 113
Ben-Gurion, David 158
Bercovici, Conrad 57–59
Beregi, Oscar 166
Berliner, Trude 97
Bessie, Alvah 107, 111
Blind Spot: Hitler's Secretary 187
The Blue Angel (film) 12–14
The Blue Angel (novel) 12
The Blue Light 31–33, 131, 132
Bogarde, Dirk 172–173, 174
Bond, Ward 46, 82
Boormann, Martin 116, 129, 130
Bottome, Phyliss 45, 49
Boyne, John 187
The Boy with the Striped Pajamas (film) 187–188
The Boy with the Striped Pajamas (novel) 187–188
The Boys from Brazil (film) 183
The Boys from Brazil (novel) 183
Brando, Marlon 57, 141, 185

Brecht, Bertold 25, 41
Breen, Joseph I. 4, 50, 80, 93, 95, 96, 99
The Bridge 137, 144
Bromberg, J. Edward 77

Cabaret 179–180
Canaris, Wilhelm 136
Carrel, Dr. Alexis 70–71
Carl Peters 100
Carradine, John 91–92, 96, 184
The Cat People (1942) 76–77
Cavanaugh, Hobart 94
Chaney, Lon, Jr. 77
Chaney, Lon, Sr. 9
Chaplin, Charlie 56–59, 176
Churchill, Winston 61, 119
Clary, Robert 182
Cloak and Dagger (1945) 25
Cobra Woman 78
Cohn, Harry 5, 150
Cole, Lester 153–154, 155, 156
Confessions of a Nazi Spy 4, 5
Council of the Gods 117
The Cross of Lorraine 60
Cuhna, Richard 149, 141
Curtis, Alan 91, 92
Cushing, Peter 184

Dailey, Dan 46
Daluege, Karl 89
The Damned 172–173
Daniell, Henry 107
Dantine, Helmut 103, 107, 111
The Day the Clown Cried 176–178
Dead Snow 188–189
Dead Snow, Red Vs. Dead 189
Denton, Charles 176, 177–178
The Desert Fox 122, 136
The Devil's General 137
Dietrich, Marlene 12–14, 128
Disney, Walt 39, 115
Dmytryk, Edward 79, 80–81
Dollfuss, Englebert 18, 47
Donath, Ludwig 97, 98
Downfall 138, 187

Dulles, Allen 104–105, 185
Durning, Charles 182

Education for Death 78, 80
Eichmann, Adolf 116, 119, 151–153, 158
Eisenhower, Dwight D. 114, 156
Emerson, Faye 107, 111, 112, 113
The Enemy Below 138, 140
The Eternal Jew 4, 52, 59–61
Everson, William K. 22, 113
Ewers, Hans Heinz 26–27

Fahrmann Maria 101, 148
The Fall of Berlin 117–118
Fanck, Dr. Arnold 12, 31–33, 131, 132
Farmer, Frances 79, 94
Farrow, John 103, 161
Fest, Joachim 187
Feuchtwanger, Leon 50–51, 54
Fiend Without a Face 166
A Film Unfinished 190
Ford, Henry 33, 71, 115, 116
The Formula (film) 184–185
The Formula (novel) 184
Forsyth, Frederick 115, 180–181, 182
Fosse, Bob 179–180
Frank, Hans 36
Franken, Steve 175, 177
Freeman, Howard 95, 96
Frees, Paul 143
Friedrich, Otto 20
The Frozen Dead 167–169

Ganz, Bruno 187
Gavin, John 142, 145
George, David Lloyd 119
Geray, Steven 107
The Gleiwitz Case 158–160
Goddard, Paulette 58
Godfrey, Peter 106–107
Goebbels, Dr. Joseph 4, 14, 17, 21–24, 30, 34, 52, 61, 67–68, 99, 101, 123, 132

201

Göring, Hermann 62, 71–72, 137
Goldman, William 183
Granville, Bonita 46, 79, 80
Gray, Charles 172
The Great Dictator 57–59, 120, 176
Grey, Joel 179
Grieg, Edvard 188
Grudgens, Gustav 52
Guinness, Alec 138, 187

Hale, Alan, Sr. 107, 113
Hall, Jon 78
Hall, Porter 103
Hangmen Also Die 25, 89, 90–91
Hans Westmar 29–30
Hardwicke, Sir Cedric 77
Harel, Isser 158
Harlan, Veit 50–51, 52, 55, 131
Healey, Myron 175
Hepburn, Katharine 74
Herzberg, Colleen vi, 181
Heydrich, Reinhard 54, 59, 72, 84–89, 152, 153, 158
Hicks, Russell 82
Himmler, Heinrich 54, 85, 86, 105
Hindenburg 182–183
Hirschbein, Peretz 90
Hitler (1962) 160–164
Hitler, Adolf 18, 36–38, 40, 62, 97, 119–120, 130, 147
Hitler: Beast of Berlin 38
Hitler: Dead or Alive 82–84, 121, 160
The Hitler Gang 6, 91, 102–105, 160, 162
Hitler's Children 79–82, 96
Hitler's Madman 89–96
Hofer, Johanna 91, 126
Hoffman, Dustin 183
Holmes, Oliver Wendell 70
Holt, Tim 79, 165
Homecoming (1941) 68
Hotel Berlin 105–113
Hotel Berlin '43 106, 112
Hugenberg, Alfred 11, 12, 14
Hutton, Jim 143
Hymer, Warren 82

The Incredible Mr. Limpet 166, 174, 175
Ingalls, Laura 73–74
Invisible Agent 77
Isherwood, Christopher 179
It Happened on July 20th 137

Jannings, Emil 12, 15, 62–63, 67–68
Jew Suss 52–54
Junge, Traudl 138–187
Jurgens, Curd 137, 138, 139

Kaiser Wilhelm II 10, 16
Keeper of the Flame (film) 74–75

Keeper of the Flame (novel) 74
Kennedy, Joseph 72
King, Andrea 107, 109, 112
Kinski, Klaus 145
Kirst, Hans Helmut 169–170
Kitchener, Horatio Herbert 63
Klemperer, Werner 154, 155, 157–158
Knotts, Don 166
Koch, Marianne 137
Kortner, Fritz 91, 97, 98, 99, 102
Kosleck, Martin 102, 116, 160, 175
Krauss, Werner 53
Kreuger, Kurt 97, 108
Kruger, Paul 62–64

Laemmle, Carl 17–18
Lang, Fritz 19–21, 22–25, 50, 91
The Last Act of Adolf Hitler (The Last Ten Days of Adolf Hitler) 137, 187
Leder, Herbert J. 166–167, 168
Lederer, Francis 103
Lee, Ruta 155
Leiser, Erwin 38–39, 151, 160, 161, 162
Lewis, Jerry 174–176, 177–178
Lewton, Val 76–77
Lindbergh, Charles A. 69–74
Litvak, Anatole 170
Lockhart, Gene 89
Lorre, Peter 9, 60, 77, 107, 109, 111 122–123, 124, 125–128
Lugosi, Bela 77
Lynch, Richard 184, 185

The Magic Face 120–122
Mahoney, Jock 142–143
Man Hunt 25, 50, 91
Man-Made Monster 77
The Man Who Killed Hitler 50
Mann, Heinrich 9, 11, 12, 14
Mann, Thomas 9, 12
The Marathon Man (film) 183
The Marathon Man (novel) 183
Marian, Ferdinand 53, 54, 63, 64
Marin, Edwin 77
Marlene 14
Martin, Dean 174
Mason, James 122, 136
Massey, Raymond 107, 109
Mate, Rudolph 78
Mayer, Louis B. 5, 47, 49
McCalla, Irish 140, 141
McNally, Stephen 116
Mein Kampf (film) 38–39, 151, 160, 161, 162
Mendes, Lothar 52
Mengele, Joseph 116, 183
Menzies, William Cameron 78
Merton, John 92
Metropolis 19
Milestone, Lewis 15
Miller, Sidney 175

Milton, Joyce 57, 58
Ministry of Fear 25
Minnelli, Liza 79
Mitchum, Robert 138, 139
Montez, Maria 78, 116
Morgan, Frank 46, 47, 50
Morgan, Ralph 91
Morison, Patricia 91, 92
The Mortal Storm (film) 45–49
The Mortal Storm (novel) 45
Mrs. Miniver 5
Murray, Jan 174, 175, 177

Nasser, Gamel 180
Naujocks, Alfred Helmut 158, 159–160
Nebenzal, Seymour 24, 90, 94
Netanyahu, Benjamin 2
The Night of the Generals (film) 170–171
The Night of the Generals (novel) 170–171
The Night Porter 173–174
Norris, Kathleen 72–73

O'Brien, Joan 176, 177–178
The Odessa File (film) 171–173
The Odessa File (novel) 115, 180
Ohm Kruger 4, 62–68, 101
Olivier, Sir Lawrence 183, 184
Oppenheimer, Joseph Suss 51–53
Operation Eichmann 153–157, 158, 160
Orr, William T. 46
O'Toole, Peter 171, 172, 173
Ouspenskaya, Maria 46

Pabst, G.W. 131, 137–138, 187
Palk, Anna 167, 168
Pandora's Box 137
Patton, George S. 156
Paulus, Friedrich 146–148
Peck, Gregory 183
Peiper, Joachim 171
Pleasance, Donald 172
The Plot to Kill Hitler 137
Pommer, Erich 12
Powell, Dick 116, 117
Power 51–52, 52
Preiss, Wolfgang 149
The Producers (film, 1968) 174
Professor Mamlock (film) 40–45, 49
Professor Mamlock (play) 40–42
Putin, Vladimir 2

Raiders of the Lost Ark 185
Rains, Claude 103, 116
Rampling, Charlotte 173–174
Reinl, Harald 130–131, 132–133
Remarque, Erich Maria 14–15, 96, 141, 144
Return of the Vampire 77
Reynolds, Gene 46, 49
Rhodes, Cecil 63, 65

Index

Riefenstahl, Leni 12–13, 14, 19, 31–37, 38–39, 129–130, 131–134
The Road Back 38
Robinson, Edward G. 116, 118
Rogues' Regiment 116, 117
Rohm, Ernst 35, 36
Rommel, Erwin 122, 136
Roosevelt, Franklin D. 69, 72, 105, 111
Roschmann, Eduard 180, 182
Rubin, Benny 175
Rumann, Sig 103

Sanger, Margaret 70
Saville, Victor 49
Schaffner, Franklin 183
Schell, Maximilian 14, 182
Schindler's List 3–4, 185
Schmitz, Sybille 99, 101
Schunzel, Reinhold 22–23, 89, 102
Scott, George C. 183, 184, 185
The Sea Chase 137
Selpin, Herbert 100–101
Seven Miles from Alcatraz 80, 81
Shagan, Steven 184, 185
Shariff, Omar 172
She-Demons 140–141
Ship of Fools (film) 164
Shirer, William I. 120, 121
Shock Waves 184
The Shop Around the Corner 50
Simon, Simone 76–77
Siodmak, Curt 77
Siodmak, Robert 77, 78
Sirk, Douglas 84, 89, 141, 143, 144, 149
Smith, Kent 80
Soderbaum, Kristina 52, 53, 55–56, 63
Son of Dracula 77
Sondergaard, Gale 97

Speer, Albert 37
Spiegel, Sam 170
Spielberg, Steven 3–4, 185
S.S. Girls 173
Stack, Robert 46
Stalin, Josef 40, 111–112, 117–118, 119, 147–148
Stalingrad: Dogs, Do You Want to Live Forever? 149–150
Stevens, K.T. 78
Stewart, Donald Ogden 74
Stewart, James 46, 47, 48, 49
Stossel, Ludwig 91, 97
The Strange Death of Adolf Hitler 97–99, 120
Strange Holiday 116
The Stranger (1946) 116, 118
Streicher, Julius 33, 36
Sullavan, Margaret 46, 48, 49
Swing Kids 185–186

Tangiers 116
Taylor, Kathrine Kressmann 78
The Testament of Dr. Mabuse 19–24
They Saved Hitler's Brain 173
The Three Comrades 38
The Threepenny Opera (film) 137
Tiefland 129–133, 134–135
A Time to Love and a Time to Die (film) 141–146, 148, 149
Time to Love and a Time to Die (novel) 141
Titanic (1943) 99–101
Tracy, Spencer 74
Triumph of the Will 4, 30–31, 33–38, 119, 129

Udet, Ernst 137

Valkyrie 137
Van Eyck, Peter 93
Veidt, Conrad 51–52, 82

Der Verlorene 124–129
Verne, Kaaren 122
Victory of Faith 35
Vidal, Gore 172, 174
Voight, Jon 181
Von Braun, Werner 115, 116
Von Harbou, Thea 23–24
Von Hindenburg, Paul 103
Von Ribbentrop, Joachim 61
Von Stauffenberg, Claus 107, 108, 137, 162, 171
Von Sternberg, Josef 12–13

Wachsberger, Nathan 176, 177
Warner, Jack L. 106, 111, 113
Watson, Bobby 83, 102
Wayne, John 138, 139
Wegener, Paul 27, 29
Weill, Kurt 41
Welles, Orson 116, 118
Wessel, Horst 25–29
Wexley, John 89
Which Way to the Front? 174–176
Whitney, Peter 108
Whorf, Richard 75
Wicki, Bernhard 137, 144
Wiesenthal, Simon 156, 182, 183
Winchell, Paul 175
Wisbar, Frank 146, 148–149, 150
Wolf, Friedrich 40–45
Wolff, Karl 104, 105
Wyler, William 5
Wylie, I.A.R. 74

The Yesterday Machine 165–166
Young, Loretta 116, 118
Young, Robert 46, 47
The Young Lions (film) 143–144
The Young Lions (novel) 141–142

Ziemer, Gregor 78–79
Zilzer, Wolfgang 112

www.ingramcontent.com/pod-product-compliance
Ingram Content Group UK Ltd.
Pitfield, Milton Keynes, MK11 3LW, UK
UKHW050526150426
5217IPUK00026B/1818